Horror
F

Special Paperback Edition

Published by Crystal Lake Publishing
www.crystallakepub.com

Edited by Joe Mynhardt
Co-Edited and Proofread by Emma Audsley

"Without literature, life is hell."
– Charles Bukowski

"As an author, I've never forgotten how to daydream."
– Neil Gaiman

"But words are things, and a small drop of ink, falling like dew, upon a thought, produces that which makes thousands, perhaps millions, think."
– Lord Byron

~Table of Contents~

Dirty Deeds (Being a Writer)

Hiding the Body (Career Advice)

FOREWORD

Mort Castle

This book is titled *Horror 101.*

Its subtitle is *The Way Forward.*

I'm adding a sub-title to the subtitle.

That's because I think it a good marketing ploy, and want to help out Crystal Lake Publishing's Joe (not to be confused with America's Joe the Plumber, who's plenty confused himself). It'll be helpful for branding, something to get the limited-moment-attention of the Facebook, Twitter, WordPress, Wattpad, Hohah and Ho-boy cyber dazed crew ...

No!

I'm adding a sub-subtitle because it tells the truth:

'Horror 101: The Way Forward'

A Book in the Spirit of J. N. Williamson.

"Oh, sure, Jerry Williamson!" I'm hoping that's your reaction.

But it's not impossible that you might be responding with ... *Who is J. N. Williamson?*, and, that's sad and in case you're feeling a tad too sluggish to Google him on your tablet, I-phone, or the LCD InfoFlasher you recently had implanted in the cat ...

Gerald "Jerry" Neal Williamson was a horror writer who published more than 40 horror novels, of which *The Banished* and *The Book of Webster's* are just as good as you can get, and he published short stories, of which "They Never Even See Me" and "The Sudd" are just as good as you can get, and he edited the *Masques* anthology series, with contributors such as Stephen King and Charles Beaumont and Richard Matheson which are just as good as you can get (and here's my bully-brag, I was in every one of 'em). Jerry and Stephen King both were given the HWA's Lifetime Achievement Award for 2002.

But the most pertinent aspect of Jerry Williamson's life and work for our purposes –

Jerry helped people.

He helped people who wanted to write horror. He helped people who wrote horror.

One of those he helped was me.

Return with us now to those slower and perhaps saner days before email and texting and 4G spots and...

I buy and read a Williamson paperback called *The Houngan*.

I'm impressed with *Houngan*'s somewhat Fitzgeraldian elegance of language, I'm impressed with the research that obviously went into crafting this voodoo story. I'm impressed with the fact that this guy, this J. N. Williamson has a horror novel out there, and, well, truth to tell, after the "sorta success" of my *The Deadly Election*, a comic thriller with great reviews and lousy sales, I'm not having any luck publishing a horror novel. I've been trying, at this point, for about four and a half years.

So I write Jerry a letter. I tell him I like *The Houngan*. I tell him I'm a working writer (no, novels weren't flying, but I was selling two or three short stories a month and making the mortgage payment thereby, therewith, and so there!), and could he maybe give me some advice as to how to crack the horror novel market ... Sure, he wrote back.

Okay, I sent Jerry the first 60 pages of a novel that

hadn't sold. When I'd asked my agent why it wasn't getting a "Yes," he said, "Damned if I know."

I waited about two weeks or so.

Then the mail brought back my much marked up manuscript and Jerry's comments. Ten pages. Single-spaced.

The near verbatim opening of the critique: *Mort, you're an established pro, and I respect your professionalism, but I have to say, I have seldom seen a bigger bunch of crap coming from a pro. There's too much that's wrong ... so let's work at setting it right.*

Needless to say, I embraced his diplomatic forthrightness. I read through his elaborate notes on such manners as auctorial distance, pacing, point of view, diction, etc., and, as I recall, I said aloud — indeed, loudly aloud – something like: "What the hell do you know, anyway!?! You miserable old bastard!?! (Jerry was 14 years my senior!) You live in goddamn Indianapolis, for Chrissake!"

Then when I calmed down, I more objectively went over his remarks. He wasn't right on all of it. Hell, he probably didn't get more than 97 out of 100 points right.

But what he said that was right was real right. And what he gave me as a bonus, instruction on how to outline a novel, is a technique I use to this day and teach my students.

Using his guideline, I ~~revised~~ totally re-wrote the novel.

It sold. With the title *The Strangers* the novel eventually came out in 1984. It had a couple printings. Then, later, Overlook Connection published a signed hardcover that sold out in about a day; Overlook's trade paperback is still in print. Then Tim O'Rawe's screenplay based on the novel got optioned by Whitewater Films. Then, still later, the novel was published in Poland and landed on the Polish *Newsweek's* list of "10 Best Horror-Thriller Novels of the Year."

Jerry, you see, was my Horror Teacher. He was no less a teacher for David Niall Wilson, James Kisner, Gary Braunbeck, Judi Rohrig, and so many others. You had a question, needed advice, craved a word of moral or morale support...

Jerry Williamson, gracious, unselfish, giving, was the Horror Community's Sensei-Welcome-Wagon-Comrade-in-Arms.

And he brought his style of kind-hearted teaching to literally thousands of others.

Yeah, thousands. In one of our late night telephone conversations (they always lasted hours — this being back in the time when long distance cost money!) I suggested Jerry put together a book on writing...

He did. The book became *How to Write Tales of Horror, Fantasy & Science Fiction*, published by Writer's Digest Books in 1987. It had contributions from Dean Koontz, Robert McCammon, Ray Bradbury and Robert Bloch won critical plaudits and stayed in print for 12 years. More than a few of today's horror professionals cite the book as the touchstone for their writing careers.

Jerry died in 2005. I wish I could say he died having seen big sales and earning big money, but alas, alas ... Doesn't always work that way, no matter the promises of all Oprah's spiritual gurus and gamesters.

What he did have, however, was the satisfaction that his bigheartedness had given so much to so many others: The horror writers of the world — and their readers.

Now we have *Horror 101: The Way Forward.* It's a book in the tradition of the work I edited, *On Writing Horror,* and Michael Knost's *Writer's Workshop of Horror*, books in the tradition of *How to Write Tales of Horror, Fantasy & Science Fiction.*

Horror 101. A reference book. A book of advice, how-to, technique, philosophy and attitude.

An idea you encounter in these pages might make you say, "Hey, I never thought of that!" An opinion might reinforce a conjecture of yours. A suggestion could lead to your thinking about a "same old thing" in a "brand new way." Why, it's even likely you'll hit a statement that will earn your "What a load of prune whip!" — and that's okay, too.

But there's no question, *Horror 101: The Way Forward* is a *teaching* book.

Come. Learn.

"Enter freely, and of your own will," Count Dracula famously said, when introducing a certain J. Harker to ... horror.

It's what this book says and what I say to you now. It's what Editor Joe Mynhardt says. Jack Ketchum, Edward Lee, Graham Masterton, Lisa Morton, Shane McKenzie, Robert Walker, Rocky Wood, Tim Waggoner and all the diverse contributors to 101, voices the invitation.

And you don't have to listen too hard to hear the warm welcoming voice of J. N. Williamson in that chorus.

After all, this is –

A Book in the Spirit of J. N. Williamson.

Mort Castle
April 2014

v

A Word from the Publisher

Welcome, horror fans, to the totally unplanned and unexpected paperback edition of Horror 101: The Way Forward.

I'd like to thank everyone who made this second part of the project possible, from the authors who donated their essays, once again, to the crazy fans who threatened to riot if we didn't present them with a paperback; that's so important to small presses & shows how much you all support us. We really appreciate it.

This edition offers readers a physical book to write, underline and take notes in, to refer back to whenever the need arises. A physical copy you can take to writing workshops till it falls apart and you buy a new one. There's even an autographs page at the back.

So get one for a friend, hell, get a couple to hit your friends with writer's block over the head with. Just use it! Horror 101 is not meant to gather dust on the shelf.

Please take note that this is a special edition, which means there are a handful of essays in the eBook edition that are not available in this paperback (Jack Ketchum, Glenn Rolfe and Don D'Auria), just as there are essays in this paperback you won't find in the eBook (Adam Nevill, Charles Day and Kevin Lucia).

So sit back and enjoy the ride. Be open to advice and unexpected new journeys. Don't let fear hold you back, we are horror writers, after all. We should be experts on fear and use it well!

Joe Mynhardt
June 2014
Bloemfontein, South Africa

"We make up horrors to help us cope with the real ones."

– Stephen King

"Why are you trying so hard to fit in when you were born to stand out?"

– Ian Wallace

"It is the writer who might catch the imagination of young people, and plant a seed that will flower and come to fruition."

– Isaac Asimov

"Efforts and courage are not enough without purpose and direction."

– John F. Kennedy

"Still round the corner there may wait, A new road or a secret gate."

– J. R. R. Tolkien

"Some men see things as they are and ask why. Others dream things that never were and ask why not."

– George Bernard Shaw

"You can't wait for inspiration. You have to go after it with a club."

– Jack London

"The difference between the right and the nearly right word is the same as that between lightning and the lightning bug."

– Mark Twain

The Serial Killer in You (The Horror Genre)

Graham Masterton was born in Edinburgh in 1946, the grandson of John Masterton, the chief inspector mines for Scotland, and Thomas Thorne Baker, a world-renowned scientist who was the first man to send news pictures by radio.

After joining his local newspaper at the age of 17 as a junior reporter, Graham was appointed deputy editor of Mayfair the men's magazine at the age of 21. At 24 he became executive editor of Penthouse.

His career at Penthouse led him to write a series of best-selling sexual advice books, including How to Drive Your Man Wild in Bed, which solid 2 million copies worldwide and 250,000 in Poland alone, where it has recently been reprinted.

After leaving Penthouse he wrote The Manitou, a horror novel about the vengeful reincarnation of a Native American spirit, which was filmed with Tony Curtis in the lead role, and also starred Susan Strasberg, Burgess Meredith and Stella Stevens. Three of Graham's horror stories were adapted by the late Tony Scott for his TV series The Hunger. Over the years he has published five collections of short stories, several of which have won awards.

Graham has also written historical sagas like Rich, Maiden Voyage and Solitaire, as well as thrillers and disaster novels such as Plague and Famine. The newest disaster novel Drought will be published in May 2014.

In 1989 Graham's Polish wife Wiescka was instrumental in his becoming the first Western horror novelist to be published in Poland since World War Two, and his sex books have not only won popular success in Poland but acclaim from the medical profession.

He was a regular contributor of humorous articles to the satire magazine Punch, as well as scores of articles on sexual happiness to American women's magazines.

He has encouraged younger writers in several countries, including France, Germany and the Baltic States. For the past 13 years, he has given his name to the prestigious Prix Masterton, which is awarded annually for best French-language horror novel. He was the only non-French winner of Le Prix Julia Verlanger for best-selling horror novel and he has also been given recognition by Mystery Writers of America, the British Fantasy Society and many others.

He edited an anthology of short stories by leading horror writers, Scare Care, in aid of children's charities, and has been honoured by the Irish Society for the Prevention of Cruelty to Children for his fundraising.

Recently he has very successfully turned his hand to crime writing, although his murder scenes are as stirring as anything he has written in the horror genre.

Drawing on the five years in which he and his late wife Wiescka lived in Cork, in southern Ireland, he has created a series of novels featuring Katie Maguire, the first woman detective superintendent in An Garda Siochána, the Irish police force – White Bones, Broken Angels and Red Light.

He currently lives in Surrey, England.

What is Horror?

Graham Masterton

Believe or not, I have never thought of myself as a horror writer. Horror to me is just a category which book retailers put your books into because they happen to have violent or supernatural content, or both. I have never made any distinction between horror fiction and any other kind of fiction. Fiction should always challenge what you believe in, and make you think hard about what it is to be a human being.

I started writing fiction at a very early age, inspired by Jules Verne and Edgar Allan Poe in particular. I would write three or four page stories and read them out to my friends during lunch break at school. Some of them were horror stories, but I also wrote science fiction, and war stories – even some humorous stories with a character like a modern-day Mr Pickwick.

Some of the horror stories, though, made a lasting impression on my friends. Twenty-five years later, a school friend told me that even though he was now a city manager, he still had nightmares about a man with no head who used to walk about the house singing *Tiptoe Through The Tulips*.

What almost all of my stories shared, though, even at that age, was my feeling that fiction should take readers right to the very edge of human experience. Reality is strange, exhilarating, and tragic. Sometimes reality is well beyond our understanding. But I always believed that fiction should take us even further, right to the very boundaries of our humanity.

4

When I was 13 I wrote a 400-page horror novel in which the sole purpose of a mysterious sect of vampires was self-destruction. At 15, I discovered the Beat writers like Jack Kerouac and Allen Ginsberg and William Burroughs, who were taking both the style and the content of their writing to an extreme. William Burroughs wrote a novel called *The Naked Lunch* which caused an uproar when it was published in 1962 because of its political and homosexual content and its open discussion of drugs.

William was living in Tangier at the time but I wrote to him and we kept up a regular correspondence until he came to live in London in 1965. By then I was deputy editor of a new men's magazine called Mayfair. William wrote for Mayfair regularly and we spent many evenings in his apartment in Duke Street discussing revolutionary writing techniques. With William's encouragement and involvement I wrote a novel myself, *Rules of Duel*, the manuscript which I recently discovered after forty years and which my good friend David Howe from Telos Books published last year.

The writing that William and I did together was difficult, often obscure, and pushed convention and accepted taste right to the very limit, and beyond. You probably won't be able to grasp much of what *Rules of Duel* is all about. But William had some very good lessons, not just for a horror writer but for any kind of writer who wants to take writing to the very edge.

The writer should not appear in his own work. He should be El Hombre Invisible, the invisible man. Learn how to construct sentences so balanced and rhythmical that your readers are scarcely aware they are reading at all. This takes painstaking practice, especially with dialog, and a complete understanding of the mechanics of grammar. You need to be able to take your work apart and put it together again like a motor mechanic.

When you're writing, don't look at the page in front of you (or the screen, these days.) Be there. Feel the wind on your back and hear the noises all around you. Take your characters by the hand so that you can physically feel them.

And never be scared to say anything. Ever.

Several times, I have purposely taken my work beyond the boundaries of accepted taste. I suppose it started with my novel *Ritual*, which was a jolly story about gourmet cannibals.

The Celestines were a religious sect who believed that they would eventually get to see God by devouring their own bodies. They kidnap the son of our hero, who rather appropriately happens to be a restaurant critic, and in his attempt to rescue the boy, the critic joins the sect.

To be accepted by them, though, he has to show that he is prepared to consume part of himself. He cuts off his own finger, fries it and eats it.

Other stories that have gone right to the edge and over include the notorious *Eric the Pie*, which was the cover story for the first issue of *Frighteners* magazine, and was considered to be so disgusting by WH Smith that they banned it from their retail outlets, leading to the magazine's very sad demise after only two issues. You can read Eric in the fiction section of my website *www.grahammasterton.co.uk* and make up your own mind.

Eric recently reappeared in a chapbook called *Tales Too Extreme for Cemetery Dance*. Cemetery Dance also published a chapbook called *Sepsis* which I deliberately wrote to go right to the limit of what readers could swallow. A story called *Epiphany* was sadly but understandably dropped by my publisher from my recent collection of short stories *Festival of Fear* (Severn House) because of its sexual content.

I have a new extreme story coming out in *Figures of Fear* next year, called *Beholder*. If you can stomach *Beholder* you can stomach anything. All I'm going to say at the moment is that it's about eyes.

A favourite device of mine is to make ancient and mythical threats re-appear in the modern-day world so that ordinary people like you and me have to find a way to deal with them. The reason why legendary beings can be so frightening is because they were devised in days when people had no understanding of disease, or natural disasters, and so they attributed them to demons and ghosts and vengeful gods. Why did your cattle die? Because creatures came in the night and sucked the blood out of them. What caused cot death? Witches who crept into your house when you were asleep and stole your baby's soul.

But again, I don't consider this to be "horror" fiction. It's just stories as stories have always been told. Stories to make you think who you are. Stories to help you to come to terms with your mortality. All of us who are alive at the moment are like a city, with its millions of lights sparkling in the night. One by one, though, the lights are extinguished, and then there is nothing but darkness. There lies the horror.

Edward Lee is the author of over fifty books and numerous short stories and novellas. Several of his properties have been optioned for film, while HEADER was made into a movie in 2009; THE BIGHEAD is in production now. Lee has been published in Poland, Germany, England, Romania, Greece, Austria, and Japan. Recent releases include Bullet Through Your Face and Brain Cheese Buffet (story collections), Header 2, and the hard-core Lovecraftian books Trolley No. 1852, Pages Torn From A Travel Journal, Going Monstering, and Haunter of the Threshold, the latter being what Lee considers his hardest-core work to date. Currently he is working on a new novel as well as making his own low-budget horror movies. Lee lives in Largo, Florida. Visit him online at edwardleeonline.com and cityinfernalfilms.com

Bitten by the Horror Bug

Edward Lee

I was bitten by the horror bug long before I became a writer or even thought of becoming one. But now that I've been fortunate enough to have accumulated some level of success (in essence, my "dream" coming true), I'm asked multitudinous questions regarding my motivations, just as any author is. Foremost among these queries revolves around my choice to write in the horror genre. It's difficult to explain objectively why I actually never *had* a choice; horror chose *me*, in a manner of speaking.

I suspect that many horror writers would affirm that. But in a broader and less abstract context, fans, critics, regular folk, etc. (and particularly relatives!) have a habit of asking me why I write horror fiction. I have this notion that, hidden between their lines, they're really asking "Why do you write that horror dreck instead of literature?" Of course, when aspiring horror authors ask me, in not so many words, "I really love horror fiction and want to be a writer. But everyone tells me horror is dead, horror is disreputable, horror is garbage that will hold you back when you're ready to write your big breakout mainstream bestseller. What should I do?" My answer is always the same: "Write horror. Don't let *anyone else* tell you how to conduct your muse. They're all sour-grapes, wannabe, no-talent bums who *wish* they had your skill and motivation. So go forth, my son, and write *horror*."

As to the fear that horror will hold back new writers from future opportunities, consider, for example, a 1980 horror novel entitled 'Virgin' by a barely known writer named James Patterson. Doesn't look like a horror novel in his past held him back, huh? There are many similar examples. But it is a worthwhile interrogative: why horror? Why not something bigger? Why not something else? Several decades ago, novelist extraordinaire Jack Ketchum told me, just after I'd made his acquaintance, "Only write what you love to read, and don't listen to the criticism of others. To Hell with them."

This is fairly universal advice but it had much more impact on me, coming from so significant a name in the field; and it assured me that I had taken my creative feet on the correct path because by that time I'd only had two novels out, 'Ghouls' and 'Coven'. It was monumental instruction for my Babe in the Woods psyche. Moreover, I believe horror fans and horror writers all possess an intricate interest in any and all aspects of fear. We write about it because it's imbued in us, we read about it because it's intriguing and even self-revelatory. It's also, I believe, quite primordial.

The Great God Zeus of Horror, H. P. Lovecraft, could not have been more correct when he claimed the greatest fear we can experience is, not the fear of the dark, or the fear of death, (or, for that matter–though not in *his* words!) fear of mutilation, rape by monsters, impregnation by para-dimensional abominations, trans-vaginal evisceration by fireplace tongs, or what have you, but the fear of the unknown. The Unknown–*that's* main ingredient to the Stew of Horror Fiction that we all feast upon. No genre transfigures this fear more potently to the reader than the horror genre. Even in great "literature," I'll contend. True, great literature often exists on a much more important level than horror (though not always!) but it seems to me that horror *must* stimulate the reader's mental pressure points more effectively and more consistently than other genres. It's *must*!

And with that mental stimulus comes the provocation that makes us ponder our inner-selves as well as the world around us. Provocation is the key, and it can be just as legitimate in horror as any other field of creativity. I very passionately appreciate the works of, say, Faulkner, Kafka, Sartre, Marquez, etc., and regard their literary contributions as paramount as and more significant than even that of the most astute horror writers. Ah, but horror is so much more fun, isn't it? And more memorable. And more impacting. And the provocation of thought that it induces in us is just as functional. That's why I was bitten by the horror bug, because my undeniable curiosity about the nature of fear made me ripe for its bite. E.C. Comics when I was five years old, sneaking into the back door of the local movie theater to see such forbidden movies as 'Mark of the Devil' and 'Blood Feast'; brazenly disobeying my parents in order to creep out to the living room in at midnight on Friday and Saturday to watch Creature Feature, and the like.

When I was six, my parents went out to dinner and left me with a babysitter named Freddie. *Five minutes* after my parents had left, Freddie's greaser pals pulled up in their Buick convertible, threw me in the back, and drove straight to Palmer Drive-In, where I received the privilege of watching 'Psycho'. I distinctly remember Freddie and his tough-guy greaser pals covering their eyes and yelling aloud during the final basement scene. But not me. I was giggling. My point: the horror bug finds us via whatever reason, environment, formative observation, etc., and I suspect there are also many other more innate and psychological–even genetic–reasons.

But if you're reading this, you no doubt have been bitten by the horror bug too. And if you're an aspiring horror writer, write horror and you will succeed. It worked for me, and if it worked for me, it can work for anybody!

Siobhan McKinney has a happy disposition in real life but in writing explores the nastier things she prefers to avoid. Horror is all around. It's in your head. A former teacher and lecturer, Siobhan's stories explore paranormal and natural phenomena, and everyday paranoia. Everyone's frightened of something – ask her children or her former pupils. Resident in Northern Ireland, Celtic mythology and a tradition of storytelling provides plenty of inspiration through much-loved ghosts and legendary warriors. Things you read in her stories might be fiction... but they might be true too. Contact her here, @ballysio

Reader Beware

Siobhan McKinney

How much horror makes a horror story? Horror, by any dictionary definition, includes the word 'intense' in the description of the feelings horror evokes: repugnance, fear, shock, revulsion. Being 'unpleasant' isn't enough, though horror is a wonderful field that can span several other mainstream genres. Dark and creepy, gruesome, chilling, and unnerving probably belong in the world of psychological horror. Just like active spectators strike the penalty ball, or jump the fence with the rider, an engaged reader will get tingles and goosebumps when they recall the horror of what they read. It's hard to beat a good mind-freak which leaves the reader disturbed long after they've set the story aside. Spooky, eerie and frightening are more than likely to be found in tales with a supernatural element where ghosts, ghouls, ghastlies and devils feature strongly. Soul-possession always guarantees considerable discomfort when written well.

As a cross-over genre, horror lends itself to creating mayhem with fantasy, thrillers, paranormal, mystery, suspense, science-fiction . . . Cut! Horror is an entity in its own right through which any story teller with a deft touch can create terrifying imaginings for their readers. 'Ew' to 'Arrgh' is a long continuum and responses will depend on the reader's mind-set and experiences. It is the author's responsibility to tease you into turning the pages, fearful of what might be revealed, but you do it anyway. Horror writers manipulate their readers with finesse. Loading characters and situations with taboos or universally accepted phobias, even if they do not themselves possess such fears, authors force audience empathy with the poor sucker who has to go through the dread and terror.

It is difficult to sustain those feelings of horror over the length of a novel, and short stories, in my opinion, serve the genre best. Horror, in children's literature, is probably defined more through horribleness and nastiness. Gross descriptions with a high 'yuck' factor elicit a visceral response and is often vocalised. Many authors balance any scariness by providing a happy ending where the young protagonist triumphs over evil or fear. Children love horror stories because they are immediately engaged in a world where their fears are safely explored second-hand. As a teacher, I have found that they listen intently and recall many more details of a horror story or a cautionary tale because they readily identify with the subject matter. Fear is something within their experience and, as we were all children once, we have a reference point for those unnerving feelings from our collective childhoods that make horror an enduring delight.

Some horror, with particularly graphic descriptions of gore or torture, might be regarded by some as 'hard core' in much the same way erotica crosses the line when weird or obscene become pornographic. Perhaps more disturbing though, are stories that play with your head and suggest with immense subtlety that something similar could happen to you. Hints and nuances embedded within wholesome characterisations reveal insidious players whom the reader either roots for or prays for their demise, preferably in the most despicable way. And therein lies the strength of the horror story. It allows villains and nasty characters to play the lead role, to be the protagonist. Bad is often good and good bad, things are turned on their head as the reader explores the murky world of the unknown. That unknown is described with such detail, the reader will feel they have entered that place – and wished they hadn't.

Psychobiology of Trauma explores the issues that affect people both physically and mentally when their 'fight or flight' response is triggered. It mirrors closely how people react to chills and thrills. Imagine a rollercoaster ride with its ups and downs, tight turns and frightening speed. Most people will feel their stomach lurch and the bladder threaten to empty, yet they laugh while they scream and will pay over hard-earned money to do it again . . . and again. Agony and ecstasy are closer companions than you realise. They share physiological responses such as those displayed when a person is experiencing fear, anger or sexual arousal, although the emotional responses differ to these stimuli.

Even when you know what to expect, the thrill never fails to please or terrify. Authors of horror can take advantage of this either by building up heart-stopping anticipation to the point of near collapse or they can take you by surprise and shock you into apoplexy.

Raised on Grimm's fairytales, and some gruesome Celtic legends, I developed an appetite for horror at a young age. Whether the author makes the reader voyeur to the action or participant doesn't matter, as long as they prompt a reaction. I can remember devouring stories from The Pan Book of Horror and scaring the bejaysus out of myself while reading Dennis Wheatley during the UK's 1974 three-day week. Baby-sitting, with homework completed and TV broadcasts over at 10.30pm (in the days before videos and DVDs) my teenage imagination went into overdrive as I read until the wee small hours, jumping at every radiator shudder and house-cooling creak when the central heating went off. Ghosts, rats, demons – they were all out there in the dark waiting for me.

Warped, weird or twisted, the characters and their actions in horror stories should make your heart give a harder thump as it tries to shift the blood frozen in your veins. Unlike other genres, this torture will continue throughout a horror story – it's not just a guest appearance – and when you reach the end, satisfying as it might be, you could be sorry you did. Reader beware.

"There's a fine line between genius and insanity. I have erased this line."
— Oscar Levant

"Not all those who wander are lost."
— J. R. R. Tolkien

"Horror is the removal of masks."
— Robert Bloch

"Jump, and find out how to unfold your wings on the way down."
— Ray Bradbury

"Where there is no imagination there is no horror."
— Arthur Conan Doyle

"You get what anyone gets. You get a lifetime."
— Neil Gaiman

"If words are to enter men's minds and bear fruit, they must be the right words shaped cunningly to pass men's defenses and explode silently and effectually within their minds."
— J.B. Phillips

"I long to accomplish a great and noble task, but it is my chief duty to accomplish humble tasks as though they were great and noble. The world is moved along, not only by the mighty shoves of its heroes, but also by the aggregate of the tiny pushes of each honest worker."
— Helen Adams Keller

Choosing your Victim (So What are Your Choices)

Taylor Grant is a professional screenwriter, author, actor, award-winning filmmaker and copywriter. His work has been seen on network television, the big screen, the stage, newspapers, comic books, national magazines, anthologies, the web, and heard on the radio.

He is co-author of the critically acclaimed, bestselling horror comic Evil Jester Presents, along with horror luminaries Jack Ketchum, Jonathan Maberry, Joe McKinney, and William F. Nolan. His dark fiction has been published in two Bram Stoker Award nominated anthologies: Horror Library Vol. 5 and Horror For Good, as well as Cemetery Dance Magazine and multiple anthologies.

Taylor is the Co-Founder and Editor in Chief of publishing company Evil Jester Comics, and is an Active Member of the Horror Writers Association. Learn more about Taylor's dark imaginings at:
http://www.taylorgrant.com

Balancing Art and Commerce

Taylor Grant

Each time you begin to write a horror story, you are harnessing the power of your imagination. But have you considered leveraging that same power in your career? If you are open-minded, I believe that when it comes to professional writing – regardless of genre or medium – you are only limited by your imagination.

I'm one of those writers you don't hear much about –

the working stiff. While I am neither rich nor famous, I have been fortunate enough to make a living as a writer and creative professional for the greater part of my adult life. Most recently, I've found a terrific balance between creative fulfillment and paying the bills with my words. If this is something you'd like to accomplish too, here are some insights that you may find helpful.

The Power of Diversification

"If you wrote something for which someone sent you a check, if you cashed the check and it didn't bounce, and if you then paid the light bill with the money, I consider you talented." – Stephen King

Over the past twenty years, I have written for the majority of mediums that exist: film, television, stage, radio, video games, comic books, newspapers, national magazines, and the Internet. And within those mediums, the range of material has been extremely varied.

To better illustrate, here are some examples: traditional animation, web animation, live action episodic, big budget features, short films, music videos, treatments, taglines, show bibles, TV/radio ads, articles, ghost-writing, blog posts, musical theater, white papers, websites, case studies, brochures, catalogs, short stories – the list goes on.

Within specific industries there are also a myriad of possibilities. For instance, as a writer of fiction, I have tackled horror, science fiction, comedy, action, drama, military thriller, and literary stories. My non-fiction writing has included entertainment, health and wellness, beauty, telecommunications, news, finance and more.

These credentials are not listed to impress you, but to impress upon you the idea that there are more ways to earn a living as a writer than you might imagine. Not all of my writing is horror-related, of course, but more of it has crossed over than you might expect.

FILM

- Hired to write two horror feature film projects; one for Imagine Entertainment, and the other for Lions Gate Films.
- Wrote, directed and produced my own horror film.

TELEVISION

- Created a horror-themed animated series that aired on the Fox Family Channel.
- Wrote several animated series episodes with horror/comedy elements.
- Wrote several live action series episodes with horror/comedy elements.

PRINT

- Co-authored a bestselling horror comic.
- Sold horror stories to anthologies and magazines (Pro and Semi-Pro).

As you can see, horror writing includes a lot more than writing novels. And the pay scale on that list of gigs ranges from zero, to a few thousand, to a year's salary.

I realize that I'm an extreme case and that you may not be interested in exploring all of the options that I have over the years. But don't limit yourself to the areas of writing that I list in this article either.

For instance, other examples of how to supplement your income include writing script coverage for film studios, marketing copy for movie posters, DVDs and Blu-rays, travel articles, grant writing, product reviews, speech writing, press releases, greeting cards, hell, fortune cookies – whatever works for you. These days there are countless writing opportunities to explore, particularly web-related jobs. If the work is solid and pays the rent, then you are a professional writer. Congratulations.

Obviously, of the various opportunities I've mentioned, film and television are probably the most difficult to break into if you're not living in Los Angeles, New York or whatever large city in your country has a film industry. But there are exceptions to every rule and if you are determined to earn a living as a screenwriter, you can't pay attention to the odds. There are certainly writers outside of the major hubs that have sold screenplays.

The power of diversification is that it removes the burden of trying to make a living at any single form of writing. I can tell you from personal experience that having the financial freedom to write what I want to write has been a dream come true. There is nothing worse than the desperation of having to pay the rent with creative fiction if you're just starting out – or even have a few sales under your belt. I have lived through that experience and it was a nightmare, and I am one of the fortunate ones who have made a living writing creative fiction.

So, what does that diversification look like? On a single day, I have simultaneously worked on a horror feature, a big budget rap music video, and marketing copy for a skin care company. There have been times when I paid all of my bills exclusively as a screenwriter, and other times when I solely wrote marketing/advertising to bring home the bacon.

Over the past twelve months I sold five horror stories, wrote advertising and marketing copy for a large telecommunications firm, wrote a short film I was passionate about for no money at all, and co-wrote a #1 Amazon bestselling horror comic.

There really are no rules.

Most recently, I have designed my life so that writing marketing/advertising serves as the foundation of my annual income. This is a strategic choice that I made to free me up creatively as a fiction writer.

Some people have a hard time getting their head around the fact that I willingly chose to give up full-time screenwriting, along with representation from one of the biggest talent agencies in North America. But it was the best decision I've ever made.

While I could certainly return to being a screenwriter at any time, the reality of writing for the studios is something I am not interested in doing full-time. My priority as a wordsmith is creative control and ownership of my properties, two things in short supply as a Hollywood screenwriter.

These days I am the captain of my own ship. In fact, one of the driving forces behind my decision to co-found Evil Jester Comics, publisher of comics and graphic novels, was because I desired creative control and ownership of my work.

However, it was my multiple skills as a writer that empowered me to do this. It has given me the financial freedom to create work that I truly care about. It has enabled me to take more artistic risks in my work and bolder moves in my career. It is why I have the freedom to create films on my terms, write the stories I want to write, and even start my own comic book publishing company.

If I had all of the money in the world, I would still continually explore writing in different mediums. Not only is it a sound business strategy, it also helps you to grow as an artist.

Your Inner Entrepreneur

Diversification is the first part of the equation. The next is to nurture your inner entrepreneur.

For some writers, this is a hard pill to swallow. I swallowed it kicking and screaming. But the actual craft of writing is only one aspect of your career. You must also learn about how to run, market and promote a small business—that business being you.

It's important to note that most of the professional writing I've done was a direct result of pounding the pavement, both virtually and in the real world. These days I am in the enviable position of having others solicit me for my work; this never would have happened if I hadn't spent years approaching my career as an entrepreneur.

It is important to continually keep your eye out for opportunity and check your ego at the door. What I mean by checking your ego is that having success in one field doesn't necessarily translate into another. I wrote for several children's television series which aired on major networks, as well as music videos for international superstars, but that didn't mean much when

I first tried to break into the feature film industry. And the fact that I had been a full-time screenwriter working for major Hollywood studios didn't win me any points trying to get a gig writing white papers or case studies (both which can be quite lucrative, by the way).

It's likely you'll have to start at the bottom when you enter a new field of writing. But if you take the measured steps to build your business in one field of writing, you will gain the financial stability to take more risks – like working for a lower wage to get your foot in the door in a new field. And so on.

Remember, each time you are hired to write, you are building your portfolio. And the more impressive your portfolio becomes, the more money you can demand.

I'm not an expert on the current landscape of online job sites, but I can tell you that there are more websites dedicated to freelance writing opportunities than you can imagine. Many of these gigs don't pay that much, but they provide the necessary experience you'll need to demand more down the road.

I can't stress this enough. Sometimes it's worth it to do a job for free, just to get your foot in the door in a brand new industry. While I don't advocate working for free for any length of time, there are certain circumstances when building your credibility is worth much more than a few dollars up front.

When I first started out, there was no Internet. So I scoured the streets for Want Ads. I searched the backs of animation trade magazines, the classified ad section of the Hollywood Reporter, newspaper classifieds, wherever I could find writing opportunities.

I sent out my resume for freelance gigs constantly, even if I was gainfully employed. Some seasoned writers would never stoop to answering lowly classified ads. But I landed a high-paying gig as the head writer for comic book legend Stan Lee through a classified ad, as well as my first job writing music videos for MTV. In other words, I checked my ego at the door and it paid off – big time.

Networking is Win-Win

The third important aspect that can make or break your career is networking.

Now I can hear some of you groaning even as I write this, and as an admitted introvert this is not something that came easy to me.

A lot of writers shy away from networking, but you can't build a career from a silo. Sitting in a room banging on a keyboard, mailing out your manuscript in the hopes that an agent or manager is going to discover you and run your career is a myth.

I cannot tell you how impactful Facebook and Twitter have been to my horror-writing career. Not only have I met hundreds of other writers and learned of rare opportunities, but I've also met editors that I ended up working with directly. These relationships have not only led to horror story solicitations, but they were also the catalyst for starting my own publishing company. Without networking, the horror fiction part of my career would have been severely hobbled.

Relationships are important in all industries, but they are absolutely critical in the writing profession, which requires us to remain in solitude and isolation for so much of the time.

I think one reason networking is anathema to some writers is because they think it means forced relationships with a hidden agenda, or worse – being a used car salesperson. I assure you this is not what I'm suggesting. Networking to me means supporting others as much as they support you.

As far as I'm concerned, we're all in this crazy business together. And there is room for all of us. I don't see competition, I see comrades in arms. Writing is one of the most difficult careers that exist; we should celebrate those who have success. It is an inspiration to us all!

I spend a fair amount of time on social media liking my friends' Facebook and Twitter posts, offering my moral support, and even offering free advice when I have time. Many of these friends happen to be writers, editors and publishers. This makes networking a win-win.

People are sophisticated and can tell if you're only out to get something from them. Be nice. Be supportive. Build organic relationships with people online, through conventions, writers groups, classes, etc. When you are helpful or supportive to others, you'll be surprised at the good things that can happen.

If you're an introvert like me, keep your relationships online. I have built many wonderful relationships with writers/editors/publishers in the horror industry that I've never met in person. The horror writing community is one of the most open and non-competitive industries I've ever experienced. After swimming with the sharks of Hollywood for so many years, it was refreshing to

Another challenge I had recently was writing comic scripts. I was approached by Zenescope Entertainment to write the Scarecrow issue of their Tales From Oz series. The main problem I had was that I over explained everything, described everything with too much detail. I'm used to using words to paint pictures in my reader's head.

What I didn't realize was that a comic is a collaboration between the writer and artist. I had to teach myself to hold back on certain things, let the artist add their flavour to it.

Something else I discovered was how 'showing' the images could be. I would write caption boxes or dialogue that was unnecessary because the artist showed it in the drawings. For example, I had an exchange between a man and his fiancée, and he was explaining to her how scared he was, how he wasn't sure if he had made the right decision. But the artist was able to show this with the character's expression, his body language. His fiancée was looking right into his face, telling him everything would work out, and his eyes were pointed at the floor.

Another thing I didn't consider was making my dialogue and caption boxes too wordy. Again, as a novelist, I have a tendency to want to explain everything, either through narrative or dialogue between my characters. Not only does the art speak for itself most of the time, but if I have long, drawn out conversations, the text bubbles themselves are going to cover up a lot of the artwork. And we can't have that!

No matter what it is, a novel or a screenplay or a comic book, it's still just storytelling. If you can tell a good story, then it really doesn't matter what medium you use. If you've been drawing pictures your entire life with a sharpened pencil, you're going to get pretty comfortable with that. If someone asks you to draw a picture for them, and then hands you a box of crayons, you've still got the tools you need to draw that picture, it's just going to look and feel slightly different.

You can always learn and adjust.

Paul Kane is an award-winning writer and editor based in Derbyshire, UK. His short story collections include Alone (In the Dark), Touching the Flame, FunnyBones, Peripheral Visions, Shadow Writer, The Adventures of Dalton Quayle, The Butterfly Man and Other Stories, The Spaces Between and Ghosts. His novellas include Signs of Life, The Lazarus Condition, Red and Pain Cages. He is the author of such novels as Of Darkness and Light, The Gemini Factor and the bestselling Arrowhead trilogy (Arrowhead, Broken Arrow and Arrowland), a post-apocalyptic reworking of the Robin Hood mythology gathered together in the sell-out Hooded Man omnibus. His latest novels are Lunar (which is set to be turned into a feature film) and the short Y.A. book The Rainbow Man (as P.B. Kane). He has also written for comics, most notably for the Dead Roots zombie anthology alongside writers such as James Moran (Torchwood, Cockneys vs. Zombies) and Jason Arnopp (Dr Who, Friday The 13th).

Paul is co-editor of the anthology Hellbound Hearts (Simon & Schuster) – stories based around the Clive Barker mythology that spawned Hellraiser, The Mammoth Book of Body Horror (Constable & Robinson/Running Press) featuring the likes of Stephen King and James Herbert, A Carnivàle of Horror (PS) featuring Ray Bradbury and Joe Hill, and Beyond Rue Morgue from Titan, stories based around Poe's detective, Dupin. His non-fiction books are The Hellraiser Films and Their Legacy, Voices in the Dark, and his genre journalism has appeared in the likes of SFX, Dreamwatch and DeathRay. He has been a Guest at Alt.Fiction five times, was a Guest at the first SFX Weekender, at Thought Bubble in 2011, Derbyshire

Literary Festival, Edge-Lit and Off the Shelf in 2012, plus Monster Mash and Event Horizon in 2013, as well as being a panellist at FantasyCon and the World Fantasy Convention. His work has been optioned for film and television, and his zombie story 'Dead Time' was turned into an episode of the Lionsgate/NBC TV series Fear Itself, adapted by Steve Niles (30 Days of Night) and directed by Darren Lynn Bousman (SAW II-IV). He also scripted The Opportunity, which premiered at the Cannes Film Festival, Wind Chimes (directed by Brad '7th Dimension' Watson and sold to TV) and The Weeping Woman – filmed by award-winning director Mark Steensland and starring Tony-nominated actor Stephen Geoffreys (Fright Night). You can find out more on Twitter at https://twitter.com/PaulKaneShadow , and over at his website www.shadow-writer.co.uk which has featured Guest Writers such as Dean Koontz, Robert Kirkman, Charlaine Harris and Guillermo del Toro.

Writing About Films and *for* Film

Paul Kane

My route into writing for a living was a fairly unusual one I think, so while I'm not sure it will be of any use to aspiring writers out there – for one thing the climate has changed so much in almost twenty years – it might at least show that even a working class lad from a mining community can see his dreams come true...if only a little bit.

I've always loved film, and TV – though I shouldn't

really, I tend to lump them both in together; TV, after all, tends to recycle filmic ideas. Mostly genre stuff growing up, as I'm sure a lot of people reading this will be able to appreciate, but just good drama in general if I'm honest. There was something about going to the cinema to see a movie that just captivated me. I remember being taken to see the big spectacle blockbusters like *Star Wars*, *Indiana Jones*, the *Bond* films. It was a fascination that never really left me, and when I went to art college to do a Foundation course, I ended up doing some bits and bobs of Film Studies thanks to a tutor called Eric Popplewell – he was taking a degree in it himself and knew I was interested, so passed stuff on. I was even given the opportunity to make and edit a couple of low-budget shorts on video, which was fun.

Off the back of this, I applied to do filmmaking at university, but sadly didn't get on that course. I sometimes wonder what would have happened if I had. Instead, I wound up on a purely academic course studying History of Art, Design and Film. It was a hard course, with a 70% drop out rate, but I learnt a lot, especially about studying movies: everything from analysis of scenes to auteurs. Plus I got to see so many films on the big screen that I wouldn't have had the opportunity to otherwise, including *Alien*, *Blade Runner* and my favourite film of all time, *Hellraiser*. I was also given a grounding in the history of cinema which took me from the early days through to the Hollywood system and European movements like German Expressionism, Italian Neorealism and the French New Wave, as well as Hammer and other studios at home. I must have enjoyed all this, because I went back a few years after graduating and paid to do a Film Studies MA!

Another thing my course allowed me to do was choose modules outside of my core units. For two of them I picked Screenwriting and Professional Writing. I wasn't very good at the former back then, though that might have been down to a pain in the arse tutor. But I took to the pro-writing one like a duck to water, again thanks to a brilliant lecturer by the name of Pete Wall. Naturally, I gravitated towards writing about film and television shows, but to get my credits I had to actually contact newsstand magazines and papers to get feedback on my reviews and articles. This included – gulp – *The Mirror* and *Dark Side Magazine*, and I have to thank Jaci Stephens and John Martin here for getting back to me with such positive comments. It was doing this that allowed me to eventually start up as a freelance writer when I left university in 1996, working for magazines like *Eclipse*, *Boy's First*, *Classic TV* and *Area 51*. I also ended up doing film reviews for my local newspaper, getting to see the latest movies at press screenings and meeting other journos, all of which stood me in good stead for future work. In the years since, although it hasn't been my main source of income, I've kept my hand in with the non-fiction, and have worked for some of the big boys, like *SFX*, *Fangoria*, *Rue Morgue*, *GoreZone*, *DeathRay* and *Dreamwatch* to name but a few. The analytical stuff that I learned was also invaluable when it came to writing my first non-fiction book, *The Hellraiser Films and their Legacy*, one of the publications I'm most associated with to this day.

So, that was how I got into writing *about* films (and TV). What about the other side of things, actually writing *for* the medium? Well, that came after I met my future wife Marie and by way of the British Fantasy Society. Let me just say right now, that if you're thinking of going into any kind of writing, the BFS is a Godsend. You get to meet up with other like-minded souls, chat about the genre, and make contacts that will stay with you for life. I'd been in touch with Marie prior to attending the BFS' annual FantasyCon – my first, ten years ago now – as I'd read her writing, loved it, and wanted her to be a Guest Writer on my site. We met for the first time at FCon, though, where Marie was pitching some scripts to a Film & TV agent.

As well as meeting the love of my life there, it also got me thinking about getting back into writing some scripts myself. I'd met a few directors doing reviews, and being a part of documentaries, so I decided to give it a go and maybe send scripts to them. I wrote one original 20 minute script called *Confidence* which gained some interest, but is yet to be made; the rest I adapted from stories I'd had published, making sure they wouldn't need too much of a budget (couple of characters, limited locations). I figured they'd give me enough of a template to follow, especially as I was only just starting out. The first one to get made was *The Opportunity*, which came about through an ex-student of mine – I was also teaching creative writing by now. Clare (Coleman) happens to also be a very talented actress, and was going out back then with Lewis Copson, another actor who wanted to try his hand at directing something short. They read the script and the next thing I knew funds had been raised, and they were filming locally in Matlock. They'd even secured the rights to shoot from the famous cable car there for establishing shots. I'll never forget the night we visited the set one February; it was freezing cold but we had such a lot of fun. Shot in black and white, and starring Clare as the main female character, it turned out really well and had its premiere at the Cannes Film Festival. I only wish I could have gone along and seen it screened.

That gave me enough of a boost to keep on pitching other scripts to directors, but in the meantime I was actually lucky enough to have something optioned and made by LionsGate for NBC. This was an adaptation of my story 'Dead Time' from *The Lazarus Condition*, which Mick Garris had introduced and really enjoyed. He was looking for a zombie tale for his network follow up to *Masters of Horror*, called *Fear Itself*, and suddenly Steve '*30 Days of Night*' Niles was scripting it as 'New Year's Day' and Darren '*SAW II-IV*' Bousman was directing. Even though I had nothing directly to do with any of this, it still looked good on my CV, plus I'd also been involved in a *Hellraiser* fan short as executive producer... So when I approached the award-winning American director of *Peekers* – Mark Steensland – about working together, he asked me what I'd got.

I showed him a couple of scripts, and he really liked *The Weeping Woman*, based on a story from my very first collection *Alone (In the Dark)*. Once again, everything happened very quickly, as Mark took the project and just ran with it. In the space of just a few months, he'd got funding from the likes of *Cemetery Dance*'s Richard Chizmar, had managed to attract not only Tony Award-nominee Stephen Geoffreys from the original *Fright Night*, but also famous Lucio Fulci collaborator Fabio Frizzi to score the piece (only recently in London, Fabio played the music as part of a Halloween concert, which made my year!).

Atmospherically filmed against the snowy backdrop of northwestern Pennsylvania and starring Melissa Bostaph as the titular Weeping Woman, the film received its World Premiere at Motor City Nightmares in Detroit in April 2011. I couldn't be there for that one, either, but did get to see it screened at FantasyCon that same year…and see the positive reaction of the audience. The film also directly led to my working on an adaptation of Graham Masterton's bestselling novel *Tengu* for Mark, though sadly this fell through down the line – something you should get used to if you want to work in the film industry.

The other short film I've had produced came about when I met a director/producer team at ChillerFest where Marie and I were interviewing famous horror names for a magazine (some of which later found their way into our book, *Voices in the Dark*). Brad Watson and Janice Willis were part of Revolt Films and had a stall there promoting their low budget vampire feature, *Asylum Night* – available on DVD and also screened on the Horror Channel. We got talking and I realised Brad and I had a lot in common, particularly when it came to influences. I also found out he'd been working in the industry quite a while and had tons of experience. I took a copy of the film away to review it, and loved it! Then Brad sent me his show-reel and I cheekily sent him a few scripts to look at. The one that caught his eye was *Wind Chimes*, a subtle ghost story that had appeared in prose in the *Read By Dawn* anthology – a spin-off of the popular Scottish Dead By Dawn film festival.

At a meeting in London, Brad made me promise not to sell the script anywhere else until he had a window of opportunity to make it. For my part, I didn't really *want* anyone else to make it, as I could see Brad had the talent to do it justice. It took a few years to see this made, a period in which Brad made another successful feature called *7th Dimension*, and I'd been working on a few more novel projects – one of which, *Arrowhead* (a post-apocalyptic version of Robin Hood), Brad and Jan came very close to adapting for the big screen. But, once more, suddenly it was all systems go and *Wind Chimes* was filming over the summer of 2012, with its premiere due at FCon in September. It's one of my favourite adaptations, not least because of the stunning performances by Robert Carratta and *Wallander* actress Joanna Ignaczewska, but also because I was right to trust in Brad's sensitive handling of the script. He even came up with the moving score. The film has since enjoyed another life – it's sold to TV, and has appeared as a DVD extra in my *Ghosts* collection from Spectral, which includes the original script and an intro from Brad himself.

Like everything else, the story doesn't end there and after more meetings, Brad, Jan and I have ended up working on a feature adaptation of my novel *Lunar*. It's my first full length script, and has gone through lots of revisions, but I like to think I did an okay job on it – the short film scripting having given me enough experience to tackle it. At time of writing, I've also done some TV scripting and have started a second feature script, plus I have more exciting short movies in the pipeline.

The best advice I can give to someone wanting to start out in either reviewing, writing articles or writing for film/TV, is just to do it. Contact magazines that say they're open to submissions, gain experience – even if it's only in exchange for a copy of a small press magazine, it's still a credit – and basically make things happen. Look for people who are actually making shorts, contact them and see if they might want to work on something. It's a good way to build up your credits and you'll be surprised what a snowball effect it all has. It's like I always say, if you don't ask you don't get...

So, good luck, and enjoy it. And who knows, maybe one day you'll be the fan who gets to write about the movies you love... or even write some yourself!

Lisa Morton is a screenwriter, author of non-fiction books, Bram Stoker Award-winning prose writer, and Halloween expert whose work is described by the American Library Association's Readers' Advisory Guide to Horror as "consistently dark, unsettling, and frightening." Her most recent books are the Bram Stoker Award-nominated Malediction (Evil Jester Press) and Netherworld (JournalStone), and forthcoming is Zombie Apocalypse: Washington Deceased (Constable & Robinson). She lives in North Hollywood, California, and online at www.lisamorton.com.

Screamplays! Writing the Horror Film

Lisa Morton

Part 1

Your novel is due in a week, you've got a month of work left on it, and you wisely decide you need a break, so it's down to the mall to check out the latest big-budget shocker at the Cineplex, or to pick up the new no-budget cheesefest on DVD. You're halfway through this cinematic masterpiece when you think, *Cripes, my last grocery list was better written than this! That's it – I'm going to save the horror film industry by turning my genius to screenwriting (and conveniently make a ton of money in the process).*

All well and good, until you realize – you don't know anything about screenwriting. Well, hey, you've published 42 short stories, 5 novels, and some film reviews, so how hard can it be?

Unfortunately, screenwriting is as different from prose as, say, waxing a car is from painting a house; sure, both require similar hand motions and both are about making something that looks nice. However, they require radically different tools, and more different talents than you might realize.

Let's start with the nuts and bolts: No other form of creative writing is as rigidly formatted as screenwriting. Not only must the writer create a compelling story with a solid plot, interesting characters, and memorable images, but the writer must also possess the technical skills to put these into movie terms. Remember, as a screenwriter you're part of an entire movie team, a team that includes a director, actors, a cinematographer, set designers, sound designers, special effects wizards, and more. They'll all be using your script as their blueprint, and so you need to be able to speak their language. Words like "exterior", "interior", "fade", "dissolve", "cut", and "reveal" must become as natural to the screenwriter as rotting is to a corpse. The screenwriter needs to know how to break his story into small scenes, how to balance dialogue and description, and how to pace his action; he also needs to learn to be comfortable writing in present tense, since a screenplay written in past tense is guaranteed to be rejected by page 2.

So, does our hypothetical prose writer need to put everything else aside so s/he can go back to school for four years just to get a film degree? Hardly (although it wouldn't hurt...). The first step in a screenwriter's education is simply to watch a lot of movies, and most horror writers are inveterate movie buffs; for one thing, probably no other genre of literature is so intertwined with its cinematic equivalent as horror, where a hit movie can fuel a literary sub-genre for years. And many horror writers have probably done a fair amount of reading about movies, too, especially in this media-savvy age; our Joe/Jane Writer probably already possesses a fair knowledge of movie lingo.

So, what's the next step? It's probably obvious, but I'll say it anyway: If you're going to write scripts, you need to read them first. Get a hold of some scripts and study them. I know there are plenty available for free download on the Internet, but I'd avoid those – they tend to be typed up by fans, and are often based on the finished movie (what might be called a "continuity script" in the biz), rather than the other way around. And don't just buy a book that reproduces some scripts; again, these tend to be cleaned up for publication. You need the real thing; you need to see exactly how it looked when it was bought by a producer and studied by a cast and crew. Buy some from ebay; borrow 'em from friends. Whatever; just get yourself a few feature screenplays to examine, preferably from films you've seen. You'll be able to not only see the way the formatting of the screenplay works, you'll also be able to see how it translated to the finished product (and be warned - the results may leave you well horrified).

Now, you may be asking: What about writing books? There are hundreds out there on crafting screenplays, and a number are by respected gurus, like John Truby or Robert McKee. Well...while I don't want to say I think these books are completely useless, bear in mind that most are targeted towards people who simply don't know how to write *anything*. At all. They'll discuss things like creating characters and "story arcs" and plotting and genre. If I was going to recommend a single screenwriting book, it would probably be *Screenplay: The Foundations of Screenwriting* by Syd Field; it includes plenty of useful formatting and technical information as well as the more traditional writing instruction, and good cheap used copies are easy to find online.

The next question our aspiring screenwriter will probably ask is: To software or not to software? The answer to that question will depend on one thing: Do you want to be a professional screenwriter, or are you just messing around? If the answer is choice B, then stop reading now and go be happy. But chances are you want something you can actually shop around once it's finished, and so I'm afraid I have some bad news for you:

You need software. And it ain't cheap.

About a dozen years ago, producers started wanting their screenplays delivered on diskettes, and they were happy with something typed up in Microsoft Word; but then perhaps a decade back, an insidious little thing happened to the industry, a little thing made up of two words:

Final Draft.

The Final Draft screenplay software is now the accepted standard throughout the film business. Even though other programs have been better, they've all fallen by the wayside like Beta did to VHS. You don't necessarily need the most current version of Final Draft (which retails at a whopping $289.99), but be prepared to drop well over $100 even for a used older version. You might also consider something like Movie Magic Screenwriter, which retails for slightly less than Final

Draft ($249.99), and offers the ability to export in Final Draft format. These programs are available in either Windows or Mac formats.

The good news is that the software programs really will do a lot of the formatting work for you; they know just where to start dialogue, for example, and they'll automatically capitalize character names for you. They'll even put in scene number for you, although that's a bad idea unless you've had a producer ask for 'em.

Now, our writer has the basic knowledge and the tools they need to get started...and uh, how does that getting started part go, exactly?

This is the part where I get to create suspense, because you'll have to wait until the next instalment, when I'll discuss more of the actual mechanics of screenwriting, including dialogue, scene descriptions and act breaks.

Until then – go back and finish your novel!

Part 2

I've talked about the nuts and bolts of writing horror screenplays; this time we move on to the power tools. Get those chainsaws revved!

Screenplays (and, perhaps, all other forms of creative writing) are made up of two basic components: Description and dialogue. However, there are some pretty big differences between how you use these basic elements in screenplays and how you use them in novels (or short stories).

First off, let's look at description. You know what that is, right? It's all the stuff in a novel that would set the scene; it's where the author might really go nuts with similes and metaphors, just revelling in her/his own voice. You, as the author, will probably want to involve your reader as thoroughly as possible and may describe not just sights and sounds but smells, tastes, sensations, and historic background. Maybe you'll show off a little here, employing use of poetic language and letting a description go on over numerous paragraphs or even pages.

Do that in a screenplay and you're dead.

Bear in mind that a screenplay is a written blueprint for a movie; movies are meant to be seen and heard, not read. Craftsmanship in screenwriting consists in finding the *visual* equivalent to similes and metaphors.

For example: Let's say you've got a scene set in a graveyard. The dead will soon be rising in this particular necropolis, but you want to evoke some mood before that happens. In a novel, you might wax lyrical and describe the cemetery as "colder than the dead heart of the lover who just left", along with several more paragraphs of prize-winning prose.

Pretty, perhaps…but it won't translate to screen. In a screenplay, you might opt instead for a visual metaphor: A dead animal discovered near a grave, or a deceased tree that's rotted and split open, all described in a few brief, succinct lines.

"But," I hear you saying, "why can't I do *both*? Why can't I include visual metaphors for the eventual audience, but make it a great read for the people who might be considering whether to buy this script or not?"

If you're lucky enough to get your screenplay to someone who can seriously advance it – a producer, an agent, even a script analyst – then you need to be aware of several things: 1) Quite frankly, Hollywood people don't like to read; the first time they see so much as a simple metaphor in your scene description, their eyes are likely to glaze over in incomprehension and they'll slap your front cover down with a definitive "*Nope*"; 2) the producer or analyst will probably be looking at your script to see how it breaks down in terms of budget and time, and will skip over large chunks of your description on first reading anyway; 3) since you've written a horror script, said reader may just flip through to the first death or scare; and 4) did I mention that Hollywood people don't like to read?

Let's talk example here. See if you can recognize this excerpt, taken from the final draft of the screenplay for a phenomenally successful 1979 horror/science fiction film:

INT. AIR SHAFT

Dallas senses a movement...
Looks toward the Alien...
Dallas blasts.
Blasts again.
Then again.
Moves forward.
Comes to a large junction.
Stands...
Looks around...

(From Walter Hill and David Giler's June, 1978 draft of
ALIEN)

No finely detailed prose there, right? No breath-taking metaphors, no poetry. Just get-the-job-done bare bones description.

While I don't completely advocate making your description quite *that* terse, I think it does serve well to illustrate how stripped down action should be in your script.

Speaking of action...let's say you're writing a big fist fight scene, or a car chase, or a werewolf transformation. How much description should you include in a scene like that? How much will your special effects wizard need to know, or your stunt choreographer?

You're probably best off erring on the side of under-describing. If it's important to your plot later on that the hero threw a *right* jab, then note that; if the antagonist's car crashes during the chase, certainly you'll mention that. But you don't need to describe every swing, kick, turn or wiggling whisker. You may even run the risk of describing something that's incredibly expensive (unbeknownst to you). Keeping it simpler is less risky.

Now, here's a perpetually tricky one: What about camera movement? Should you include none, some, or tons?

Most screenwriting gurus will tell you absolutely none...but my own experience has been that most producers actually will *want* you to put some in (they may even give you very concrete suggestions for a second draft). So my answer is this: Indicate camera movements sparingly, just enough to show that you know what they are. You're probably safe writing in a tracking movement, or a pull-back-to-reveal; but don't indicate very complex camera movements, and don't do it on every page. The only exception to this, of course, would be if you're also directing the script yourself (in which case I highly recommend that you look at any early screenplay by George Romero – they may run 300 pages for a two-hour film, but they break down *every shot* on paper!).

Dialogue in a screenplay is probably easier for a fiction writer than description, because dialogue is actually fairly similar in novels and screenplays. If you can write decent dialogue in prose form, you can probably do pretty well in a screenplay. Chances are you haven't given a character in your book a two-page monologue, and you're not going to do that in a script, either. Just as in a novel, you probably shouldn't overdo things like dialect or spelling out accents.

Explaining your plot through dialogue can become trickier in a screenplay than in a novel. In a book, you might reveal key clues through scene description or a character's interior monologue; however, in a screenplay you don't have the luxury of the printed page (and see the David Lynch screenplay of DUNE for an example of why interior dialogue doesn't always work on film!). It's easy to end up with some of those awful "Here's what's happening" expository dialogue passages if you're not careful. If your plot is very complex, you'll need to either simplify it for film, or find some way to convey information visually. One of the best examples of visual information is found in Ted Tally's magnificent adaptation of Thomas Harris's THE SILENCE OF THE LAMBS: In the book, Clarice has a long interior monologue as she examines Frederica Bimmel's room and slowly pieces together the dead girl's connection with Buffalo Bill. With the option for interior monologue removed, the screenwriter could have given us a lengthy conversation between Clarice and Frederica's father...but instead he opted for a quick, silent scene in which Clarice found photographs of the poor victim apparently modelling for her killer. It was faster and more visually interesting than a dialogue sequence would have been.

The last thing to know about dialogue and description is how to mix and match in a screenplay. Nothing will get a producer to throw a script into the "Pass" pile faster than flipping through it and seeing two or more solid pages of description or dialogue. One good rule of thumb is to simply never have an individual scene that goes longer than two or so pages; an ideal screenplay would probably have no scene that's longer than one page, and even scenes that are only a few lines of description are fine. I once had a script with a dialogue passage between several characters that went on for three pages; I thought all the dialogue was necessary, so I actually faked cutting up the scene by simply having the characters moving through various rooms while they conversed (and each room constituted a new scene description). A cheat, but it worked.

Now you know how to use the power tools on those nuts and bolts – you studied some scripts, you've bought the software, you've got some idea of how to make dialogue and description work, and you're ready to start writing…or are you?

In the next article we'll talk about scenes, length, and a few of the other things you need to know to become the next William Peter Blatty. Because goodness knows we could use a few more of those, couldn't we?

You can read parts three and four of Lisa Morton's screamplays at *www.lisamorton.com/screamplays3.htm*

2013 was a brilliant year for author / director / editor Dean M Drinkel. First up, was the 'Tres Librorum Prohibitorum' series of horror anthologies for Western Legends Publishing: The Demonologica Biblica was published in March, garnering rave reviews; The Bestiarum Vocabulum was released late fall.

For Static Movement, Dean has compiled / edited Cities of Death (May), which will be followed by Demonology - mid 2014.

2014 also sees the sequel to the 2011 smash Phobophobia entitled Phobophobias, by Dark Continents Publishing.

DCP also published Dean's own short collection of stories Within A Forest Dark.

Dean contributed stories to the Horror Society's Best Of anthology and Fear The Reaper (Crystal Lake Publishing).

The Alchemy Press will publish Dean's anthology 'Kneeling In the Silver Light: Stories From The Great War' during the summer of 2014.

Any spare time Dean has left is spent securing funding for his short film scripts Bright Yellow Gun and Splinter (which won the 'Best Action Screenplay' at the respective Monaco International Film Festivals of 2012 and 2013) and on his horror screenplay set in Paris entitled The House Of The Flowers.

More about Dean can be found at: http://deanmdrinkelauthor.blogspot.co.uk/ or Issue #331 of Fangoria magazine.

Screenplay Writing: The First Cut Is the Deepest

Dean M Drinkel

Right, before we go any further, let's just set our stall: when it comes to writing screenplays, shoot any kind of writing actually, people don't know shit about what they're talking about.

Controversial.

Yes, they might tell you that they do, that they won this award or that award; that the film made from their original script made a billion dollars at the box-office; that so-and-so actor or actress had never read anything like it before and the moment that it landed on their doormat they just knew they had to make it.

What a load of bullcrap.

And you know what's worse – I know even less than they do.

Now, I'm not going to give you any advice or assistance, I'm sure you don't need me to do that – after all, no doubt you've got the next hottest screenplay either right in front of you, over there on that shelf, on your laptop / pc or even tucked away in the drawer alongside that great novel, collection of short stories or even (god forbid) poems that you've written – so fair play to you, I'll tip my hat in your direction, you obviously don't need me, so I'll bid you farewell – I'll join you in the pub later.

Oh you're still here, even still reading? Cool – perhaps Facebook or Twitter aren't loading right now, has your Broadband run out– you're sticking around?

No worries then, let's chat you and I, we've both got time to kill after all. Shouldn't we be writing? I mean that script isn't going to write itself is it? Have you dusted the breadcrumbs off, wiped that wet coffee ring off the cover? Good, let's procrastinate some more...

It's funny that earlier today, as I was planning this piece for Joe (and what a great honour it was to be asked, someone else must have been busy – though if you haven't already then you should check out Crystal Lake's brilliant anthology *Fear The Reaper,* of which I contributed a story and probably made a right royal pain in the ass of myself by doing so), I had the idea for a new script – which in itself is handy because as I'm writing this it's only about six weeks until I travel down to the South of France for the annual drinkandscrewfest which is commonly known as the Cannes Film Festival. It's called *Milou* which is about an Englishman who visits Paris to teach people how to write whilst he's got he has his own writer's block on his book *Wild Vanilla* – life imitating art, love it.

Cannes. Two weeks in the sun.

Let's digress for a moment. I've been lucky to get down there for a couple of years now and every time has been a right blast – I thoroughly recommend it to anyone who gets the chance – just make sure you bring plenty of cash – take it from me, you'll need it!!! Anyway, anyway, I've also had a couple of short films screen there too, films that I've written and directed – so let's talk about them as no doubt I have to be professional about all this.

The first was very loosely based upon the E.A. Poe story, *The Imp of the Perverse.* We shot this in an old squat in Vauxhall, London. Downstairs was a vegan restaurant, upstairs there were a number of rooms for 'hire' with all sorts of mayhem going on – one time the local druids were chanting and dancing, an elderly man walked in whilst we were rehearsing and asked, "Is this the music?" before doing an about turn and marching off.

At that time I had been busy writing / directing in the theatre but really wanted to make a film. So one weekend, I knocked up a script (see how easy it can be if you put your mind to it?), grabbed some actors and went off to make this film. A week or so later, I looked at all the footage and tried to make sense of the story but eventually all good things came together, I threw out the original script, worked with the editor on what we had, added some strange effects and music and to our honest amazement, we had quite a polished short film. A month or so later we went down to Cannes, had a few drinks, went to a few parties, got the train back to Paris and then went... damn, wonder how the film went?

Oddly, worse was to come. We shot a very odd film called *Cenobite* (yes, my work is heavily influenced by Clive Barker) which was chock-full of very eerie sequences and was actually quite 'chilling' – we entered that into the New York Horror Film Festival. Now, anyone that knows me knows I bloody hate flying, but that was the only way I was going to get there. So I hear the film is screening, cool. I book a flight and cheap hotel in NYC – get an early morning flight from Heathrow as I'm only planning on being there a couple of days. I land in JFK having read several books on the journey over (as well as having more than a few drinks – I really don't like flying did I say?) when I get accosted by a seven foot Immigration Officer who demanded that

I strip almost butt-naked in front of him and the other passengers whilst telling me he absolutely loves horror movies – problem is his whole term of reference is Boris Karloff and "that Dracula guy".

After bending over and taking one for Queen & Country, he pats me on the rump and sends me on my way. Probably because of this experience, I become totally disorientated and end up going on the booze for four days – I met up with an old artist friend of mine who I hadn't seen for a number of years so we get proper on it, so much so that we went to Soho House and I ended up buying a shot for everyone in the damn place – and guess what? On the plane back – I realised I missed my film again!

After these two experiences, I promised myself to stay a bit more sober – but I'm a writer and that didn't quite work. I wrote / directed a short film entitled *Sete* which, if you don't know, is Italian for 'bitten'. This was a two hander, set in that same house in Vauxhall, between two very talented actors – it was a very tongue in cheek vampire film which we shot at normal speed but then slowed it right down to make it look 'creepy'. There was a proper script and everything, ha ha – we entered that one into Cannes too. I almost co-directed this with a seven year old French lad that we found wandering around the squat who just kept shouting "Accctiiiioooonnn", until his mother appeared an hour or so later thinking that we were the hired entertainers. Clowns? Perhaps she had a point.

Next up was a film called *Midnight Wired*. This was just a directing gig for me, working from a script written by a very talented actress. We had some brilliant locations all over London including nightclubs, saunas, strip joints, college laboratories etc. It wasn't our fault that when we did a lot of the exterior stuff, England were playing a major rugby match only a stone's throw away and that on the weekend shoot, both the lead actor and myself went out and got absolutely plastered after the first day. We didn't get any sleep but did return (almost sober) for the next call and probably did some of our best work.

We had such a blast editing it on a Mac – but it did go right to the wire (see what I did there?) and we didn't know whether we'd get it finished in time, but by God we did. The film was shot in colour but we screened it in B&W which made it very look very atmospheric, even if none of us had a fucking clue what it was about – including the writer / actress. I watched it the other day – some of it is really good, I do have a soft spot for this one.

After this I went back to directing my own stuff. We had been staging a number of plays about the mysterious Crump family – based a little bit I guess on Fred and Rose West but with plenty of humour mixed in. The plays had been quite successful, so we decided to shoot one of the easier stories and make a film called *The Crumps* (natch).

I think thus far this is my favourite film because it's just so anarchic – all three of the actors really got the vibe and deep into their particular characters, which is definitely captured on camera. When it was cut / edited / finished, I remember screening it for my father who sat there, looked at the tv, then at me, then back at the screen.

"Dean, what the fuck was all that about?" he asked, a very perplexed look upon his face.

Which was probably the best thing anyone has ever said about my work, no, I tell a lie, what was that review someone wrote of one of my short stories not so long ago? Oh yes: "That was the most disturbing descriptions of semen I have ever read". High praise indeed.

What was even better for me was that I was recently able to bring my beloved characters back to life, albeit in a new medium, when they appeared in a short story I wrote for Western Legends' anthology *The Unnatural Tales Of The Jackalope.*

I fancied a go at animation so we followed up *The Crumps* with *East Of The Son, West Of The Moon* – this was a heartbreaking tale of a boy haunted by a moon-like-creature on the eve of his grandfather's funeral. It was a very poignant piece and I'll be forever grateful to the actors who did the voices (Ed Ward, Lainey Shaw and Graham Townsend) and Justin Miles for the animation. It did go down a storm.

Finally (for now) was a short called *Ruby*. This was based upon another play that I'd staged in London, at the Cockpit Theatre. It had been so well received that lots of people wondered if I would make it into a film, so why disappoint? I got some money, we spent a couple of weekends up in a church in Worcestershire (fine, except that the locals thought we were filming *Midsomer Murders* and kept asking us where John Nettles was) and in a 'prison cell' in London. This was a restrained piece and the version we screen is quite a short, tight cut, but there is so much additional footage that we are currently investigating releasing a redux / extended version – even my scenes (I play a policeman) might survive the knife this time (you see what I did there – i.e. check the title of this piece).

I promise that one of these days we'll put all these films up on our website (*www.ellupofilms.com*) or at the very least on YouTube. They do deserve a bigger audience and they actually aren't that bad – even *Midnight Wired*. They were made with honesty, care and attention.

So, I did say you had come to the wrong place if you were looking or advice – oh hang on, I'm having a brainwave... if you don't know, I was runner up for the *Sir Peter Ustinov Screenwriting Award* (which is given out at the prestigious International Emmy Award Ceremony) for my feature script *Ghosts,* and then in both 2012 and 2013 I won 'Best Action Screenplay' at the Monaco International Film Festival for my scripts *Bright Yellow Gun* and *Splinter,* so I must know something about what I'm talking about, right?

Wrong.

Didn't you take any notice of what I said earlier? No? I'll recap for you then, after all, you're only the writer.

When it comes to writing a screenplay that is successful, no-one knows shit. Most of the time, it's just down to pure luck, no matter how much blood, sweat or tears has gone into it. Sure, like me, you've probably read a couple of "How to write a screenplay" textbooks and yes, they're good at telling you how to format (but even then there's no set hard and fast rules) and yes, they might tell you about different structures that work... but for me, all that matters is you are honest in what you write – write what you want to write. Sod structure. Sod format. Write. Write. Write. When you're satisfied that you've got the story you want to tell written down on paper, *then* you can worry about how it looks and what to do when it's ready to send out.

But hey, that's for someone else to wax lyrical about... me? I've got to have a drink... I mean write that screenplay I was telling you about... there's only so many cats you can look at on Facebook...

... good luck with your screenplay.

You're going to need it.

PS – See you in the Petit Majestic in Cannes – mine's a Kronenburg if you're buying....

May I Update? (6 June, 2014)

Wow – that was a blast. Ten days of pure mayhem and boy, so much drink was drunk. I even lost my Karaoke virginity. The French really do love me – in fact, after a couple of bottles of wine *everybody* loved me – that's how I see it anyway. I think there are some photos somewhere; look for the red Englishman with the orange coat, straw hat, blue shorts and purple shoes – colour co-ordination isn't my strongpoint, I will admit.

Forget that for the moment, the question on your lips is – how did I get on? Once I remembered what I had planned to do, the first thing I did every day (after waking up obviously and making sure I still had ten fingers, ten toes and that all my faculties were in place) was sit out on the balcony and get sun-burnt – NO! – have a bowl of hot chocolate, a croissant with jam and wrote (as well as trying to get through the previous night's hangover!). I even bought a new pad, two pens (one red, one black) and two pairs of sunglasses for that very task! Ten pages of pure brilliance was being created on a daily basis so by the time I came back to London I had a completed screenplay, albeit Draft One, of approximately 140 pages – something that can be knocked into shape pretty quickly. *Milou* had been but a dream three weeks ago but now it was a reality. Something... sorry, *someone* inspired me so the words flowed easily – thank you Milou (you know who you are!).

What I also did for the fun of it was come up with a dream cast of whom I imagined playing my characters and realised that a lot of them I bloody well know personally; a heady mix of both French and English actors. Most of them I think would probably jump at the chance of being involved in this amazing film as well! This really could work, I told myself. I'm onto a real winner here if I can keep myself out of the pub for at least a couple of days a week I'm sure.

Even though my plan is to direct it myself, I met up with some well-known French and Belgian directors (yes, they do exist), spoke to them about the story, and the feedback I got was very, very, positive. On the train back to London I certainly had a smile on my face, this could really happen. There are even a few producers both side of the Channel that are starting to ask questions about budgets, cast, locations. It's getting a life of its own. Real momentum. Buzzing.

What happens now then? Writing this piece has inspired me to start a 'film-diary' which will be called 'From Cannes to Can: Let's get this damn movie made can we?' (or something like that, I'll give it some more thought after a couple of pints later tonight) and I'll be providing regular updates on how the project is coming along – probably on my blog *or* even in book form – if I can find a kind enough publisher, hint hint!

My ultimate aim for the script and then finished film is to be screened at Cannes next year or, if too soon (yep these things can take time I know, I know, let's not get too excited just in case) then definitely the festival after! There are a couple of competitions I'll probably enter the script into, as winning awards does help with funding and attracting 'talent'.

Right, I'm taking up too much room in this book as it is and the pretty barmaid is just pouring me a cider so I'd better make a run for it.

But listen, if we are successful, I certainly know where this journey started – with you, dear reader – so thank you, raise a glass to me next time you're down at the pub – and always remember: anything is possible!

I'll make sure I thank you all when I read the Palme d'or and a massive great deanhug to my little babymilou – you really are special...

With a week or two since Cannes then, what's my advice to you gentle reader and wannabe screenplay writer – well, *you* can write that screenplay. It isn't difficult and doesn't have to be daunting. Set yourself a daily task and then stick to it, no more, no less.

Remember for your first draft you can be as bold and beautiful as you want – why limit your imagination? It's as you redraft / draft / redraft that you can start thinking about the restraints / constraints that may be set on you when you start meeting with producers / directors / actors and as your amazing script starts to move from development to pre-production to production. And with that in mind, the biggest piece of advice I can give a screenwriter is this: watch as many films as you can and be where films are seen – go to the festivals, join organisations (Writers' Guild etc.) and get your name out there! Sadly no-one is just going to knock at your door with a bag full of cash...oh, hang on... damn doorbell's ringing...

Simon Marshall-Jones (aka The Tattooed Head) is editor/publisher at award-nominated Spectral Press, a writer, reviewer, columnist and blogger: a book lover, of course, but also likes French cheeses rather too much, as well as wine, port and rum, a collector of vintage car and motorcycle magazines, enjoys scale-model figure making in his spare time and is heavily covered in tattoos but still has nowhere near enough yet.

Publishing

Simon Marshall-Jones

So, you've been a fan of horror/sci-fi/fantasy/literary/whatever fiction from the very moment you learnt to read, and you have avidly devoured just about every book you've managed to get your hands on, or you have begged, stole or borrowed those tomes you missed or which are now out of print. Over all the years, each has given you pleasure to one degree or another, filling your imagination with wonders which you will never experience in real life. You have your favourite authors, and your bookshelves are lined with those signed first editions of their work. But, for some reason, this still isn't enough – there must be something more you could do to become even more involved.

Indeed, some go on to dive into the heady world of fandom, while others sit down in front of a computer and start writing their first story. Still others compile semi-regular 'zines, devoted either to their particular scene or a favourite author. And others, like myself, decide to go beyond the publishing of 'zines and journey into the industry itself, in my case the owner/editor/publisher of an independent imprint called Spectral Press.

So, why did I become a publisher? Two reasons, mostly: a) I'd already had some limited experience of publishing back in the early nineties, when I ran a music fanzine called Fractured, so more or less knew what was involved, and b) I'd already tried my hand at writing but was always left dissatisfied with my efforts. That's not to say I wasn't any good at it, it just didn't fulfil me as I had hoped. So, in my infinite wisdom, I deemed the next best thing would be to ask others to write for me and publish them.

So, what prompted me to take the plunge? It was a visit to my first ever convention, FantasyCon, back in 2010. I was a book reviewer at the time, and I was handed a couple of chapbooks by publisher Nick Royle to review, and as I read them back at home, I realised what a perfect platform the format was to showcase and promote an author's work. In the next few weeks, the amorphous matter swirling around in my head finally coalesced into the idea of Spectral Press, which then released its first chapbook, *What They Hear in the Dark* by Gary McMahon, in January 2011. Having that little book in my hands was one of the proudest moments of my life.

Okay, things had moved on ever so slightly since my fanzine-editing days – for instance, back then soliciting submissions was done by either advertising in a magazine, or sending letters to people you thought might be interested in contributing. Then those who were willing would send you something by return of post –

which also meant that any edits needed would be marked up on the actual manuscript, sent off to the writer for his perusal and then sent back with the corrections. As to the layouts, they were done physically and posted off, rather than mocking them up on computer and sending the files to the printer. You also had to be aware of page order when laying the sheets out: in other words, on the first A3 sheet you had to put your A4 page 1 on the right-hand side and the last page on the left, then to ensure continuity you pasted page 2 on the left and the penultimate page on the right on another sheet, and so on until the whole thing had been completed. Incredibly time-consuming, as you can imagine and, on occasions, very frustrating if you'd realised you'd got it wrong. This is probably one reason why I no longer possess any hair. Nowadays, though, publishing is much easier in the Digital Age. An article can be sent, edited, sent back and resubmitted in a single day, all without moving from the house. The same goes for graphic design work, artwork commissions, ordering, invoicing, and paying.

BUT (there's always a *but* somewhere along the line, isn't there?) – if you *do* want to become a publisher, let it be stated here and now that it's a lot of hard work, despite the advances of technology and computers. When I set up Spectral three years ago, I was regularly spending fourteen hour days in front of the computer, sending out emails, soliciting submissions, handling enquiries, sourcing suppliers, finding printing companies, publicising the imprint, promoting individual books, etc., etc., all essential aspects of the job. And remember, there's just one of me, albeit with a little help from the wife here and there. I managed it, but I was often exhausted at the end of the day.

Luckily, all the hard work paid off, as the first publication did well, and established the name very firmly in the minds of potential customers. But here's where things can go wrong: if you hit upon a successful idea, or you have a successful product, there's always the temptation to rush more product out as quickly as possible to capitalise on it. Bad idea. Building a business up slowly is the secret here – start off small and gradually add things when you deem it the right time. In my case, I started with chapbooks in the first year, then added novellas and an anthology in the second, and in year three expanded Spectral's remit with the first single-author collection and the launch of a non-fiction offshoot, Spectral Screen. The point is, don't rush – that way lie the seeds of failure.

It's an extremely rewarding project, conversely it can also be incredibly frustrating and annoying. Timetables don't always get strictly adhered to, because circumstances beyond anyone's immediate control can have serious knock-on effects. Sometimes there are printer's errors, or mistakes made in compiling files, or things inadvertently get wiped off the hard-disc (which, luckily, hasn't happened yet), or illness gets in the way, or life does. For instance, we moved recently – and I can't tell you just how much disruption it caused in the smooth running of things. Everything's back on track now, thankfully, but it took a bit longer than expected or wanted. Major publishing companies also experience these glitches as well, but they have the manpower to cover them - when you are the only one responsible for doing everything, those problems become magnified.

On the positive side of the balance sheet, there can be nothing better than when your work and ethos are recognised by not just your customers, but also by the very people whose writing you are promoting. It's great when people get it, when the reviews are positive, and the critics recognise what it is you are trying to do. It's even better when a book or two is nominated for an award, or a story is reprinted in an annual year's best anthology, or, as happened last year to Spectral, one of the novellas you published wins one of those awards. It's at that moment you realise that every shred of hard work you've invested into the project, all the long hours, along with the occasional disappointment, was more than worthwhile.

It's safe to say that one will never become a millionaire by being an independent publisher but, in all honesty (and with hand on heart), it isn't about making money – for me, it's about giving back to the scene/genre what it has given to me, allied to an ethos of giving the customer what they want as well as value for money. We may be an irrevocably earthbound species, but literature of all sorts has transported me to all manner of distant worlds, given me delicious shivers in the safety of my own comfortable abode, and shown me vistas impossible on this planet of ours. And there are so many great writers out there who deserve more recognition than they presently get, and so I am doing my part to get their names out there, in however limited a manner. The bottom line, when all else is said, is that despite all the trials and tribulations I absolutely love what I do. And that is all anyone can ask of their job.

Charles Day is the Horror Writer Association's Mentor Program Chairperson, Co-Chair for the NY/LI Chapter, and a member of the HWA Library committee. He is also a member of the New England Horror Writers Association, the American Library Association, and the Young Adult Library Services Association.

He is also the Bram Stoker Award® nominated author of YA series,' The Legend of the Pumpkin Thief'. He's also published his first adult novel Deep Within (Alter Press,) and the first book in his Adventures of Kyle McGerrt trilogy, a YA western heroic fantasy, 'The Hunt for the Ghoulish Bartender' (Blood Bound Books.)

His forthcoming publications and projects in development for 2014 include his first co-authored novel with Mark Taylor, 'Redemption' (April, 2014) a comic book series based on 'The Adventures of Kyle McGerrt' trilogy, 'The Legend of the Pumpkin Thief' comics series, and his first middle-grade series, 'The Underdwellers', and his third YA novel, 'Immortal Family'.

On the publishing business side of things, Charles is co-owner with Taylor Grant at Grant-Day Media Inc. with corporate offices in Hollywood, and New York, which houses the successful imprints Evil Jester Press, Evil Jester Comics, and Hidden Thoughts Press (Mental Wellness Collections,)

He's also an artist and illustrator who's passionate about creating the many characters he's brought to life in his published, or soon to be published works. You can find out more about his upcoming writing projects, check out his illustrations and art, or find out what he's cooking up next with that evil dude-in-the-box, the Evil Jester, by visiting his Facebook page or blog:

http://charlesdayfictionwriter.blogspot.com/
or www.facebook.com/charles.day.92

I Want to be a Small Press Publisher Too

Charles Day

So, you're considering starting your own publishing company. A small press designed to cater to novels, novellas, anthologies, and perhaps short story collections by single authors? You've seen small presses popping up all over the social media venues and you figure, cool, I can do this too. *I can start my own press.*

Well, you can. It's easy to start a small press. You don't need to run an office from inside a building, or rent space in some commercial storefront; you can set up your own virtual publishing company right in your kitchen if you like. Me, although I have an office downstairs at home, I find I spend most of my time with the evil Jester at our dining room table. We spread out all our projects, to do lists, and submission manuscripts, mail packaging, take out laptops to open our database full of authors, close to 57 already, and we get down to performing the duties of a publisher.

Are you going to be able to quit your day job, hopeful you'll get rich? Not likely. Of course there are some success stories, but the majority of us small press publishers are more involved out of passion than making a million dollars. Why, it's just because unless you can set your publishing company up like the major commercial publishers with print runs and thousands and thousands of dollars to take out ads on TV and in the major magazines throughout the country, and be able to pay professional advances to the big authors or celebrities, you'll more than likely find that your income will be lower than what you make at your full time job.

Now I'm certainly not out to discourage anyone who wants to start a small press. Bottom line is the more you put into the company you want to build the better chances you'll have of becoming a success. I'm working extra hard at trying to find ways to improve sales, build capital, get better promo, and of course search for the next bestseller. And that is the most important. If you happen to stumble upon the next best seller, you can do exceptionally well with profits for both you and the author, but again this is not easy to obtain, unlike the major publishing houses who can take a good book and produce ample sales with investing in capital. We've had a sleuth of great authors published. From Joe McKinney, Jonathan Maberry, David Morell, Peter Straub, Jack Ketchum, William F. Nolan, David Pierce, Eric Red, Jeff Strand, and so, so many other authors who've gone on to become mid-list or higher authors.

And above all, always remember, you can have all the great authors in the world with your publishing company, but the key to returning customers are carefully selected stories that resonate with your readers and quality. Making sure your books are sent through a rigorous editorial process, and that you take the time and invest the money in book covers and careful proofreading and formatting before bringing your titles to publication.

That said, I will share that Evil Jester Press, Evil Jester Comics, and Hidden Thoughts Press (non-fiction) have all seen both great and not so great months. And I was there. I tried to run the company full time, leaving a cushy job after being employed with a steady paycheck for over 25 years, only to find out that although I made great strides in building the business and retaining more staff (currently at around 10 dedicated authors, comic script writers, editors, executive staff, and an art director and book formatter), I still needed to go back to having a steady paycheck every other week.

One other thing to keep in mind when getting your small business off the ground, is the little things that can help you save money, like checking out the tax issues in your own country, registering for an EIN number if you're located outside the US, so you don't lose 30% to Amazon or Smashwords etc. Making sure you divide up the royalty profits fairly so that the publishing house retains a percentage comfortable for reinvesting into your business for use with marketing, promo, taking out ads, etc. You will also want to build up a list of reviewers, bloggers and other contacts for the future. And don't forget, it's all about exposure and getting your business noticed, so the best place to start would of course be an awesome name and a logo.

So, I say if you want to run a small press, go for it. Go for your dreams. Take what inspires you and run with it, especially if you're passionate about what you do. Just bear in mind that owning a small publishing company is a ton of work, hundreds of hours a month that will be needed to produce some profit. You'll need to do the math and decide if you can solely do this at home or as a second income to a more secure day job. Either way, I wish you the very best at it.

Award-winning author and graduate of Northwestern University, Robert W. Walker created his highly acclaimed Instinct and Edge Series between 1982 and 2005. Rob since then has penned his award-winning historical series featuring Inspector Alastair Ransom with 'City for Ransom' (2006), 'Shadows in the White City' (2007), and 'City of the Absent' (2008), and most recently placed Ransom on board the Titanic in a hybrid historical/science fiction epic entitled 'Titanic 2012 – Curse of RMS Titanic'. Robert's next title, 'Dead On', a PI revenge tale and a noir set in modern day Atlanta. More recently 'Bismarck 2013', an historical horror title, 'The Edge of Instinct', the 12th Instinct Series, and a short story collection entitled 'Thriller Party of 8 – the One that Got Away'. Rob's historical suspense 'Children of Salem', while an historical romance and suspense novel, exposes the violent nature of mankind via the politics of witchcraft in grim 1692 New England, a title that some say only Robert Walker could craft— romance amid the infamous witch trials. Robert currently resides in Charleston, West Virginia with his wife, children, pets, all somehow normal. For more on Rob's published works, see www.RobertWalkerbooks.com, www.HarperCollins.com and www.amazon.com/kindle books. He maintains a presence on Facebook and Twitter as well.

Weighing Up Traditional Publishing & eBook Publishing

Robert W. Walker

In any non-traditional publishing as in eBook publication, there is no such thing as 'an advance against royalties'. In Traditional Publishing as we know, now often termed DTB's by our younger generations, ie. Dead Tree Books, the 'advance' has always been there. This is a significant difference. For the older generation, my generation, the first phrase that comes to mind for the author is 'an advance against royalties' and what this means is the author gets a lump sum 'loan payment' to start work on the process of crafting a book or novel. However, in eBook non-traditional publishing wherein everything is lower case, there are NO advances. In fact, in 'non-publishing' as some like to call it, there are a lot of '*no's*' to the traditional model.

However, before we get too far afield, an advance against a royalty of $100, 000 is a thing of beauty on the surface. No doubt about that. A writer can rejoice. However if it is for four books to be written over four years, that's pretty much slave wages or $25,000 a year, which if one is independently wealthy makes for nice pen money. Not so with most people who are attempting to make a living (no joke) at writing.

To the midlist author who wins this arrangement or spin of the publishing wheel, 25,000 a year does not go far. It's about minimum wage if that. Whereas in eBook publishing, there are NO advances and no paying back of that 25,000 a year either. On the one hand, your publisher grants you a 'loan' to be paid back via your royalties (if royalties even occur); on the other hand, every cent of an advance must be paid back to the publisher via your royalties, and until that hundred thousand is worked off by your royalties (if at all) you see no additional funds from royalties. Should your sales be too low to return that advance to your publisher, you are both left with a bad business loan, and your name or reputation as a writer is mud thereafter.

The above is one area where traditional and non-traditional publishing go in very different directions. But there are far more differences for the writer as businessman as well. Below are some of the glaring differences other than no advances.

Traditional Publishing
They contract for all rights including eBook
Your royalty rate for paper is 10 percent/12 hardcover
Chance of having returns is 100% & remainders too
Your chance of getting a rejection letter 90 to 100%
Prestige of publishing with 1 of the big six...
Professional, topnotch editorial help at no charge
* Author pockets 10-12% of a $25 book
9 months to 2 yrs. from acceptance final MS till pub date
Publisher provides overworked PR person
Publisher determines everything on cover
Publisher writes copy/description of book
Publisher can/often does change title
Publisher determines price of book
Publisher dictates/curtails length of book
Publisher's royalty statement routinely confusing
Publisher's royalty statement not seen for 6-12 months
Royalty statement/payment confusing 90% of the time

Publisher may/may not find review outlets

EBook Publishing
Author pockets 70% of 2.99/3.99
Editorial help at your expense
Little to no 'prestige'/much criticism
No rejection letters
So few returns, negligible/no remainders
Your royalty rate is 70 percent
You are in a partnership with Kindle/other
Author publishes when s/he wishes
You seek out reviewers
Payout arrangement clear
EBook statement daily report
EBook gives clear daily sales report
Author determines length
Author determine price
Author determines title
Author writes copy/description
Author decides all cover art matters
You are PR or you hire PR

* This means an author makes more on each $2.99 eBook than each $25 traditional book.

Allow me to add some other hard-won lessons regarding the above points. Publisher determines design matters such as single or multiple volumes or a series, and in eBook publishing, the author has control over such issues as series, stand-alone, or three volumes in one.

These differences are due in large part to the medium. The medium is the message. What I can add is that with traditional publishing comes 'traditional' notions of prestige, as in 'real book publication' grants a writer a certain prestige among readers, critics, and other writers. However, a new attitude is being seen, an attitude among readers and writers that says the text is of tantamount importance, not the way a book is delivered. While this notion and eBook publishing have been around now for approximately thirty to forty years, young people, new generations, are embracing it completely. The idea that a book delivered in sixty seconds on a Kindle reader is as viable a piece of writing as if it is delivered between the covers of a hardbound book—or can be. This is something of a radical shift not in publishing but in readers.

Many traditional publishers either do not get this or simply wish to fight for the old standards of 'proper' format and delivery of books. In the past and now, many people believe that a book showing up in hardcover is a better book, better vetted, better edited and certainly written better. However, we have all encountered hardbound books riddled with problems from grammar to concept. More and more, readers are learning about the struggle that goes on behind the writing of a novel, the research, the rewrites, the editing, vetting and more rewrites that go into the creation of an eBook by a writer, and while some eBooks display a lack of talent, nowadays more and more display genius 'outside the bun' or in this case 'outside the covers'. Never judge a book by its cover takes on a whole new meaning, despite the fact eBook cover graphics has spawned a whole new 'industry' as has eBook digital platform and editing services.

Publishing with a major traditional publisher certainly can win one respect and sometimes critical acclaim, neither of which are automatically going to increase sales, but awards and accolades are a wonderful thing. However, the drawbacks can be many for the author, not the least being a far smaller percentage (12% vs. 70%). Notably, traditional publishers, since the state-of-the-art Kindle device has skyrocketed in sales are suddenly insisting contractually that authors turn over their electronic rights to the publisher. Some authors have been savvy to maintain their eBook rights regardless. However, traditional publishers holding your eBook rights—especially the majors—as a rule will set your eBook price far too high to the detriment of eBook sales.

E-readers are savvy and will turn away in droves if an eBook is priced too high. Several of my books are saddled with this problem as the publisher set the price, while eBooks priced by me are selling a thousand books a month nowadays. In short, the e-reading public will seldom to never purchase an e-novel or e-book priced at the same or nearly the same as the paper or hardbound book. Not to mention that an author will always make more money putting his eBook rights to work on his own rather than through a publisher.

Working directly with Amazon.com, the author is basically given-at no charge-the opportunity to become a franchise. Most midlist authors are given no advertising budget, no coop monies, nothing as any ad dollars go for the stars alone. With Amazon/Kindle and other eBook publishers, every eBook an author places on digital platform gains instant distribution (distribution with traditional publishers presents both publisher and author with stripped, returned books, a nightmare in bookkeeping, and a sure path to remainders). Reading a royalty statement from a traditional publisher is always a guessing game; reading the daily 'ticker' on each eBook with your name on it is as easy as reading the stock market and about as addictive. Going back to EBook distribution. Distribution is advertising is distribution in the eBook world. It is entirely virtual and online. With Kindle ads going out on national TV and Kindles being used as props in major motion pictures, the author can only benefit more.

There are no doubt many other comparison points between traditional and non-traditional publishing, but you know what? Non-traditional modes of publication are getting to be part of the mainstream and hardly *non* anymore. Many authors are going the Indie Author/Publisher route as it makes perfect economic sense to do so. This is especially true for authors with large backlists of otherwise dead books known as out of prints. Already edited and vetted books that have seen returns, remainder days, used bookstore days—all of which pulls money from the pocket of authors. Now such lost titles are working for authors to the tune of thousands going back into the author's pocket.

I hope this little compare/contrast article has been of help to you personally if not professionally. Hope to see you on Facebook, twitter, and elsewhere online.

Chet Williamson has written in the field of horror and suspense since 1981. Among his novels are Second Chance, Hunters, Defenders of the Faith, Ash Wednesday, Reign, and Dreamthorp. Over a hundred of his short stories have appeared in such magazines as The New Yorker, Playboy, Esquire, The Magazine of Fantasy and Science Fiction, and many other magazines and anthologies. He has won the 2002 International Horror Guild Award, and has been shortlisted twice for the World Fantasy Award, six times for the Horror Writers Association's Stoker Award, and once for the Mystery Writers of America's Edgar Award. Nearly all of his works are available in eBook format at the Kindle Store and through Crossroad Press (http://macabreink.com/). A stage and film actor (his most recent appearance is in Joe R. Lansdale's film, Christmas With the Dead), he has recorded over 40 unabridged audiobooks, both of his own work and that of many other writers, available at www.audible.com. Follow him on Twitter (@chetwill) or at www.chetwilliamson.com.

Audiobooks: Your Words to Their Ears

Chet Williamson

Just as eBooks have completely transformed publishing, so too has modern technology transformed audiobooks. In ye olden days, if you wanted to hear a book read to you rather than read it yourself, you had to spend a large amount on a vast pile of cassette tapes (and later a vast stack of CDs), or take those cassettes and CDs out of the library. Then you had to hump that media around, changing cassettes or discs as you jogged or worked or drove in your car. It's a little known fact that more people died as the result of tape-changing related auto accidents than perished in the entire Boer War.

Then along came downloaded audio files, which you could magically slip into your iPod, iPhone, iPad, Blackberry, or Blueberry. The prices dropped, Audible.com took over the market, and audiobook sales surged. No longer did a book have to be on the New York Times bestseller list to be economically viable as an audiobook. Soon thousands of authors saw their books becoming audiobooks. And every other author wondered, as you may be now, how they could get in on the lucrative action.

In truth, it may not be all that lucrative. But when you consider that your book or books are already written, and that all you have to do is provide an e-copy to the prospective narrator or audiobook producer (*and possibly pay to have it produced, but we'll get to that*), it looks like whatever you make will be money that you didn't have before, and that's always nice, right? Well, maybe. It depends on how much money you have to put out initially.

Before I get into too much detail, let me tell you a bit about my own experience with audiobooks. Before becoming a writer (and if you haven't read my works, go over to the Kindle Store and check out my eBook backlist of titles originally published with Tor, Avon, Cemetery Dance, and others) I was, and still am, an actor, and have been a member of Actors' Equity Association, the professional stage actors' union, for many decades. One reason I became a writer was because I thought it would be fun to create a scenario in which I played *all* the roles instead of just one, including scenic designer and director.

David Niall Wilson, who resurrected my backlist through his Crossroad Press, was starting to produce audiobooks as well as eBooks, and I mentioned my acting experience, which also included film, video, and voiceover work. He offered me the chance to audition as narrator for my own work, and liked what he heard. As a result I've narrated over forty audiobooks. Along with five of my own, I've recorded works by Clive Barker (*Cabal*, and my favorite Barker story, *In the Hills, the Cities*), Joe Lansdale (*The Magic Wagon*) , Jack Ketchum (*The Woman*), John Skipp and Craig Spector (*The Light at the End*) , Irving Wallace, Michael Moorcock, and many more. I learned as I went along, and the first thing that any writer who desires an audiobook needs to consider is which of two ways you want to proceed.

The first is to be your own narrator. The second is to get outside help. But no matter which option you choose, the most efficient course is to produce your audiobook though Audiobook Creation Exchange (ACX) which will distribute your audiobook through Audible.com, Amazon, and iTunes. You could stop reading this right now and go to ACX.com, where you can get all your questions answered. But in short, there are two ways to produce your audiobook. You'll list the book as open for auditions, which means that prospective narrators will see it, record the sample text that you post with the audition, and send you sample auditions, which you'll then listen to and choose the narrator who you think will best do justice to your book. When you post that audition, however, you have to decide which way you want to go:

The first is to pay a one-time fee for production, which is usually figured on a PFH (Per Finished Hour) basis. $100 per hour is pretty much the bare minimum you can expect to pay. So if you have a book that takes ten hours to read, you'll be paying the producer $1000. Depending on your name recognition among audiobook listeners, it can take a long time to earn back that investment.

The second option is to find a producer/narrator (narrators often produce as well) willing to create your audiobook through a Royalty Share in which you, the writer, split your royalty 50/50 with the producer/narrator. You pay no money up front, but everything you make on the book is shared with the producer/narrator. Don't forget that ACX, as your retail distributor, takes a hefty percentage from every sale. That percentage has been changed recently (*increased* in ACX's favor, of course), and may be again, so I suggest you check the ACX website for up-to-date figures.

The difficulty with trying to find a narrator/producer (who I'm just going to call the producer from now on) to accept a royalty share deal is that if your work isn't very well known, it may take a long time for the producer to see any reasonable financial return. As the author, it's all gravy to you, but the producer has to prepare the book, record it, edit it in order to meet ACX's audio requirements, and submit it to ACX, all of which can take many days. On a royalty share, there's no up-front money for the producer, so don't be insulted or disappointed if only a few people (or none at all) audition. I've recorded works by writers who are quite well known in the horror field that have, over a long period of time, sold less than ten copies in audiobook format. Yes, you read that right. Ten. Less than. But at the same time, I've done audiobooks that have sold very well.

Now let's look at the option of being your own narrator/producer. There are folks out there who, for a large amount of money, will show you exactly how you can make big bucks narrating and producing audiobooks (including your own) with no previous voiceover or acting experience, regardless of what your voice sounds like. 'Tain't so. At first it sounds simple, particularly if you're the author. After all, who knows better what your characters should sound like than you? The problem is, can you express that with your voice? And would you expect a listener to listen to your voice for more than ten hours? *And* are you willing to expend the time, effort, and money to narrate yourself and do a professional job, as well as be your own editor and sound engineer?

Let's look at the physical requirements. You're going to need a microphone, and a good one, which should cost you at least $300. You'll also need a mic stand (I prefer to record standing, as it opens up my lungs and lets me talk longer without having to take a breath) and a pop filter so your P's, B's, and S's don't pop and hiss. You'll need a professional pair of over-the-ear closed headphones, *not* earbuds or any open headphone. You'll need a sturdy music stand to rest your reading materials on. And you'll have to have a Kindle, Nook, iPad, or other e-reader with a touch screen, unless you want to stop recording every time you turn a page because of paper rustling.

Do you plan to record directly into a computer? If you've got a PC, forget it. *Any* fan noise is too loud. Apple, sure. I'm not an Apple guy, so I use a dead quiet Tascam digital recorder, which costs about $300, and a hundred dollar pre-amp. Decent cables (I like Monster brand) will cost you another fifty bucks. Add to that a punch pedal that lets you edit on the fly.

Do you live in a city? Do you have extraneous noise from the outside? That good mic will pick it up. I live in the suburbs and work in a dead corner of my basement which is pretty well soundproofed. When I record, I turn off the heat in the winter and the A/C in the summer. When a really loud truck or motorcycle goes past, I have to stop and rerecord.

Does your stomach growl? If it does, the mic will record it, and you'll hear it, and so will any unfortunate listener. But the main enemy is your own mouth. The mouth is filled with saliva and that bothersome, always moving tongue, which pops and clicks at the most inopportune times. You have to learn to phrase, you have to learn to breathe correctly.

And I haven't even gotten into characters yet. The larger the cast, the more individual voices you have to create to differentiate each character. You'll find scenes which are dialogue-heavy, and in which lines pop back and forth between several different characters, and you have to make sure the listener knows exactly who is talking when.

And this brings us to preparation. You can't just read a book cold, even your own. You've got to go through it carefully, making notes about voices and personalities. You don't want to record nearly an entire book and find on the last page, "Rolf's German accent thickened even more as he raised the butcher knife," when you've been reading him as an American throughout. Pronunciation is important as well, particularly place names. You've got to do the research.

But even without prep time, most professional narrators find that they spend at least two hours to come up with one finished hour. For a ten-hour book, that's at least twenty hours, and that doesn't include final editing time (I don't do my own final edits – too tech oriented for me. If you want to, that's one more complex skill you have to master). I've found that I can satisfactorily turn out a finished hour and a half a day (that takes three hours to record) before my voice tires and concentration flags – when you narrate, you have to *always* be on, every second.

So if you're really considering doing your own narration (or, God help you, going into the business as a narrator of other people's work), go to ACX and see what their professional audio requirements are, and if you can live up to them. If you think you can, go for it. It's nice to get both the author and narrator share of the royalties.

But when that audiobook is finished, and ACX distributes it, it's up to you to promote it. Audible.com is fast becoming like the Kindle Store in terms of a vast wealth of material, much of it good, much of it not. In order to rise above that ocean of titles, you've got to self-promote (I'm *so* sick of that word). So go ahead, use Facebook, Twitter, your website, Pinterest, and the rest – just don't be obnoxious about it. And don't post it on *my* Facebook page, unless I've narrated it. I've got enough crap of my own to shill. So good luck – keep your prose clean and your voice clear. And *enunciate*.

Lawrence Santoro spent thirty years as a director, producer and actor in theater and television before devoting himself full-time to writing.

In 2001 his novella 'God Screamed and Screamed, Then I Ate Him' was nominated for a Bram Stoker Award. In 2002, his adaptation and audio production of Gene Wolfe's 'The Tree Is My Hat', was also Stoker-nominated. In 2003, his story "Catching" received Honorable Mention in Ellen Datlow's 17th Annual Year's Best Fantasy and Horror anthology. In the 20th, his novella, 'At Angels Sixteen', from the anthology A Dark and Deadly Valley, was similarly honored.

Larry's first novel, 'Just North of Nowhere', was published in 2007. A collection of his short fiction, 'Drink for the Thirst to Come', was published by Silverthought Press in December, 2011.

Since its inaugural show in January, 2012, Larry has hosted the weekly horror podcast, "Tales to Terrify", sister-show to the Hugo Award-winning StarShipSofa. In 2013, 'Tales to Terrify' was named Podcast of the Year by thewebsite, 'This Is Horror'.

In October, 2013, his story, 'Instructions on the Use of the M-57 Clacker' was published in 'Fear the Reaper' from Crystal Lake Publishing. His Lovecraftian tale, 'Jars', appeared that November in CANOPIC JARS: TALES OF MUMMIES AND MUMMIFICATION from Great Old Ones Publishing.

Larry lives in Chicago and is working on a new novel, 'A Mississippi Traveler, or Sam Clemens Tries the Water', as well as adding to a linked collection that spins off from his steampunk novella, "Lord Dickens's Declaration."

Stop by his blog:

http://blufftoninthedriftless.blogspot.com/ or listen weekly to *Tales to Terrify, http://talestoterrify.com/*

Writing Aloud

Lawrence Santoro

For me, reading my work aloud feeds the writing. Here's a story. It's mostly true.

I grew up being read to. My grandfather—called Pop-pop—my mother and my father, all read to me. I snuggled close to their wool, silk and flannelled bodies, breathed their personal scents—dentures, talcum, tobacco—closed my eyes, listened and made what I felt, breathed and heard into worlds. I loved those worlds.

We lived in a large house from the previous century. At night, the place squeaked, shuddered and cracked. By age six or seven I was already given to the joys of bedtime terror. Maybe Pop-pop's reading of Poe, Lovecraft and others inclined me in that direction, but I embraced our house's living noises, its dusty basement and attic smells and the dark old places that waited for me. I carried those senses and memories to bed with me.

Once upon a time, a cricket got into the wall between my room and the stairway. Mother, father and Pop-pop said, "Just a cricket."

Sure...

The noise was bigger than "just a cricket" and, if bigger, who knew how *much* bigger? His sound filled the wall, and if it was *that* big—and that was a big wall—what could this thing in my wall really be?

"A cricket?" A cricket that might eat its way into my room? Sure. One that could chew wires, swallow electricity, suck light from the bulbs, voices from the radio, cold from the refrigerator; it could make everything stop... Or maybe start a fire, burn the house—and us—in the middle of the night. Happened to *The Reading Rug Company* a block away, across the street from the cemetery on that summer night when I was four?

Of course it might.

"A cricket?"

Sure.

I was that kind of kid.

I told Hebhardt, Mahler and Johnny Keegan about the cricket. Each telling ramped up the apocalyptic possibilities. No one thought a cricket in the wall was scary but my buddies did like my "exaggerations," as my mother would have called them, about death-bringing crickets.

My friends knew it was a lie and they liked it. "And jeeze, anyway," said Missie and/or Trissie, the Talking Magpies (named for two cartoon birds we liked), "crickets are good, they bring luck," facts the Magpies knew because their father had been in Japan after the War.

Hold that thought about telling tales to your chums, and let me tell you about the playground at Third and Spring.

Summers where I lived, in Reading, Pennsylvania, you either hung out in the alley, you climbed to the Pagoda on Mount Penn where you ate sandwiches and looked down on Reading, or you went to Third and

Spring playground and the big guys pounded you.

Well, you can only climb Mount Penn so many times, and even tormenting the sister 'witches' who lived at the bottom of the alley got boring after a week. That left going to Third and Spring playground which, luckily, had upper and lower levels. The lower was a couple of baseball diamonds, each supporting a crew of big guys.

The upper level had swings, slides, see-saws, a kid-propelled whirly-go-round and a field house. Swings were good. See-saws were okay and if you got Hebhardt or one of the littler kids to lie down and hang over the edge of the go-round, you could spin him faster and faster until he fell off, staggered, then puked. That was excellent.

We are about to get to the reading aloud part of the story.

The field house had no walls and an A-frame roof. The place was usually filled with little kids making lanyards, potholders or clay things. On one summer's end, when all the potholders, lanyards and clay things anyone would need in life had been made, the upper playground monitor decided to fill the last weekend of vacation with a storytelling contest. Prizes to be awarded.

"Tell the cricket in the wall story," Hebhardt, Mahler, and the Magpies said. "Go on, go on."

I didn't want to.

I wasn't nervous. At eight years of age, I'd spent every social gathering for half my life, posed by my mother on a piano bench, chair or table where I was made to recite 'A Visit from St. Nicholas', 'The Raven' or other things in front of rooms full of adults bearing highballs. I was not nervous about getting up in front of a batch of lanyard weaving little kids. No. I did not want to enter the stupid contest because that summer the upper playground monitor was a girl, a wonderful girl, a girl enduring those reshaping months between high school and college, a girl growing more beautiful every day. I was in love.

My mouth was shut on the subject, but Mahler knew. He reminded me that this loss of heart to a culottes-wearing, whistle-bearing, lanyard-making blonde was a regular part of summer vacation and if I told a really good story, it might, you know, help.

I put my name in.

My beloved reminded me this was a story-making contest. I had to tell a story of my own, something from real life or something concocted from life stuff.

"A fib?"

"A really big fib!" the goddess said.

My cricket shrank to nothing. Writers should be familiar with this effect. My cricket would not do. Neither would most things that had ever happened to me. But, as mentioned, at age eight, I was afraid of a lot of good things and fear brings joy and energy to any story.

I made a list. On my list were the black water bugs in our cellar, also getting turned around while asleep and waking up not knowing where the bathroom had gone. Cap pistols and firecrackers were on the list, snakes, pineapples, balloons, spiders, having to wear woolly pants, the idea that I'd have to take a driving test someday. There were the things-in-the-night shadows at that place where the alley narrowed and turned down toward Madison Avenue. They were really scary. There were catfish and dragons—something left over from a cartoon I saw when I was five. There were more, the list was long. Hebhardt, Mahler and the Magpies added their fears to it. Not Keegan. He wasn't afraid of anything and was about to descend to the lower level, anyway.

I took the list and, in my Big Chief tablet, wrote a tale: Two adventurers—you must start with adventurers—were walking through the deep forests of Europe. They were having adventures. One thundery night they came upon a castle on top of a mountain...

The story wound on. The castle moat was full of catfish with stinging whiskers that whipped out of the water and grabbed your feet and stung you then dragged you into the moat and drowned you. The castle belonged to the Snake King of All the Universe. The King kept a dragon, which ate whole sheep, pineapples and other things that belonged to the forest people. The castle was full of spiders who herded black bugs, there were places where darkness moved and the walls turned 'round... Eventually, the adventurers dumped salt on the Snake King of All the Universe and he shrivelled and died. That was like when the Magpies and I salted a slug by our garbage can. The forest people ate the catfish and everyone was happy.

I thought it was pretty good.

Mahler didn't think so. Hebhardt said he did, but... The Magpies shrugged, Keegan was gone.

Okay, we're almost there...

The fact was I thought the story was barely okay. I sat in a corner and read it to myself. I scratched out. Added to. Had more quiet reading time...

It was no better. Well, maybe some.

Came the day. The field house was full. Even some big guys had come up from below to hoot the losers; I think Keegan brought them.

Lanyard, clay and potholder people surrounded my beloved like a cloak. She called to us from her clipboard. One by one each did his or her story. Her pencil touched my name. She smiled. "Larry, is this something real or something you made up?"

"Ohhh. This is real," I said, "this really happened. Me and Hebhardt. It was after the war." She made a tick on her paper, nodded. I opened my Big Chief tablet, my eye touched the first line.

Now, I tell you, this was not nerves but the faces around me, my knowing that they existed and were about to hear *the thing* in my tablet, made it clear to me that *the thing in there* was not good. This, I swear, was not nerves. This was just my first experience of that moment of transition, the moment when the creator becomes the audience; when he sees in one flash what he has done and understands in a flash of blinding recognition how others will see it.

In later life, when I was a theater director, I became familiar with this moment: the first audience has quieted, the house gone dark, the curtain rises, the stage brightens and the whole of the play, worked on and perfected for six weeks, suddenly reveals all its flaws and jejune failures to you in a dam burst of understanding. All this, before the first line is spoken.

That day in the field house, the experience was new. And there was nothing I could do about it anyway. There never is. I began…

Far beyond "not good", the tale in my book was monumentally dumb, dumb as potholders, lanyards and clay things. Plot, grammar, pictures (I'd illustrated the thing), even my reading, all of it was dumb. Oh, it was bad. My character—who alleged to be me—suddenly had an English accent. Where'd that come from? No idea. Must have thought it would make me more interesting.

Less than a minute in I realized the story, as my Uncle Jim said of many things, "stank on ice."

This was me, Larry, standing before the one great beauty of all the world who was surrounded by little kids and big guys and I was making a dead fish-stinking frozen goof of myself. I gave up, gave up reading the thing, put the book down and told the story just to get through it. Facts, just story facts as I remembered them. I spoke, remembering the sweat and burn and sometimes semi-dangerous slips I'd made climbing the little mountain that loomed over Reading, of my times seeing the skitter and shine of a black water bug in the one bulb that stood between me and the darkness of our basement, I spoke of dragons and remembered the chill of a garter snake's sudden wrinkle by my hand on our lawn. I looked in the eyes of the lady with the clipboard and whispered, told it all to her.

Something happened.

What? This became one side of a conversation. The accent dissolved. While the story did not improve, something was better. I spoke shouts and whispers, paused long then dashed briefly. That was like Pop-pop. I leaped on the blood-and-explosion words, words that carried the action, words in which fear and pain stood shining bright and where courage bristled like a pig! Then I tried to make that pig squeal! Arms waved, eyes went lidded, I crouched into the dark and secret places of the story I had written in my head but missed putting down. I let my voice follow the tale as it might have been.

Yes, I exaggerate. I was eight. I was not a great actor like Randolph Scott or Kenneth Toby. But I discovered that when I read aloud, the memories inside me made the tale live in a way impossible when the writing simply sat on the page begging for eyes.

At the end there was polite applause. The big guys hooted. The Woman smiled and made a mark on her clipboard.

I won the contest. I don't remember what the prize was—not what I had hoped, that I would have remembered.

The chums were polite. "It was okay". "Yeah, yeah. Yeah". "It was all right". The Magpies asked what happened. "It was really good at first, then you went away and there was just the story".

Huh.

Later, maybe that night, maybe later still, I re-wrote the thing. Why? No idea. Not for another contest and the idea of trying to sell it didn't even occur to me. Curious, I suppose. Curious about what had happened with what had been written versus what had been told. Most of the re-writing was cutting. Even at eight, I was amazed at how much story and mood the voice carried and had revealed itself in sound. Adjectives, modifiers dropped away. The story became nouns and verbs—I didn't know what verbs and nouns were; at the time, they were simply what remained when those unnecessary words were nudged aside by my voice and the eyes of the one audient that mattered.

To this day I write aloud. I speak the words as they go down next to one another. Two things: I like to know that what I've written sounds like it comes from a human being and not a writer. That's one.

The second is, I want the world I've written to have its own vocabulary and sound. I want those who speak—and hopefully live—on the page to be specific people, people of their time and that place.

Reading the thing aloud keeps me honest, lets me hear the music.

A third element about writing aloud is that it gets the writer away from writing from the eyes only. For a long time, my impulse—and I suspect the first impulse of many writers—was to put down what is seen, forgetting there are four senses at play in any given moment.

When I read a passage aloud the oversight becomes obvious: A man in a forest at night. The trees are black shapes. There is no moon. If there are stars, they cannot be seen through the interlaced branches and leaves overhead. Maybe a distant glow is seen through the depths of the woods. A fire, perhaps? Danger.

That story-world is thin; potentially interesting, but stand-offish.

I read the passage aloud, slap my forehead and slink back to the page. I add how, for example, this forest smells on this night: dry dust in the air sucks the wet out of nose and throat? Is there a whiff of wood smoke in the night? Not a campfire, but the scent of a larger burning, one distant, unseen? That smell comes and goes on the wind. The wind touches your face, it mingles the burning and the still-fresh scents of pine oil and...yes, yes... Can you hear? Far away, there is a hiss and crackle, then, still distant, an explosion. It comes to you that a sudden, intense heat has wrapped some ancient tree so completely that that part of the forest, in an instant, became a flaming bomb. Close to you, the wind rises. You hear, you feel it on your face. The smell of burning overwhelms the fresh forest scent, the trees that had been black shapes a moment ago are alive to this dangerous wind. They creak and sigh with it. Animals, large, small, predator and prey, move quickly, together, forgetting all stealth; still unseen, they come, they flee toward you in a mass...

A few years ago I spoke with David Morrell at a convention. He put a name to what I'd been doing instinctively. He cited the writer/teacher John Barth who called the technique *triangulation* of the senses. With triangulation the writer supplies the reader with at least two other senses added to the visual; this gives the passage life and presence, puts the reader inside the moment.

Thank you, David, thank you Professor Barth.

Early in my writing life I was lucky. I fell in with a group of authors who got together every week to put voice to new material and to hear the work of their friends. This was 'Twilight Tales.' Not a writing group; we did not critique each other's stories. These were public readings. 'Twilight Tales' owed its existence to Chicago writers, Tina Jens and Andrea Dubnick.

Over the course of a few years, my first solo book, 'Just North of Nowhere', emerged as an "accidental novel" from a batch of stories I wrote and tried out, bit by bit, in front of groups ranging in size from five or six other writers, to gatherings of 40 or more readers, friends and other curious drunks who came to the upstairs back room of the Red Lion Pub. During that time I also wrote a passel of stand-alone stories, some of which became the core of my collection, "Drink for the

Thirst to Come" and others that were published here, there or were stripped for parts.

Going in front of an audience and reading those stories as they were written and re-written taught me more about the craft than any class or seminar I'd ever taken. I learned much from that flash of transition, the instant of becoming my audience and fathoming what the writer-me had done. I learned to find what was needed in a story and what could be jettisoned. I learned to find what senses could be brought into play to bring a passage to life. Thank you life and old dark house, thank you Pop-pop, Mother, Dad, blonde Goddess, thank you Twilight Tales.

The work I did because Twilight Tales prodded me, gave me a small following. I was nominated for a few Stoker awards.

Later, because Gene Wolfe recommended me to him, Tony C. Smith, editor, publisher and owner of the Hugo Award-winning StarShipSofa podcast, asked me to read a few of my stories for his show. He then asked me to read some other writers' stories. I picked up a few awards for my writing and my narrations.

Later still, Tony asked me to host a new podcast he was setting up, a weekly horror-themed show he was going to call Tales to Terrify.

I said no. Then thought again and said yes. Yes, if I could present work not only by known authors but stories by writers no one had heard of, but should!

Tony said yes.

Tales to Terrify is now in its third year, was recently the recipient of the Podcast of the Year Award by the British *This is Horror* website, and my writing time is severely curtailed by the show's production schedule.

But I'm happy with that.

I have few illusions about my place in publishing. I make some money at it but I'm not an A-list author, not even a mid-lister (if there are such creatures today). I have become somewhat known in a small niche that seems to extend around the world. I enjoy the occasional reading of my own and other people's stories we present on *Tales to Terrify*. And I still learn every time I open my mouth.

And here's a thing: Yes, public reading helps to sell books. That's good. Having your work podcast spreads the word about you and your work. Also good, especially as we watch the geopolitics of publishing thaw, melt and resolve itself all 'round.

For me though, writing aloud teaches me the work.

That is invaluable.

Oh, one more thing: reading to others…it doesn't have to be a great performance.

All you have to do is listen to yourself.

Thomas Smith is an award winning writer, reporter, essayist, playwright, and TV news producer. He writes both secular and religious horror and has been included in various magazines and anthologies including Quietly Now: An Anthology in Tribute to Charles L. Grant, Cemetery Dance, Tales to Terrify, and Diminished Media's upcoming anthology, Monsters!. He is still reeling from the fact that Charles L. Grant once read the first page of one of his short stories and said, "Damn, I wish I'd written that." His novel, Something Stirs, was one of the first two haunted house novels for the Christian market. He also hangs out on Facebook and Twitter occasionally.

Ghost-writing: You Can't Write It If You Can't Hear It

Thomas Smith

Let's talk about ghostwriting.

I don't mean the *"Listen. Do you hear those chains clanking?"* kind. I'm talking about the sort of thing where someone says "I have an idea but I don't know how to put it on paper. Can you help me?" The kind where someone pays you to write an article/essay/book/story/play/ etc. for them under their name.

Ghostwriting takes a certain facility with words. A knowledge of the craft of writing. It takes the discipline to write on a tight deadline, to write when you don't feel like it (as does all serious writing), and the ability to take a client's ideas and turn it into coherent and publishable copy. But don't pack up your laptop and start looking for clients just yet. Being able to put words on the page is just the beginning. In order to be a good ghostwriter (i.e. the kind that gets paid on a regular basis), you must be a chameleon. Just as the 160 members of the family *Chamaeleonidae* are able to change color and blend seamlessly into their surroundings, a successful ghostwriter must be able to do the same thing. They must be able to put their personal voice aside and adapt the literary and stylistic voice of their client.

And in order to do that you will need two very important tools.

Your ears.

Before the research is done or the first interview is recorded your work has already begun. Before you can begin the writing part of ghostwriting you have to be able to adapt your style and your words to that of the client. In short, you need to speak in his or her voice.

You have to become a chameleon.

Here's a case in point. I recently finished a ghosting project for a client who was forced to cut his arm off with a pocket knife or burn to death. He chose the former and once the story came out, he received international attention, including two interviews on the *Today Show* (with Matt Lauer), time on *Fox News*, hundreds of radio/TV/print interviews, national and international documentaries, a segment on *Pleasure & Pain With Michael Mosley* (for the BBC) and more newspaper stories than you could read in a week. When the demand for a book about his experience moved him to try his hand at writing, he found out he was a better road construction superintendent than he was a writer.

So, he hired me.

When the manuscript was finished, his wife looked at me and said, "Tom, this is unbelievable. It sounds just like he wrote it." High praise for a ghost. (Note: that project is scheduled for publication in September, 2014).

Why did it sound like my client? Because I listened to thirty hours of our taped interviews.

A lot.

It's also the same way I ghostwrote a one act play as part of a trilogy for a New Orleans theater group. The story about a murderer who slowly goes insane had to fit seamlessly between the two original one acts written by someone else. How did I pull it off?

I got the client's voice in my head.

But let's get back to the tools, and a pertinent fact.

Until you develop a list of clients willing to hire you to write fiction, you'll need to supplement your income with other ghosting projects. Probably non-fiction projects. But the tools and techniques are the same. Ghostwriters often work from interviews, audio, and face-to-face conversations, so a good ghostwriter must listen to his subject. And it is vital that you listen for more than information, facts, and plot points. You have to learn to listen for inflections. Word usage. Slang. Good grammar. Bad grammar. Vocal tone and timbre. A ghost will listen for cadences, rhythms, and patterns in the client's words and phrases. They will also read anything the client has written.

Does the client speak in short, choppy sentences or does she communicate in longer, more complex ones? Does he use a lot of jargon or primarily tell a long series of personal stories? These things are important because, while you have your own style and your own voice, *your job is to sound like the client.*

Remember the *Chamaeleonidae* family? It's time to join them.

And to do that, you'll need to read through a large sample of what your client has done before you came on board and you'll need to *read it out loud.*

Why?

Because the nuances of language stand out when you hear them. To train yourself to write in the style and voice of someone else, you should see what the words feel like. Plus, patterns and idiosyncrasies tend to jump out at you when you are speaking/hearing them. The fact is, as a ghostwriter it is a much smaller step from speaking to writing than it is from reading to writing.

Don't believe me? Try it.

The next thing a ghostwriter has to listen to is *the client.* Your job is to deliver the project they have envisioned. So you need to know what is important to them about the project? What do they feel is the main thrust of the manuscript they want you to write? Do they have a good grasp of what they really want? Remember: as a ghostwriter you have control over the style questions, but *they have control over the content and the focus.* It is, after all, their project. So before you sign a contract (you DO have a contract, don't you?) make sure you (1) have made the delineation between style and content clear and (2) make sure you can write comfortably within the parameters they have set.

Now that you have a basic understanding of the importance of using your ears before you use your fingers, where do you start? How do you get that first ghostwriting gig?

Some people start with collaborations. In many cases

collaboration is more about the quality of content than a seamless integration of styles. But developing the listening skills are still important because even in the case of a manuscript where the authors have two distinctly different styles, there has to be a connecting thread that holds the project together. If styles are too divergent, people can become frustrated. And once you've lost the reader, you've lost the battle.

When you're ready to move to full-fledged ghostwriting, it's OK to start small. Articles, short stories, blog posts, and other smaller jobs. Why? So you can learn to write and deliver copy based on another's criteria. And once you're comfortable with the process, start looking for larger ghostwriting projects:

Some of the best places to find ghostwriting assignments include book packagers, book publishers, agents, ghostwriting services, and small independent publishers.

Many ghostwriters find work via places like craigslist.com, journalismjobs.com & freelancedaily.net (though you have to be careful on Craigslist. Check the source thoroughly before you get too involved. Many opportunities are great, but a few are scams at best).

Note: some "experts" will recommend finding work via the various content mills that flourish on the internet. But let's be honest; if that's where you plan to look for work, then this book will be useless to you because too many of the people who run those sleaze emporiums know less about writing and editing than I do about brain surgery. And professional advice will be wasted on those who write for them. Plus, too many pay slave wages at best. So just don't go there. You've been warned.

Now, one final caveat on the nuts-and-bolts of marketing yourself to potential clients: Consider your expertise. Do you write fast? Does your work require little editing? Do you already have some level of success as a writer? Your experience and expertise can be a big asset when you're searching for the right client. If you can show specialized abilities in an area, you have an automatic edge on the competition.

And once you have that assignment locked up, what's the first thing you're going to do?

That's right.

You're going to listen.

Then you're going to join your brothers and sisters in the *Chamaeleonidae* family.

Blaze McRob has penned many titles under different names. It is time for him to come out and play as Blaze.

In addition to inclusions in numerous anthologies, he has written many novels, short stories, flash fiction pieces, and even poetry. Most of his offerings are Dark. However dark they might be, there is always an underlying message contained within.

Join him as he explores the Dark side. You know you want to: http://www.blazemcrob.com/

Ghost-writing

Blaze McRob

Difficult times call for extreme measures.

In 1986, my health was spiralling downward so fast, I had no idea what was happening. My headaches, already severe after I had taken a couple of bullets to my head in 'Nam twenty years earlier, were incapacitating me. It was hard to see or think clearly; I was often dizzy, and hated to even look at food.

None of this made any sense to me. My diet was good, and I only had an occasional beer. I was running around 100 miles a week, having been a competitive runner for ten years. In short, I was a perfect specimen of health.

No longer.

I was running an insulation company in Northern New Jersey and was down in the southern part of the state to attend a certification class. The town was close to a VA, and I decided to get some tests done while I was there. They did the usual blood work, X-rays, scans, and such. I was going to be back down in this neck of the woods in a few weeks and thought I'd stop back then and see what the story was.

A week later, I got a call from the VA telling me to come down as soon as possible. Nothing else was said. I took off from work and went down.

Ushered in to see a rather gruff doctor, he told me to sit down and look over some X-rays and other stuff. It was all Greek to me.

"What do you mean you don't know what you're looking at?" he asked.

"You're the doctor. You tell me," I said.

"You have fucking brain cancer!"

"What do we do to treat it?"

"We . . . we don't do anything. You have to deal with it. There's nothing we can do. You have six months to live at most. I wish you luck. Good bye."

Nice guy.

I understand now that that was a low time for the VA. In fact, the system came close to shutting down.

Okay. What was I going to do since everything was up to me? Did I just get painkillers and sit around like a spaced out zombie and wait for the end, or did I take an active stance in attacking the disease? The obvious choice was to take the high road and become my own doctor.

This was a time before the huge internet explosion where one can find any sort of knowledge in an instant. But there were libraries, both on the county level and in the colleges. My first change was in my diet. I went to a lacto-vegetarian diet, and I made certain I consumed plenty of anti-oxidants, and . . . and huge amounts of garlic. Why garlic? Cancer cells love to eat garlic, but they eat so much of it they overindulge, and it kills them. They literally explode. Gluttony is not kind to cancer.

My second step was to increase my running to 160 - 180 miles a week. It hurt, but I did it. And my third step was to write a book. A story had been floating around in my head for years and it was time to act on it. I had written things in the past, but they were, for the most part, training manuals and such. This obsession was a novel. I *had* to write it.

My health improved dramatically, without the help of the so-called medical profession. I needed no further tests to tell me the cancer was on the run. And my novel? It was completed within a few months and I was writing another one. I had no idea what I was going to do with these books, but I liked what I wrote and was hooked.

During this period, my wife, who was a manic-depressive person, actually told me she was glad I was sick because now I would understand her pain. Nice attitude.

I had taken to running a particular route because it veered away from the busier roads and was serene. On many days, I would meet up with an older gentleman and we would run together. He was retired and simply loved to run. One day I mentioned my books and he perked up.

"What do you write?"

"Horror."

"Are you any good at it?"

"Damned if I know."

"Do you mind if I read it? I was in the publishing business before I retired. Granted, most of what I did was with magazines, and ones for women, Redbook for example, but I have friends. Who knows?"

What did I have to lose? I had no aspirations of being an author, but it would be nice to know if anyone else besides me liked what I wrote. We arranged a place to meet, one of the local running races, and I handed him my hand written manuscript. Two months went by, and he gave me a call.

"Penguin wants your novel. How does $100,000 advance sound?"

"Holy shit! You gotta be kidding me."

"No, they love the story. We need to meet and go over things."

A hundred grand was three years pay for me. And if the book really sold well, I would make a lot more than that.

John, my running buddy and new agent, met me at my lawyer's office. I hated to tell John I had a change of heart, but I had forgotten a very important thing: in addition to my wife's mental health problems, she had a bad gambling habit and spent far too much money. I had to hide money from her so I could pay the bills. This new source of income would no doubt be totally wasted by her if she ever found out about it.

"How can you pass this up, Bob?" John asked. "This is the opportunity of a lifetime."

"Sure it is, but not if my fucking wife spends all the money."

"I have a solution," said Larry, my lawyer.

"What, man?" I asked.

"You have a daughter. Put the money in a trust fund for her. If you don't spend any of the money, your wife can't either."

"What if she sees my name and author bio on the book? The cat's out of the bag then."

"Ah," said John, "be a ghost-writer. You write, a famous author needs another book, and you two work out a deal and split the money."

"Do I have a say in the matter?" I asked.

"Of course," John said.

"The advances are mine and we split the royalties evenly."

"After you have earned out the advance."

"That's my deal. I'm sticking by it," I said. "You two hammer out the legal stuff. What does an agent receive, John?"

"Ten to fifteen percent."

"You get twenty."

We all shook hands and I left the office, returning when Penguin agreed to the deal. What did they have to lose? Nothing. They won and the authors won. They were expected to write two novels a year, but sometimes life gets in the way: an author or family member gets sick, divorce rears its ugly head, or maybe writer's block attacks. I always had a novel ready. I was quick and would write four to five a year.

Everything worked well for a while. My daughter had a baby, then three more. I changed the trust funds around to include them. My wife still had the mental illness and gambling disease, so even though I wished I could tap into some of the funds, I didn't do it.

My wife had a stroke. Not even that stopped her from gambling. Once she was able to use a phone again, she would call a cab while I was at work and hit the Bingo parlours. Think you can't spend much at Bingo? Think again. She dropped hundreds in a night.

The trust funds continued.

My wife died soon after we moved to Wyoming. I no longer had to worry about hiding the money from her. It was my daughter I had to watch. She had inherited my wife's mental health issues and got addicted to drugs, sex, and alcohol. Her children went to the father of two of the children and she departed for parts unknown. I tried, with no luck, to get custody of the children. Her man was not any better than her when it came to drugs and booze so I couldn't give him the money. Fortunately, his parents are watching the kids.

My lawyer watches the situation for me in New Jersey. I have a new lawyer in Wyoming who does the same thing. You see, I was foolish and married a woman who only wanted to be kept and did not want to work any longer. We had seven children together. The money from the new trust fund I set up goes to my children and to a worthy children's charity. Once more, I never spent a dime of the royalties, and even if my ex-wife found out about it, there is nothing she could do.

Now, I am free from all worries as far as my past novels are concerned. I wrote and shared 75 novels with other authors. For one author, I wrote more of his novels than he did. I have to laugh when people tell me I have a style like so and so. Wrong, they have a style like me.

Yes, I stepped into some good stuff to get into this writing business. In the present world of publishing, this would be a lot tougher. I made my deals. If an author didn't like them, they didn't get my books. No one knew we existed then. The cat's out of the bag now. Take the case of the author who published eleven novels last year, made $65 million, and didn't write any of them. You know who he is.

I don't ghost-write anymore. There are a number of reasons. The Big Six, now the Big Five, are going down the tubes. Adios. My agent died a few years back. Penguin had some wannabe waiting for me. I told him to get fucked and walked out the door. There is no reason to have an agent any longer. You want the glory of writing for a big name publisher, go for it. Waste your time. Swim with the rest of the stupid schools of fish thinking this means prestige and is the right way to do it.

Am I angered at the system? No. I'm just stating fact. I am at the stage in my career where I want to be known as Blaze McRob and not some writer who is putting out crap now. Sorry, but it's all about the story. If you can't write, then don't. No matter how big a following you once had, an author is only as good as their last book.

I am proud of the novels I wrote when I was a ghost-writer. Even though they were not in my name, I brought pleasure to many readers. That makes me happy. But now, times are different. We all need to adjust.

Remember, though, as long as you write a great book, you will be a success. People will find you. And best of all, you can be your own person.

Happy writing!

Rocky Wood has been President of the Horror Writers Association since 2010. A freelance journalist since 1978 he has won the Bram Stoker Award ® twice, for Stephen King: A Literary Companion in the non-fiction category, and for Witch Hunts: A Graphic History of the Burning Times in the graphic novel category. He is recognised as one of the world's leading experts on the works of Stephen King and lives in Melbourne, Australia. His website is rockywoodauthor.com

The Horror Writers Association - the Genre's Essential Ingredient

Rocky Wood

Horror is a very distinct genre in fiction. Easy to define at its core, it also embraces wider tales of dark fantasy and the occult. If you are seeking a literary career that includes writing horror, dark fantasy or the occult, either as your primary genre or with a good percentage of your output there, you must consider joining the genre's peak group of your peers – the Horror Writers Association (HWA).

Established in 1987 the HWA had around 1250 members in late 2013. These members come from all parts of the world – North America, the UK, continental Europe, South America, Asia, Africa and Australasia. They write tales that cross all the sub-genres of horror fiction – from ghosts to zombies, vampires to werewolves and everything in between.

One of the great aspects of the HWA is that it

welcomes aspiring and new authors of horror fiction and non-fiction, including screenplays, young adult fiction and graphic novels. This inclusive stance appeals to many of those just starting out in the genre. It can be a daunting time, when writers feel alone, with little guidance and aware they face a huge learning curve to improve their writing, get published and build a career. That is one the reasons the HWA introduced 'Supporting' memberships in 2010 – to allow these writers an easy path into the genre, a place to network with publishers, editors and fellow writers. Supporting members have all the benefits of other levels of membership, excepting access to a very small part of our online forum.

The next level of membership is 'Affiliate' – with a minimum requirement of one $25 short story sale, it is easily attainable. The professional level is called 'Active' and there you will find members who have sold three short stories at professional rates, or received an advance/royalties exceeding $2000. Members such as Stephen King, Peter Straub, Ramsey Campbell, Joe Lansdale, Robert McCammon, Chelsea Quinn Yarbro and Anne Rice.

In the seven years I have been a member I have seen many previously little known writers progress to the point that they are *New York Times* bestsellers, have won Bram Stoker Awards ® and signed multiple book deals with mainstream and specialty publishers. These include writers such as Jonathan Maberry, Joe McKinney and Lisa Morton. And many more members have developed their careers to the point they are regularly published and are building brands of their own.

The HWA also administers the Bram Stoker Awards,

the premier awards in the horror genre – encompassing the following categories – Novel, First Novel, Young Adult Novel, Fiction Collection, Anthology, Graphic Novel, Long Fiction, Short Fiction, Non-Fiction, Screenplay and Poetry Collection.

Of most interest to new and aspiring writers of horror fiction will be these benefits of HWA membership:

A mentor scheme

- Ability to recommend works for the Bram Stoker Awards. One of the major adjuncts to that right is that members are offered literally hundreds of horror works for free each year, that they can study and learn from (not to mention save money!)
- Multiple promotional opportunities through our public blog, our social media and our Forum
- Access to our Members Only Forum, where you can discuss or learn from discussions about the horror writing business
- A monthly online Newsletter crammed with regular columns on horror writing, aspects of the business, markets, etc.
- Access to our Membership Directory
- Two scholarships are offered each year, valued at $2500 each!
- From time to time we publish anthologies in conjunction with mainstream publishers. They pay professional rates, generally offer royalties and the works are chosen *solely* from member submissions
- The Bram Stoker Awards Banquet each year is a

chance to network with the cream of the industry – from agents and publishers, to editors and fellow writers. They are held in conjunction with either the World Horror Convention, or HWA's stand-alone Bram Stoker Awards Weekend

- We have many Chapters that offer members a chance to meet with fellow members locally
- We pay for booths and tables at literary festivals, conventions and the like – members are welcome to attend, help man the booths and are allowed to promote and sell their books
- We hold regular online Round Tables, where industry experts discuss important aspects of the horror writing business
- We have a dedicated website for Young Adult Horror fiction
- We have a dedicated website for Horror Poetry
- We have a Grievance Committee and a Hardship Fund
- The Members Only section includes lists of Agents, Markets, a list of Libraries interested in horror and appearances by horror writers; and
- A dedicated Member Handbook to help you access all these benefits!

So, if you are interested in building a career in horror writing the place to kick-start that career is the Horror Writers Association. Visit our website at *www.horror.org*.

Ellen Datlow has been editing science fiction, fantasy, and horror short fiction for over thirty years as fiction editor of Omni Magazine and editor of Event Horizon and SCIFICTION. She currently acquires short fiction for Tor.com. In addition, she has edited more than fifty science fiction, fantasy, and horror anthologies, including the annual The Best Horror of the Year, Lovecraft's Monsters, Fearful Symmetries, the six volume series of retold fairy tales starting with Snow White, Blood Red, and Queen Victoria's Book of Spells: An Anthology of Gaslamp Fantasy (the latter anthologies with Terri Windling).

Forthcoming are Nightmare Carnival, The Cutting Room, and The Doll Collection.

She's won nine World Fantasy Awards, and has also won multiple Locus Awards, Hugo Awards, Stoker Awards, International Horror Guild Awards, Shirley Jackson Awards, and the 2012 Il Posto Nero Black Spot Award for Excellence as Best Foreign Editor. Datlow was named recipient of the 2007 Karl Edward Wagner Award, given at the British Fantasy Convention for "outstanding contribution to the genre" and was honoured with the Life Achievement Award given by the Horror Writers Association, in acknowledgment of superior achievement over an entire career.

She lives in New York and co-hosts the monthly Fantastic Fiction Reading Series at KGB Bar. More information can be found at www.datlow.com, on Facebook, and on twitter as @EllenDatlow.

What a Short Story Editor Does

Ellen Datlow

There's a big difference between editors and copy editors. I have nothing but respect for copy editors, but I become rabid when I read articles and off-hand remarks mixing up the functions of editor and copy editor. I'm primarily a short story editor, so that's the kind of editing I'll concentrate on, although there's certainly some overlap with novel editing. I'm going to use the word magazine to include both print magazines and webzines.

First of all, a short story editor solicits fiction. This may sound easy but it isn't always so. Some writers write short stories because they love the form. Others do it because they believe (correctly) that writing and publishing even a handful of excellent stories can bring quicker recognition than novels. One of the biggest problems a short story editor has is keeping her best writers from moving exclusively into novel writing. Many writers, once they begin producing novels, no longer feel they have the time or energy to write short stories because of the (usually) lousy pay. Very few venues considered professional by SFWA pay more than ten cents a word for a story. Some pay up to twenty cents a word but most pay between five cents and eight cents a word. So short story editors have to regularly cajole and nag writers to write short stories rather than novels. A good editor is pro-active, searching out new talent and encouraging established writers to produce short fiction.

A magazine's fiction editor begins by reading the manuscripts that come in. When I've edited magazines I'd first look through all incoming submissions and skim the cover letters, separating the unsolicited manuscripts or "slush" from non-slush. "Slush" is the term used for submissions by people who have never published anything anywhere nor have attended a recognized writing workshop (such as one of the Clarion workshops or the Odyssey workshop). All the slush goes to the "slush" reader—someone hired (or otherwise compensated) to read those submissions—if my reader likes a story in the slush pile, she will pass it on to me.

Editing an original anthology is different. Before I can sell an anthology proposal, I have to round up some "names"—writers whose confirmed participation will help sell the book—to a publisher and to the reading public. I draw up a wish list of writers I'd like in the book—this will include writers with whom I've previously worked, other established writers whose work I admire, and also talented newcomers whose work I'd like to encourage. Only the most recognizable names will actually be in the proposal.

If the anthology sells, I send out invitations, explaining in more detail the anthology's theme, outlining the submission parameters, the due date, and the payment. I encourage potential contributors to work as broadly as possible within the theme. I (and most other anthologists) ask for more story submissions than I can publish because I know that some writers won't be able to make the deadline, or won't be able to come up with an appropriate idea. Also, of course, I inevitably have to turn down some of the stories—not necessarily because they aren't good, but sometimes because a story is too similar to one I've already bought. An anthologist's task is to choose stories that work well together, making the volume work as a whole.

As I edit a specific anthology, what I'm looking for evolves. Initially, I'm wide open to a variety of types of stories. As the anthology fills up, I start to weigh what I've got in terms of word length, theme, point of view, type of story, type of characters, and structure, and the needs of the anthology become narrower as I try to fill in the remaining spots with something different from what I've already bought.

Because there is always an anthology deadline, the editor stays in touch with the writers to remind them of that deadline and prod. Then the submissions come in. The editor will read and rejects the story straight out, or may accept it immediately (sending out a contract and when that's signed and returned, paying the writer. There are varying schedules for payment but that's a whole different topic). The third possibility is that the editor tells the writer that she likes or loves the story but feels it needs work before she can commit to buying it. This is possibly the most important part of the whole process, and certainly one of the most satisfying to me—working with the writer to make a good story great, or as close to great as possible.

An editor often works with the writer both before committing to buying a story and after actually buying it. Throughout my career I think I've read possibly only three or four submissions that needed absolutely no editing whatsoever. Very few stories are so perfect that they cannot use the critical eye of an editor.

So the bulk of the stories that I like or even love will need work—from a light line edit (more on this later) to a major rewrite. I may suggest, push, and cajole but I'll never do the actual rewrite—that's not my job. I *will* try to help the author communicate what she intends to in her work by asking questions: What do you mean by this? What happened here? Why did this happen? I tell writers that *they* need to know what's going on in their story—even if this information never appears in the final text. A writer may know her world so well that she believes the reader will *get* it but that's not always so—as the "idea" reader it's the editor's job to ask for clarification of certain points, when necessary. I often go through several revisions with writers if I like the story enough to begin with—this includes suggestions for consistency in character behavior, asking for clarification of paragraphs/sentences/phrases so that the reader can comprehend what's going on—especially if the narrative is complicated and/or the language dense. I might suggest different wordings. If the ending doesn't work the writer and I will discuss why this is so and try to work out a way to fix it.

I edit in stages: the first go-through questions and attempts to address any major problems in the story (that is, of course, if I like the story enough to invest my time and energy in the first place). Then, I'll see if the author's rewrite fixes those problems. There will usually be a few follow-up questions or suggestions. Next I'll concentrate on the more detailed issues during which there's a flurry of correspondence until the writer and I are both happy with the result.

Then the story will sit in my inventory or in my anthology file folder until I'm ready to schedule it for an issue (for a magazine) or when all the stories for the anthology are accepted. This could be up to a year, which is actually a good thing because by this time both the writers and editor can look at the story one more time with almost-fresh eyes. Before a story manuscript goes into production, I give it one more very careful line edit—that is, I go over the manuscript line by line and check for redundancy, inconsistencies, overuse of words, misuse of words, final questions on logic, and yes...if I happen to catch them—correct typos or errors in punctuation that I missed earlier.

An anthology editor creates the front matter that is to be provided for the anthology's publisher. This includes the Table of Contents, with the stories and their authors listed in final order, a copyright page, individual author bios, possibly individual afterwords, and an overall Introduction.

Then the anthology goes into production. This is where the copy editor comes in. Fiction copy editors check the manuscript's punctuation, go over it for consistency, spelling errors, and otherwise "clean up the text," hopefully catching anything the author and the editor miss. She will also query factual or other errors. The anthologist then goes over the copy edit to ensure that nothing important has been changed without the permission of the author (some writers are easy-going about punctuation. Others don't want a semi-colon touched). The manuscript—with my changes, made after consulting with each author—either a "stet" which means "leave as is" or "ok" or complete rewordings by the author—is then returned to the publisher and a proof-reader goes over the manuscript.

Other jobs of the editor: contracts—making sure one goes to the author for signature and three are returned to me, signed (one copy for the author, one for me, one for the publisher); payments—ensuring that the author is paid in a timely manner (by me if I'm editing an anthology or by the accounting department of whatever magazine for whom I'm working.

That's basically it, at least until the anthology comes out. But that's another article.

Iain Rob Wright is one of the UK's most successful horror and suspense writers, with novels including the critically acclaimed, The Final Winter; the disturbing bestseller, ASBO; and the wicked scream fest, The Housemates.

His work is currently being adapted for graphic novels, audio books, and foreign audiences. He is an active member of the Horror Writer Association and a massive animal lover.

Check out Iain's official website for updates at: http://www.iainrobwright.com or add him on Facebook where he would love to meet you.

Make Your Own Dreams

Iain Rob Wright

There was once a time when self-publishing meant that you were silly enough to pay some company of crooks a load of money to print several dozen poorly constructed copies of your naively written novel and then try to sell them from the boot of your car. It used to be named 'Vanity Publishing', and for good reason: the only thing it was good for was stroking a wannabee writer's ego. What it did not do was put food on their table or allow them to quit their day job. Self-publishing used to suck.

That all changed when the gadget era began. First music migrated to a digital existence via iTunes. Then films did it via Netflix. Now books are doing it via Amazon Kindle. Of course there are other players such as Apple, Kobo, etc, but I truly believe that Amazon were the ones with enough vision to truly take reading into the digital realm. They championed the rise of the eBook like no other.

Now, both aspiring and established authors can sell directly to the public. They can cultivate their own audience and grow their online business in the same way a person selling monogramed toilet seats can. For that is what the eBook revolution has truly done; it has changed the publishing industry from an old boy's club to a free enterprise where effort and talent is rewarded. Now, finally, in the same way as any other business, a person can start from fresh, deliver a good product and grow their business via positive reviews, recommendations, repeat business, advertising, promotions, giveaways, partnerships, and any other avenues an entrepreneurial writer can think of. The devoted will succeed, while the weak-willed will struggle. That's right, not everyone will make a fortune self-publishing, but at least now everyone *can*! The potential is there for everyone to have a crack at it and give it their best shot. The publishing industry is finally fair. Somebody wanting to be a writer now has the same obstacles as someone who wants to be a carpenter. Learn the craft, work hard, find customers, and succeed. Welcome to the business world. You are now a Director of your own destiny. Here are some of the experiences I had on my own path to making a good living as a writer. There is no failure anymore, just varying levels of success...

The Early Stages

The early stages are hard and prone to tears; no one can make it easy for you. As you self-publish your book, many of you will be opening yourselves up for the first time to criticism and disappointment. Well, don't be afraid, because getting told you suck is one of the most important parts of your growth as a writer. I will explain why in a moment.

Now, just to prepare you, when you self-publish your very first book – you will get no sales (well, maybe a few). Your earnings will be poor and you will shake your head and weep that you will never get to leave your horrible job. Well, don't panic, because that happens to all of us. No one knows you exist! It's not that you are no good. You could have written a masterpiece, but right now no one can see it. You need to get customer reviews, word of mouth, and also wait while Amazon (and any other vendors you have used) integrates your product into its vast website algorithms. You are at the very first rung of the ladder, and your only focus now should be to climb a little higher each week. Don't focus on how much you *want* to make. Focus on what you did last week and beat it.

Now, the first thing you need is reviews. Buying a book with little or no reviews is a risk, and customers don't like risking their money. So what do you do? You reduce the risk. For the time being, give away your book free via promotions or price it as cheaply as you can (you can charge more when your book has lots of great reviews). You still may not move a lot of copies, but you will slowly start to get some people reading your book. Some of those people will leave reviews; and that is what you need. If you're lucky, one of those people will like you and become a fan.

On the negative side, some of those reviews might be bad. They might tell you that you suck. That is good. You are not a good writer yet and you probably do suck a little bit. No one has ever blindly published a masterpiece. Mozart didn't just play the piano perfectly one day; he learned and developed. You must do the same. Bad reviews are the very best advice you will ever get – because they are harsh, unbiased, and most importantly of all, honest. You have flaws, sorry, but you do. If you write for sixty years, you will still have flaws. Charles Dickens had flaws and so do you. Bad reviews point them out to you.

When I first started, I noticed a trend in all my bad reviews (as rare as they were, ha!) was that I was identity confused. Although British, I was writing like an American to emulate all the great American horror authors I had read growing up. This led me to have a confused writing style, which included British words like 'telly', 'brew', 'git', 'bugger', 'knob-head', side-by-side with very American words like 'cookie', 'trunk', 'wiener', and 'Justin Bieber'. This led to both sides of the Atlantic being confused and distracted when reading my work. Not good. But my bad reviews made me aware of the problem. As a result, I made the effort to remain true to my British background and began writing in my own true voice. My books suddenly had a new identity. Americans began to enjoy my 'quirky' dialogue and my English fans enjoyed being accurately represented by a writer of their own. Needless to say, my bad reviews became rarer and rarer. You, too, must take heed of your bad reviews. They may be hurtful, but dag nab it they are helpful. Only a fool closes his ears to his critics. You must bend over and welcome your detractors.

Building an Audience

Now, as you get in a few reviews and sell a few books, you will find things will gather a little bit of steam. Your sales will still be few, but they should be steady. Your books may appear in searches (I always add subtitles after my book titles, such as 'A Horror novel' or 'Apocalyptic Horror novel,' as this increases the number of keywords in the title) or be recommended by people who have already read it. Time to start leveraging what you have to grow your audience.

Now the first thing to do is NOT go on Facebook and start begging readers and other authors to help you. They get this all the time from dozens of other desperate authors, and quite frankly why should they help you? You haven't done anything for them. Believe me, the path to success is not by shoving your book in everyone's faces. You should be championing yourself, not your book. If you want to make a career out of writing, people need to like *you* and follow *you* as a writer. So be a nice guy, chat to people about whatever it is that people are chatting about. Offer to share the work of another author you have seen. Do favours for others and get involved with the reading community – they'll return the favour down the road. It is much better to have someone share your book because they like you and because you did a favour for them previously. If you are a nice guy people will help you because they *want* to, not because you nagged them. Believe me, this is the way to go about things. If you need to share something about your book, do it on your own page or even on pages set up for promoting new releases (there are hundreds), but don't invade someone else's privacy, because you will annoy them.

Once you have the ground work set up and a small

following, forget about social media and start writing again – and I don't mean short stories or novellas, I mean novels. The best way to make more money and gain new fans is by writing full-length novels. The more novels you have on sale, the more chance someone has of stumbling upon you. It also means that when you are lucky enough to find a fan, they will be able to buy 2,3,4 books from you rather than just 1. That in itself equates to more money. Writing new books should always, for as long as you do this, be your *number one* priority. If you want to quit your day job you need books. The lucky writers will need but a few to make decent money, others may need a dozen, but one thing is true: the more books you write the more money you make. It will also help you grow and develop as a writer, too. More words on paper (or eInk) means more practice for you.

Now, I know lots of authors are very eager and they quickly publish a load of short stories or novellas. These are lovely for bridging gaps between novels for an already successful author, but they honestly waste the time of the writer still wishing to grow. Short stories make little money and sell far fewer copies than full-length titles (at least in my opinion). I know it is hard to have to wait so long to get a taste of what releasing a new story feels like, but you have to be patient. Commit yourself to writing a new novel and don't stop till it's done. It may take a while, but it is time well invested. Once you publish your new novel, start the next one. When you have hundreds of fans clamouring for another fix, then you can give them something shorter to tide them over. As a new writer you need to make money and find fans – novels is where it is at! Period.

Building a Brand

Once you have the basics dealt with and have built a small platform on which to grow, you need to take things to the next level. Remember, you should be selling yourself as a writer, not individual books. You want people to find *all* of your work, not just a novel at a time. You need to become a brand.

The first thing you should do is get help. People think self-publishing means going it alone. IT DOES NOT. Self-publishing means you're the boss, but even bosses need to hire out for other services. McDonalds doesn't make its own tables and chairs in a McWoodwork factory. It pays someone else. A writer does not paint his or her own covers. They pay someone else to do it. Artists, editors, website designers, and formatters are all worth the money they charge, so consider them carefully.

Use the money you earn from your books and reinvest it. When you first start to use your earnings towards investment, the first thing you should look at is artwork. Unless you have a qualification, you should not do your own covers. If money is short, you can pay graphic designers to pull something nice together from stock images, but even this should be a stopgap until you can afford to pay an original artist (I use Stephen Bryant at SRB Productions). Expect to pay around $450 dollars per cover for a top-class painter, but I promise you that the cost covers itself. Develop a relationship with your artist and develop a brand with them. Study the bestselling books in your genre and take note of what they all have in common (hint: they are usually vague and only seek to create mood. Very rarely do they give away any content of the plot or characters. Moody and vague is key for Horror, Thrillers, etc). If you have more than one book, develop a template. The individual artwork and colour scheme should change for each book, but your template should remain. Have your name appear in the same font and size on every cover. Give yourself a strapline (mine is 'Fear on every page', James Patterson's is 'The pages turn themselves.'). Make it obvious to a browser that you are more than just one book, and that you have longevity. Readers like to know that an author is writing more books (reading books is an investment and good authors are hard to find). Also, by having a consistent brand, your books will stick in a browser's mind. If they ignore your book a few times, but keep seeing the same name in the same style and font, they will start to get curious. You will have made them aware that you exist. This is the fundamental challenge of being a self-published author: being discovered. Your cover is one of the best weapons you have to hook a new reader.

Expanding your brand even further, create yourself a website and get your artist to do you a banner with the same fonts and templates as your book covers. Link all of your online sites together and your whole presence as an author will become more cohesive and more professional. The differences between you and a New York Publishing house author will become less and less. You are not less than they are, so why should you seem it. Look at the websites of authors you admire and emulate the layout. Don't get too fancy. You're a writer not an online casino. Join up to as many social media sites as you can and link to them from your website. Make it easy for fans to contact you, but don't waste your day on Facebook because it is folly. You should be writing books, remember? If you are lucky enough to have a fan contact you, then you better bloody well get back in touch with them. Love your fans and they will love you. They are family now and you need them!

Expanding

Once you have a few books out and a cohesive brand, you should be making enough money to get butterflies in your belly. You might be able to buy a new flat screen TV with the money you have earned, or even start being a little rude to your boss at your day job (you will be able to stick your fingers up to him one day soon if all goes well).

The last part of the puzzle is to expand, expand, expand. You need to write new novels, I cannot stress that enough, but you should also make sure that in addition to eBooks, you also publish paperback copies through Createspace (formatting is tough, so pay someone), and look at publishing audiobooks through ACX (doing a royalty split with the narrator means no upfront cost). You can also look at foreign publishers, comic book artists, and more. Each of these things will only earn a small income, but if you do it with all of your books, then that small income will become not unsubstantial. It also has a benefit besides income: it makes you look professional. When a reader sees your book and then notes eBook, paperback, audiobook, and German, it tells them that you are the real deal, and that you take this seriously. Just make sure to exploit every money-earning opportunity that you can. Succeeding as a self-publisher is not about writing one big hit, it's about writing lots of books and maximizing the profit each of them makes. It's a business and books are your products. You need to sell them.

The future

I don't know what the future holds (people like J.A. Konrath and Barry Eisler are better prophets than me), but I can say that my fortunes keep increasing as a self-published author. I started at zero, with no publishing credits and no friends in high places. Now I feed my family and love my life. Self-publishing gave that to me. It took me out of my crappy, low-income job and gave me a life I love. It may not happen for you, I am sad to say that, truly, but there is no reason that it shouldn't. The best thing the self-publishing revolution has given us is an equal chance. You have as much chance of succeeding as anybody else. So give it your best damn shot, buddy. I hope to see you at the top.

Kenneth W. Cain is the author of The Saga Of I trilogy (These Trespasses, Grave Revelations, and Reckoning), The Dead Civil War, and two acclaimed short story collections: These Old Tales and Fresh Cut Tales. His short stories have been published, and are forthcoming, in several anthologies and publications. He lives in Chester County, Pennsylvania with his wife and two children.

Self-Publishing: Thumb on the Button

Kenneth W. Cain

If you're like me, you've had a good share of rejections, and at one time or another you've felt somewhat defeated by them. It's just a fact of how people work, especially creative types. You pour yourself into your writing, put everything you've got into every single word, and what do you get in return but a form letter rejection, which informs you that it isn't quite good enough.

For a while, you have enough stamina to send your story out again, and then again. You keep on sending that story out until you've accumulated quite a stash of such notices, with most of them likely being form rejections. That is often when the battle begins within one's self, the doubt and negativity that brew inside of us to the point we soon tell ourselves we aren't good enough.

At this point, some will give up. Others will find publishers who don't do much more than slap a cover on the work and then post it for sale, offering little in return. A few will stick it out, maybe find a decent enough home for their writing after a long and trying time. And still others will come up with the notion, after considering what some of the lower end publishers offer, that they can do it all themselves and be better off. So many of the latter sorts throw together an unimpressive cover, slap it on their story, and post the work to Smashwords. They then check their sales multiple times a day to see if they've accumulated their millions yet.

Trust me when I say to keep your self-publishing expectations low, as it requires both luck and skill to succeed in this business. Rarely does one offer up their book, do nothing, and still acquire many sales. Sure, you may be able to sell dozens of copies to your family members, co-workers, and friends, but so many other authors do the exact same thing, so quite often you end up lost in a sea of self-published works without standing out among them. It can be frustrating, and most of that frustration will come as a result of not taking the time to understand what a good publisher does for their authors. It is important to know what goes on behind the scenes, because in order to become successful at self-publishing you will need to know both sides of how to publish a book.

There also could be other reasons for taking the self-publishing route, and that is what I want to discuss here to some degree. My goal in this article isn't to glorify one aspect of the publishing industry over another, but to inform others by speaking of my own experience. It's my hope those of you who have been considering the self-publishing route will find some help through my familiarity that will enable you to decide if self-publishing is the right choice for you.

Understand first, I do not only self-publish my work. I believe in the traditional route and prefer that over self-publishing. But I do think self-publishing has an evolving place in the industry. Therefore, I have chosen a blended route at this point in my career, but I'd say I lean toward traditional.

Deciding when to self-publish is often the crux of the issue. For this reason, it's important to first comprehend the reasoning behind my decision to self-publish. In my particular situation, I had been laid off from my job. After over twenty years working in the high-end side of graphic design I found myself with few options moving forward, without asking my wife to leave her job and moving our family elsewhere. This is why I opted to return to my true passion, which has always been writing.

At the time, I had no idea what I'd gotten myself into or how well I would be received. There is no doubt I was ill prepared, overzealous, and out of practice. As such, I'd been forced to supplement my writing income using as much of my graphic design skills as possible.

The first logical place to start came in the form of book cover designs. It did prove somewhat lucrative for a short time, but as the rise of the eBook accelerated, more and more book cover designers popped up. Some are very good at what they do and others not so much, but the sheer volume of those offering this service drove down the low-end market. The formatting end of the business seemed the next most rational job for someone of my background to pursue. As I had no idea what that process was or how to even format eBooks, I experimented. One lesson I learned long ago will always remain true, that you do not experiment with a potential client's work.

It all happened too fast, regarding my decision to delve into self-publishing. At the time, rejection had started to frustrate for me, and I'd decided to give up. I've spoken of this before, in various interviews, that I literally threw up my hands and asked my wife, "What do I do with these old tales that nobody wants?" From those words, the concept for *These Old Tales* was born. I also explored full color formatting by creating a few children's books for my own two kids. Before long I found it easy to self-publish, as well as addicting. As a result, I jumped into several other projects under a couple of pseudonyms, and several more children's books. I became overwhelmed with a deluge of self-published projects. Therein lies the rub in my case.

These Old Tales did well, enough that a few talented authors contacted me with some thoughtful praise and guidance. To say the least, I was floored, and the success of these stories, despite my inability to find them a good home in the traditional sense, fuelled my fire going forward. So it shouldn't come as much of a surprise that I fully embraced self-publishing for a period of time afterward.

During that stretch, I self-published thirteen children books in total, all illustrated by myself. I also started three young adult series (which in their original form had been erotica) under one pen name. I put out a couple of non-fiction pieces under another pen name. And of course I published my first collection, *These Old Tales*. Many of these titles were produced in both print and digital formats, so I'd become versatile in all aspects of the formatting business.

At some point, I did find formatting work. As some of you may know, I've done formatting work for The Lovecraft e-zine and the occasional formatting and cover work for a few small publishers. Sometimes that work can be quite relaxing for someone who has some roots in graphic design, as it offers me some peace.

Flash forward, and once more I felt troubled. What bothered me was how some people lashed out against self-publishing, mostly because I had a toe or two dipped in those waters. It is interesting, seeing people generalize, and speaking of things they haven't dabbled in themselves, putting it down as though they have extensive experience in that part of the industry. Make no mistake, some who do put down self-publishing, while they may not have self-published any material, do have extensive knowledge of the subject because of their publishing backgrounds. But they also have a vested interest in the other side of the industry. I believe a good deal of those who complain about self-publishing have developed perceptions that aren't necessarily valid in regards to today's marketplace.

My passion had been reignited by these words, and I wanted to prove to myself that I could improve upon my last effort. The concept for my second collection, *Fresh Cut Tales*, altered my perception of self-publishing. I'd entered with the attitude of wanting to surpass everything I'd achieved with *These Old Tales*. While a blurb for *These Old Tales* had come as an afterthought, I sought out recommendations from a few well-known authors by supplying Advance Reading Copies in hopes of hearing back from at least one of them prior to publishing the book.

Of the blurbs I received, one came back only a couple

of days before pushing the publish button. And when I read the advice and praise that came along with the blurb, it made me rethink everything. It had floored me enough that I questioned myself and I approached a small press in hopes they would publish this new collection for me.

Now, understand I have nothing against this particular press which shall remain unnamed. I know nothing of the true reasons they lacked interest. I was told the book was too much of a risk, despite the fact that nearly all of the up-front costs had already been paid for by myself, along with securing some top-notch editing and blurbs. Frustrated by this response, I pursued a home for this collection no further and pressed the button.

Nearly half a year later, here I stand, reviewing the work I've done. In that time I've reflected on my writing career and came to the conclusion that I needed to make some changes. I've since killed off my pseudonyms. Establishing one writing career is hard enough work, so I brought all of that writing under my real name. Once I had everything in one place, I began to re-evaluate the work I'd self-published, and saw things I didn't like.

Self-publishing enabled me to parlay my experience and secure some real formatting and cover design work, which have helped to make ends meet. This keeps me sitting in my broken chair, writing full-time. And I know my skills have improved over time, which I believe is exemplified in *Fresh Cut Tales*. But my experience with *Fresh Cut Tales*, while quite rewarding, also made me more aware than ever of the parts of self-publishing I'd long been ignoring. When you choose to self-publish, you must also play the entire role of the publisher, and do all the things a good publisher would typically do for an author.

With writing being my primary concern and all that I had done to support that effort, I could not find the time necessary to promote each and every work I'd self-published, which is perhaps one of the most important undertakings to help a book succeed. There are book blog tours, reviewers, guest blog posts, conventions, author readings, and so much more. These are only some of the things a good publisher does to help the author.

To a degree, *These Old Tales* and *Fresh Cut Tales* have a certain life of their own now, which is somewhat helpful. But they still do need the same promotion and care any other book requires. Everything else I'd self-published had become stagnant due to a lack of that same dedication. If it were always up to me, I'd rather spend my time writing new stories.

Recently, the three young adult series have been picked up by a small publisher, which will help me see them through to completion, with edited versions of the existing editions. I've started to review my entire children's book line, with plans to combine books so there will be fewer to handle. Of the non-fiction I wrote, one will eventually be offered for free. The other will be rewritten for other purposes. I've even started to rewrite the stories in *These Old Tales*.

So, what have we learned from my experience?

Plain and simple, if you want to self-publish, start by doing some research on the Internet. For the most part, it's free knowledge and there is a lot of it out there. Read as much as you can prior to pushing the button. Know what others do, how they get it done, and all involved with self-publishing a book. Know your target audience and utilize that information to create a solid business plan. Yes, you can put out a book for almost nothing, but don't do that. Invest in yourself. Hire a good editor and a decent cover artist who can help make your book standout on the shelves. You'll get out of it what you choose to put into your work and many people will respect that effort if nothing else.

It isn't all about pushing a button. There is a perception out there, and if you don't have respect for the craft, why should they respect your work? Yes, people will criticize your work without ever bothering to read it. They will formulate opinions; perhaps even go to lengths in an attempt to tear you down, and sometimes just because your cover artwork looks unprofessional. Is this always the case? No, but it's out there and it does happen. And the more people who put down one author's efforts, the more this overall disdain for self-published work grows.

Know what you're getting into once you push that button. See it through another person's eyes, how your book will likely be perceived. Don't believe everyone that says it looks great, because often those who care about you tend to hold back. If you plan to self-publish, you want to put a respectable book out there that will stand out among those which have been poorly edited, have covers drawn in crayon, or any of those other obvious warning signs that tend to scare off potential readers.

Exhaust every traditional outlet, and when you feel you are at an end, keep your head up. Keep writing. Keep submitting. Be confident. When all else fails, if you truly believe in yourself and want to self-publish, do it the right way, do it with respect, and others will respect you.

I'm not certain self-publishing is for me. Despite the naysayers, though, I've created something that makes me proud. This is not to say I would or wouldn't self-publish again, but I do think the traditional route better suits my needs. I've learned over time that all those rejections aren't so bad. They build something inside of an author that helps you to become thicker-skinned and more resilient. It's a process, and eventually if you work hard enough, you start to see a means of making a better story. And that is what it's all about, the better story. As a result of persevering, I've started to see some results, shortlists and personal notes on my rejections, things I can learn from and build upon. So before you push that button, think, decide what's best for you. But know that many writers feel exactly how you feel right now, at that moment when your finger is on the button. Don't give up.

Daniel I. Russell has appeared in various magazines and anthologies such as Pseudopod, The Zombie Feed from Apex, Festive Fear: Global Edition, Andromeda Spaceways Inflight Magazine and will appear in Shadow Award winner Brett McBean's Jungle trilogy. He is the author of novels Samhane (Stygian Publications and in Germany, Voodoo Press), Come Into Darkness (KHP Publications and Voodoo Press) Critique and The Collector Book 1: Mana Leak (both Dark Continents Publications). He is the current vice president of the AHWA and former associate and technical editor of Necrotic Tissue Magazine, and guest editor of Midnight Echo. Daniel lives in country Western Australia with his partner and four children, if he includes the Xbox in that count.

What's the Matter with Splatter?

Daniel I. Russell

Gore in fiction is always an interesting topic among horror fans, be it blood dripping from the page or screen.

Just as different people have different boundaries for their horror, this also applies to splatter and the disgust factor. In a recent example, some argument broke out over an Amazon review of an anthology I was featured in. The reader clearly did not enjoy the book and was disgusted by the levels brutality and sexual violence, yet claimed to be a horror fan. What do I make of this? I agree with the reader. I completely agree. I'm not arguing that the reader is a not a horror fan, nor questioning the right to feel this way about the book. In fact, I'm sure a few of us are rubbing our hands together in a smug manner. We did what we set out to achieve. We shocked. Job done.

However, as with most internet displays of opinion, things deteriorated. In particular, I refer to a comment agreeing with the reader, with the addition that the writers and positive reviewers show how far humanity has fallen.

Yes. I admit it. I'm the reason for all the ills of the world because I wrote a story wherein a man cuts his own nose off. I think this was prophesied in the Bible, somewhere near the back.

There is a stigma around the dirtier end of the horror spectrum that those who dwell there are sick in the head, or perverts, or even worse, simply bad writers that have to resort to cheap tricks to sell books.

At a literary dinner, I was talking to a fellow writer whose books belong to a completely different genre. When discussing my work, the writer was surprised that people actually bought, and read, my stories. Whereas I would never buy and read books from her genre, simply because it's not my thing, I would never question a reader for liking what they enjoy just because it's not to my taste. Nor would I, as in the Amazon conversation above, do the extreme horror equivalent: I'm sick in the head for reading this? No, my friend. You're a pussy for not being able to take it. Completely ludicrous! Each to their own, I say.

Within horror, I feel uncomfortable with the hypocrisy extreme horror receives at times. How an author can be outraged that the literary crowd don't recognise the value of horror and then look down their own nose at splatter, in my opinion, is awful.

As long as the key ingredients are there, i.e., good characterisation, cracking plot, fantastic pacing, great use of language, etc., you're going to have a good story irrelevant of the blood, or lack of. If the gore isn't to your taste, then move on. No harm done. But to label a book as bad or poorly written solely because it has lots of gore? To me that sounds a little small minded.

So feel free to have the blood spray and splatter and coagulate! Explain the sound a serrated blade makes on bone! Or...don't. It's easy. Write what you want, write what the book is asking for. Don't worry what readers think. You can't please them all.

THE DISSECTION

So as this is a book to give horror writers a few tips on the craft, I suppose I'd better get off the ranting crate and talk technique. Should you want to have a bit of gore within your pages, how can you make it leap off the page and stand out from the crowd?

In my most recent workshop and as this topic came around, we spoke about zombie movies. Now if you take a step back and look at the horror movie genre critically, what movies would your average viewer list as extreme? I'm thinking *SAW*, *Hostel*, *Serbian Film*, etc. However, these movies, while they indeed have scenes that may push the gag reflex of some, these scenes are relatively few and far between. Body counts are not that high in these films. The gore takes up a small amount of screen time.

Now in a standard zombie movie, the body count is a lot higher, perhaps not within the main set of characters, but the 'fodder' level is high. Extras are bit, usually in a gratuitous, flesh peeling back from the bone manner. The zombies themselves are often dispatched in a variety of ways, with heads exploding and limbs being chopped off left, right and centre. Think of the helicopter scene in *28 Weeks Later*. Yet less people are concerned about these movies.

There are a few reasons for this, and each one is a step in the right direction to writing a gore scene that hits the right button in your reader. Read on, as these tips will not only help you write your gore scenes, but make you a better lover.

OVER DOING IT

If the gore is constant, even the most squeamish, light weight horror reader will quickly become habituated to it, and it will lose its impact. In addition, as mentioned earlier, the blood and guts might be considered as the icing on the cake if that is your horror writing style. There is such as a thing as too much gore, and even as a writer who loves the red stuff, I agree with this sentiment.

The basis of a good story is plot, characters, pacing etc. Too much blood will step into gore for gore's sake territory. I both hate and respect that term, as it's basically true but is overly used. If your narrative/plot is simply acting as a device to parade as much blood and violence before your reader, then the priorities are wrong and your fiction will suffer.

Quality not quantity. Don't go at it all the time, pick your moments instead and give those moments the attention they deserve. No one likes horror chaffing.

THE BUILD UP

Violent scenes can be quick by nature. If one character shoots another, I don't think it would be a good idea to use five pages to describe the moment the killer pulls the trigger to the body hitting the floor. On the other hand, if a scene such as this is too quick, the reader can gloss over it with barely a ripple. So how do you find the balance?

The movie *Hostel* is a great example of the build-up. The cut, the blood spilling might only take a moment, but the parading of the weapon, the humiliation of the victim, even the threatening dialogue all fill the scene with dread before the knife slips in. I respect a certain level of showmanship before a kill. This can also deepen your villain if they take pleasure in the acts they are about to commit.

INTIMACY

Pain is an art, and there can be a huge difference between suffering and death depending on the creativity and circumstances for a scene. For example, should villain want to kill victim with a knife, he could simply cut the throat, stab the heart, etc. Bam. Job done. However, should the scene need to be nastier, take your time and explore other avenues for that blade.

The human body is wondrous thing. Imagine your partner and the way certain parts of their body are sensitive and demand special attention! Recall how they smile, writhe and moan when you nibble an ear lobe or stroke the inner thigh…

Now imagine the noise they would make with a knife dragged over those intimate areas.

The squirm factor is a powerful tool when writing a gore scene. Consider the areas that people are generally uncomfortable with, such as eyes, feet, teeth, etc. Here's a pin. Now, where would you least like me to jab you with it? If you put yourself in the place of the victim and have them undergo your worst physical terrors, that revulsion should bake off the page.

But remember! Show the reader, don't tell the reader. The smells, the sounds, the sights! If you are to describe the pain, use similes and metaphors but don't overdo it. Get a feel for the right amount. A good editor should easily pick up on too much or too little.

TECHNICALITIES

I used to work for a law firm dealing with costing law. We'd have a wide range of files to work through, but the majority were personal injury cases and the standard procedure for an injury claim is to have a medical report prepared. Needless to say, barely a day went by without a squeal as someone turned a page and came face to face with a glossy of a severed finger or deep laceration.

Yes, Dan, but surely as a horror writer who has shed his fair share of fictional blood and guts, you'd relish such sights, you sick bastard.

Not overly. We are wired to be repulsed by blood and injury, just as we are designed to find things scary or disgusting. It's self-preservation. To find a body on the street would be terrifying, and you'd want to get away from the area fast, as what happened to that poor soul could happen to you. The amount of carnage to a body suggests more deranged behaviour, lack of respect for human life, and the extra damage trips our internal alarms further. Walking down a dark alleyway in the middle of the night, I'd rather discover a victim of strangulation than mutilation. Actually, scratch that. I'd prefer to be in bed with a good book. You can have as much mutilation in that as you want, thank you very much.

It's not just that the graphic pictures disturb because the injuries had actually happened to someone, but because they're real and not special effects make up. A real life injury provokes much more of a reaction as compared to movies and CGI effects because of the detail and the, how should I put it, factualness.

So what does this mean in a book? It means: do your homework. For the gore scene to carry more weight, more validity, the physics and biology need to be right. Would the blood spray, spurt, trickle or pool here? If my character receives a deep laceration here in the midsection, what would fall out, if anything?

Again, with balance. You don't want an action scene grinding to a halt as you jump into medical journal mode, but you need enough meat on the bones.

My favourite example of this is from Graham Masterton's culinary novel *The Ritual*, wherein, spoiler alert, the protagonist is trying to infiltrate a society that indulges in a little auto cannibalism. Part of his initiation is to cut off and eat his own finger.

This might seem pretty light compared to some of the gore scenes in a book by the likes of Edward Lee or Wraith James White, but Masterton absolutely nails it, with enough detail to truly paint a stomach churning scene. It's not often that I dread to turn the page to see what happens next. Big tip of the hat to you, Graham!

If you got this far, I thank you deeply for sticking with me. If this was one of my workshops, it would be around this time that I ask the room who drove here and if anyone fancies a post-workshop pint. Please, feel free.

Just keep writing. Keep trying new things. Keep writing what you want.

And please, keep the fresh blood flowing.

Michael McCarty has been a professional writer since 1983 and the author of over thirty books of fiction and nonfiction including 'A Little Help From My Fiends', 'A Hell of Job', 'Liquid Diet & Midnight Snack: 2 Vampire Satires', 'Monster Behind The Wheel' (co-written with Mark McLaughlin), 'Conversations' with Kreskin (co-written with The Amazing Kreskin), 'Lost Girl of the Lake' (co-written with Joe McKinney), 'I Kissed A Ghoul', 'Laughing In The Dark', 'Modern Mythmakers' and 'Dark Duets'. He is a five-time Bram Stoker Finalist and in 2008 received the David R. Collins' Literary Achievement Award from the Midwest Writing Center. He lives in Rock Island, Illinois with his wife Cindy and pet rabbit Latte.

Michael McCarty is on Twitter as michaelmccarty6.

Facebook! Like him on his official page: http://www.facebook.com/michaelmccarty.horror.

Or snail mail him at: Michael McCarty, Fan Mail P.O. Box 4441. Rock Island, IL 61204-4441

Partners in the Fantastic: The Pros and Cons of Collaborations

Michael McCarty

When people meet me at signings they often say, "You wrote that one book with that other person." It is true, I've written a lot of collaborative books.

Fiction books I wrote: *Monster Behind The Wheel* (Medallion Press) with Mark McLaughlin.

Partners in Slime (Damnation Books) with Mark McLaughlin, *Bloodless* and *Bloodlust* (both from Whiskey Creek Press) with Jody LaGreca.

Rusty the Robot's Holiday Adventures (Pie Plate Publishing) with Sherry Decker.

Lost Girl of the Lake (Dark Moon Books) with Joe McKinney.

The Scream Queen series *Night of the Scream Queen* and *Return of the Scream Queen* (Dark Moon Moons) both co-written real life scream queen Linnea Quigley.

And let's not forget about my two short fiction collections, *Dark Duets* and *With a Little Help from My Fiends* both from Wildside Press.

Or the Two-Headed Poetry Monster series, co-written with Mark McLaughlin, *Attack of the Two-Headed Poetry Monster* (Skullvines Press), *Revenge of the Two-Headed Poetry Monster* (Elektrik Milk Press) and *Bride of the Two-Headed Poetry Monster* (Wilder Publications).

Collaborating on books and short stories has always been heavenly for me. But, I've been fortunate that way. I know that for other writers, the act of collaboration can be sheer hell.

For this article, I have assembled a group of new and veteran writers who have collaborated on novels or short stories, so they could share their thoughts on the subject.

Whitley Strieber

Collaboration? Rule one: if one of the two opponents carries a gun to meetings, then both should do so.

Rule two: the one who draws first is the guilty party.

Rule three: God has announced that book-writing

opponents are exempt from the Fifth Commandment.

Rule four: But it's okay to covet each other's oxen.

Rule five: If the adversaries share the same agent, then he may be cut in half, and it's considered okay for them to fight over who has to take the top half.

Frederik Pohl

What is the secret to a successful collaboration? Tremendous patience. It's a lot like a marriage. You don't know what you're getting into until you're in it. There are inevitable conflicts in style and interest – I don't mean writing style, but in working.

Sometimes collaborations can be fatal. The one novel I wrote with Lester del Rey, which was called *Preferred Risk*, took a year out of my life. It's a terrible book; if you come across it, don't read it. It was originally published under a pen name and I used to lie about it. Then Lester's wife, Judy del Rey re-published it with Del Rey Books, and put our names on it – so I can't deny it anymore.

Terry Pratchett

With Neil Gaiman it was a genuine collaboration, and we were having such a great time doing it we didn't care much about the mechanics of it beyond the problem, in those pre-Net days, of making sure we both had up-to-date copies of the next. The other things have involved *Discworld*, and I'm the boss. That's the secret. You'd be surprised at how much of the work I do, even so. *Discworld* is mine.

Neil Gaiman

It was enormously fun for Terry Pratchett and I don't think we'll do it again; we did it once, and we did it well.

Harry Turtledove

The example I'd like to talk about is my collaboration with Judith Tarr on a time-travel fantasy novel called *Household Gods*. When I pitched the idea to Judy, I said, "Is this something you want to do? Is this something you think you can do with me? And will we be friends after we've done it?" You want to work with someone who has a different set of strengths and weaknesses from yours. With luck the book will have the strengths of both and the weaknesses of neither. I'd like to think that Judy and I succeeded in that. We're talking about doing another one together in the future.

Melanie Tem

Benefits of collaborating: the emergence of a third voice, different from that of either collaborator. Drawbacks of collaborating: potential for hurt feelings when one isn't satisfied with what the other has written.

Joe R. Lansdale

I have collaborated, and might do it again in the future, but I don't care for it a lot. Most of the time, the results are half of what each could do alone, not twice as good. Some exceptions, of course. Film lends itself to collaboration better than prose, but, though I won't say I won't do it, I'm not crazy about it. I have done it, and there are quite a few collaborative stories I've done. A few of them are okay, most are mediocre.

D.F. Lewis

I love the literal texture of words and their interconnections (particularly as naturally generated by the horror genre) – crashing gears as well as neat dovetails, direct or oblique.

All my collaborations have been free-flowing, unplanned interchanges, till one of the parties finishes it and puts it in the blender. This releases, by serendipitous brainstorming, the essential story: stories that otherwise couldn't be written. Tapping the collective conscious. This is not pretentious, but pretending – pretending with child-like fervor, in earnest and for real. (My co-collaborators may not agree!)

Drawbacks? None that I know of. Half or twice the work? It ceases to be work at all: better than sex! There is one collaborator who will not be named. In fact, he was once part of a threesome with me and then disowned the result. It has now been published under just two names. He is still a friend, though. Luckily, every other collaboration has resulted in total agreement by all parties. I recall one particular occasion where the collaboration felt as if it were taken out of our hands and was created on a different plane of existence. I was once mind-boggled by the resultant story. I was scared. I had scared myself. How often does that happen with a horror writer?

J.F. Gonzalez

Benefits are having somebody to bounce ideas off of and to provide a different perspective in order to see possible flaws and weaknesses in a piece that you might not necessarily see. Sometimes the benefits are having the initial spark of the story idea come from your collaborator, especially if you are blocked. Then once you start reacting to the idea, it becomes easier to get the muse flowing, and once you start bouncing ideas back and forth, you are collaborating.

I once surprised Mark Williams by not sticking to our planned outline at the end of our novel, *Clickers*. Things just seemed to take on a life of their own, and I went with it. His initial reaction was surprise, but then he wound up really liking it.

Mark McLaughlin

Over the years, I've collaborated with a variety of authors, including Rain Graves, Marni Scofidio Griffin, D.F. Lewis, Matt Cardin, Shane Ryan Staley, Brian Knight, Craig Sernotti, Lou Badillo, and a whole bunch of Michaels – Michael McCarty, Mike Arnzen, Michael Kaufmann and Mike Philbin, also known as Hertzan Chimera.

The best part of collaborating is that working with all those writers has enhanced my writing skills. I encourage collaboration among writers – each collaboration is like a compact writing course, and when you're done, you can sell the story and split the money.

In 2008, publishers released two collaborative books by Mike McCarty and me. Delirium Books/Corrosion

Press and Medallion Press released our novel, *Monster Behind the Wheel*, and Skullvines Press released *Attack of the Two-Headed Poetry Monster*. We were very fortunate that both were on the final ballot for Bram Stoker Awards – *Monster Behind the Wheel* in the First Novel category and *Attack of the Two-Headed Poetry Monster* in the Poetry category. We also wrote *Partners in Slime,* a short story collection from Damnation Books, and two other poetry monster books: *Revenge of the Two-Headed Poetry Monster* from Elektrik Milk Bath Press and *Bride of the Two-Headed Poetry Monster* from Wilder Publications, LLC.

I know that publishers sometimes shy away from collaborative works because they worry that the writing team may break up. So hopefully the presence of two collaborative works on the Stoker Award ballot by the same team in the same year showed some publishers that a writing team can make a positive difference.

I always enjoyed the old Dean Martin and Jerry Lewis movie comedies, and occasionally I think of Mike and myself as the Martin and Lewis of horror. But the question is, which of us is Martin and which one is Lewis? We're both as nutty as Jerry Lewis, and we both enjoy a martini as much as Dean Martin. I guess if one of us starts hosting a telethon every year, that's the one who's more like Lewis!

Connie Willis

A couple of people said, "When I saw you wrote with someone else, I just assumed it was one of those franchise things like the other authors have done."

Especially what the dead authors have done.

When the name is on a book like Asimov's *Caves of Steel* series or some of the things Anne McCaffrey has done with other people. It's not really a collaboration at all.

But with Cynthia Felice and me – these are true collaborations. We wrote alternating chapters, we brainstormed the plots together, we did the rewrites together, sat side-by-side going over the manuscripts, had some royal battles over different decisions in the books. True collaborations. I felt bad that anyone would think these were some kind of franchise – because that is a whole different kind of book.

Poppy Z. Brite

I enjoyed it, though it's not something I would want to do as a habit. I enjoyed getting intensely involved with my characters, and I wouldn't always be able to share that with another writer.

Also my collaborators have been close friends of mine – I don't think I could work with someone I didn't already know quite well. Occasional collaboration, though, has been a good way to do work I mightn't have been able to do otherwise and to have the sometimes-humbling experience of working with another voice.

My first collaboration was a short story, *Saved,* for the late Mike Baker's anthology, *Young Blood*. I'd been invited to contribute but didn't have a story idea. My friend Christa Faust wanted to submit a story she'd written years ago, but she felt it needed extensive revision, which she didn't have time to do as she was completing her novel, *Control Freak*. I liked the story, but thought I could do something very different with it, and so I did.

Christa and I decided to collaborate again when I was invited to contribute a novella to Douglas Winter's anthology *Revelations* (U.K. title: *Millennium*). The situation was reversed this time: I was working on my novel *Exquisite Corpse* and didn't feel I could take enough time away from it to write a minimum 10,000-word novella alone. Christa and I came up with the idea of a story set in the late 1930s, just before World War II, involving Peking opera, opium smugglers, and the Japanese invasion of Shanghai. Since I was busy with my novel, she did a great deal of research and wrote the first draft of the story. After that, we traded so many scenes and ideas and cross-country 4 a.m. phone calls that it's now impossible to say who wrote what. All we know for sure is that *Triads* eventually swelled to 30,000 words and turned out to be, in our opinions, one of the best things either of us had written.

William F. Nolan

As to working with another writer on a novel, it can be done, but with difficulty. Each novel is a very personal journey into one's inner self. I don't mean to sound pretentious – but novel writing is often a search for one's soul. It's tough, dividing your soul with someone else.

George (Clayton Johnson) and I tried to write a sequel to *Logan's Run* together, but it didn't work out – so I went ahead and wrote *Logan's World, Logan's Search* and *Logan's Return* on my own.

John Pelan

Two heads are often better than one – your collaborator may see possibilities that you hadn't even dreamed of. For example, Goon was originally science-fictional in nature.

The drawbacks? It is twice the work or half the work? No drawbacks, the folks I've worked with have been just great. It's a matter of leaving your ego at the door, and being willing to have something that you may think is a great wind-up being taken out.

The hardest part is making certain that whatever narrative voice is used melds seamlessly enough so the reader can't tell who wrote what. Any anecdote relating to collaborating with another writer? Just that my collaborating with Edward Lee eventually led to him moving to the West Coast. We were both so inept at sending files back and forth via e-mail, it just seemed like life would be a lot simpler if we were in the same building.

Richard Matheson

To collaborate is usually very easy in the beginning. When Richard (Christian Matheson) and I put together a story, it comes together very quickly, because we both see things the same way. The difficulty comes when you're doing the writing, because his style and my style are quite different. Actually he has become a much better writer than I am. He's brilliant.

Richard Thomas is the author of three books—Transubstantiate, Herniated Roots and Staring Into the Abyss. His over 100 stories in print include Cemetery Dance, PANK, Gargoyle, Weird Fiction Review, Midwestern Gothic, Arcadia, Pear Noir, and Shivers VI. Visit www.whatdoesnotkillme.com for more information.

The Journey of 'Rudy Jenkins Buries His Fears'

Richard Thomas

You've found your voice, you've written a few queries, so now what? What happens next? What kind of expectations should you have? What I'd like to do is walk you through one of my stories, the process of writing, editing, and submitting it. This should give you an idea of what you may have to go through in order to get a story published. Or, you could get lucky, and maybe the first market you send it to will snatch your brilliance right up. But that's not how it usually happens.

Poor Rudy

I don't write a lot of horror, but I definitely dabble in the horrific. I'm not afraid of writing dark stories, so when Jack Ketchum signed up to teach a class at The Cult, I decided to take the class. I had visions of studying under the master, and then maybe, talking to his agent about picking up my second novel, *Disintegration*. Well, I did talk to her, but that whole angle didn't work out as planned (still shopping it, unfortunately).

In November of 2010, the class started. I was thrilled to get to talk to Jack (or Dallas, if you're in the know) and see how he had been able to write such dark, violent, and powerful material. The first assignment was to write something about fear, so I penned a tale about road rage and how violence can follow you back home, and that bit of noir was entitled "Seeing Red." It was published at *Crime Factory*. The second week we were asked to write about a larger idea, a concern or social issue that was important to us. I thought about my family, and what it might be like to get divorced. I ended up writing a bit of magical realism entitled "Tinkering With the Moon," and it eventually ended up at *Gargoyle Magazine*. Week three we were asked to write about an intimate conversation between a man and a woman, which ended up being a strangely formatted story about how a serial killer is born, called "Ten Steps," which was published at ChiZine (*Chiaroscuro*). The final week got me "Rudy Jenkins Buries His Fears." This was probably the darkest of the four stories I wrote. I couldn't figure out why, in the three previous weeks, that I had written lighter stories—not the dark, rip the fetus from the belly of the woman stories that Ketchum was known for writing. But this story got me there. The assignment was to write about pain. After the three previous weeks, I thought about the most heinous and nasty storyline I could think of, what really pushed my buttons—what kind of story would be difficult for me to write? Child abuse is what I settled on, molestation even, but in the form of something different, maybe, the monster at the end of the bed, the thing that would come into a young boy's bedroom at night, and betray his trust and destroy his love. How could I empower poor Rudy, set him free, so the ending wasn't a singular note of violence unleashed upon the vulnerable? Well, he had to reveal his monster, get his revenge, and make sure it never happened again, right?

The Response

So I posted up the story and I got my feedback. Overall it was good, my fellow readers enjoyed the story. But it's inevitable that you'll get different opinions. How do you know what advice to follow? One person thought the religious references were too much. Another didn't understand a phrase or how Rudy came to glean certain knowledge. I went back and looked at my story, and felt that my choices were still solid, so I didn't make many changes. I also waited to see what Dallas had to say. When in doubt, go with the most talented, and experienced voice in the room, yeah? He helped me clean up a few sentences, including a passage where the boy has his eyes closed, and yet, still seems to be able to see the shadows on the wall. I used the word "tiny" several times, and he helped me to see that those words didn't really mean anything and in this context, were probably not correct anyway. So I replaced "tiny" with "trembling" in one place, in reference to his hands, and with "translucent", to describe his frayed underpants, in another. I know, not pretty, but sometimes you have to sit in the dark in order to appreciate the light. I wasn't doing this to give power to the rapist, but to give power to the boy. When I was done with this bit of flash fiction, I started to send it out. 900 words of brutal darkness, set in a little boy's room, and then buried in the lawn out back. Where to send it?

Submissions

I started with the obvious dark choices, places like *GUD, Shimmer, Shock Totem*, and *Shroud*, places that are open to horror. It only took three days for *GUD* to kick it to the curb, a bit longer with *Shimmer*, six days, *Shroud* at seven, and *Shock Totem* at twenty-six. Then I moved on to some lesser markets (in my opinion), places like *One Buck Horror, Dark Horizons*, and *Strange Horizons*. They all passed. Then some top markets opened back up, places like *Weird Tales, Fantasy and Science Fiction, Fantasy Magazine, Apex*, and *Orson Scott Card's Intergalactic Medicine Show*. The rejections were anywhere from four days to eighty-nine days. And I learned a valuable lesson. *OSCIGMS* only publishes what they call PG or PG-13 stories. No overt sex or violence. OOPS. Screwed up on that one, but at least I knew what they wanted now. At this point, I started to send it out to a wider audience, edgy lit magazines that I thought might somehow be open to this story, places like *Hobart, Juked, Keyhole, Caketrain, Redivider, Cream City Review, Hayden's Ferry Review, Camera Obscura, Black Clock, Dark Sky*, and *The Collagist*. The rejections kept pouring in, and I started to lose faith in this story. I was grasping at straws. 133 days, 169 days, 182 days, and still no love for Rudy—what to do next?

Second Opinions

Sometimes you need to regroup, revisit your work, really dig deep and see if you might need to kill the story that you love. I went back and read it again. I still loved it. I didn't want to change a single word. I posted it up in my private workshop, called Write Club, where I knew I would get great advice from some close friends and talented authors. They'd give me the truth, the real story, and let me know if I was just full of myself, or if this story was actually any good. They told me it was solid work, they were impressed with the way that the sentences breathed, it had a tenderness and deeper meaning, and the ending was empowering. As much as my ego was stroked, I was back to where I was before, loving a story that nobody else wanted, forced to start over, and send it out again, dig deeper, and find the right market. I held on to the kind words of my workshop peers—Eddy, Michael, Bob, Pela, Nik, Mlaz, and Chris. It went out to twenty more places. And then Cemetery Dance had a competition.

The Contest

So I found out that Cemetery Dance was running a contest, and I decided to throw Rudy into the fray. It was a wild competition, so many fantastic stories, over 100 in total, divided into eleven different groups. Only the WINNER of each section would move on. The voting started. Rudy jumped out to an early lead, and then faded. The politics of an open competition heated up and votes were bandied about, and Rudy faded back and then surged forward. Every time a post went up at Twitter or on Facebook or somebody's blog, the votes would pour in, and things would change. In the end, Rudy won his group and moved on to the final ten. Only the top three stories would make it into the chapbook that Cemetery Dance would put out, alongside some great names in horror, like Brian Keene, Douglas Clegg, and Ray

Garton. Rudy again jumped out to an early lead, this time, only the 111 authors able to vote, and sadly, only half of the authors actually did. Rudy ended up in fifth place, and didn't make it into the chapbook. I was back to square one again—depressed, angry, and so close to making it that I didn't know whether to vomit or start crying.

Destiny

What do you do at this point? I still had rejections coming in, a daily kick in the nuts. Every time I got an email, I thought, "This is it, he'll get accepted here." But no, it didn't get accepted. I started lowering my standards, over six months now shopping this story, and I was slowly going insane. And this is one of the biggest mistakes you can make. Don't ever lower your standards. Hold on to that story, wait for the right moment, something will come up, somebody will be a perfect fit for it. I heard that Dark Moon Books was putting out an anthology of horrific stories, and they were looking for flash fiction. In fact, they sent me an e-mail, no doubt seeing me someplace, maybe that Cemetery Dance contest, or the story I had in *Shivers VI* ("Stillness") with Stephen King and Peter Straub. So I sent them off my story. I'd never heard of them before, so I went to their website to look up the anthology. *Slices of Flesh* is what it was called. I wasn't sure—was it too gory? Were these guys hacks? No, they weren't. There was a list of authors that were already IN the collection. Names I knew: Jeremy C. Shipp, Gary Braunbeck, Ramsey Campbell, Tim Lebbon, and...Jack Ketchum. Ironic. I wrote this story for Jack in an intensive that he taught, spent the next seven months shopping it around, only to come back full circle to a collection that he was in. Now I wanted in. Bad. The collection was going to be released at the World Horror Convention. It could possibly get nominated for a Bram Stoker award (NOTE: It did get nominated, but didn't win). And the proceeds would go to charity. When I finally got the response from the editor, what did it say? They loved it, thought it would make an excellent addition to the anthology. I was in.

Almost Done

So at this point, I'm thrilled, but I still have to send off withdrawal notices to every single market, every magazine, journal and website. I sent them off at once. It's what you have to do. Eight withdrawals later and this time I was really done. It turned out that I didn't have that many submissions left. One submission was at *Borderlands 6*, an anthology that I really wanted to get into, one of the best anthologies out there. But by sending them the withdrawal as soon as I heard that Rudy was accepted, they told me they'd still like to see something from me—so I sent them another story, one that could still get in (NOTE: It didn't). That's how these things happen.

Final Thoughts

I show you this journey of my story "Rudy Jenkins Buries His Fears" for a number of reasons. I want you to understand that we all struggle to get our work out there. Sure, I've sent off a story and had it snatched up in a few days. But that's the exception rather than the rule. I want you to understand that you have to believe in a story, and if you do, if you fight for it, and never give up—you can persevere. Understand that sometimes you may need to look at a story again, make changes, and show it to more people. And other times, you have to hold fast and believe in your work, no matter how many people pass on it and make you feel like a failure. Read your words, find that sentence that sings, and hold onto it, and believe in your craft. And then make something happen.

Statistics

"Rudy Jenkins Buries His Fears" – Submissions: 51; Rejections: 43; Withdrawals: 8; Number of days before acceptance: 212.

Joan De La Haye writes horror and some very twisted thrillers. She invariably wakes up in the middle of the night, because she's figured out yet another freaky way to mess with her already screwed up characters.

Joan is interested in some seriously weird stuff. That's probably also one of the reasons she writes horror.

Her novels, 'Shadows' and 'Requiem in E Sharp', as well as her novella, 'Oasis', are published by Fox Spirit (http://www.foxspirit.co.uk).

You can find Joan on her website (http://joandelahaye.com) and follow her on Twitter (http://twitter.com/JoanDeLaHaye)

Writing Short Fiction

Joan De La Haye

A short story is by its very nature focused and compact. Every paragraph, every sentence, every word has to have an impact on the story. If it doesn't move the story forward – get rid of it. When writing a short story, long winded, flowering prose is unnecessary. The least possible amount of words should be used to describe the settings and characters. Your writing needs to be tight. This also holds true for novellas and novels. The tighter your writing in any situation, the better your book or story will be.

I've found that using a lot of dialogue in short stories really helps to move things along as well as with introducing and developing characters. A character can be described well by the things they say. Dialogue also cuts out on long descriptive passages.

When writing a novel, you have a few scenes to set your characters and the scene up, but with a short story you have to drop your reader right in the middle or as close to the action as possible. Your suspense build up needs to be quick, but still slow enough to build the suspense that keeps your reader guessing. It's a hard balancing act, but the art of writing a short story requires that delicate balance.

In the horror industry there are many magazines, ezines, and websites that accept short story submissions and some of them pay quite well, not enough to pay the rent but enough to buy a beer or a glass of wine. There are also a few anthologies that are regularly looking for submissions. They're a great way to get your name out there. If someone has read one of your short stories in one of those magazines or anthologies, chances are that they'll go out and get that novel you've written. Short stories are a great way to hone your craft while you work on your novel and earn some cash at the same time.

Short stories are easier to sell than longer ones, especially for newbie writers. Short stories take up less print space in magazines. Readers also have a short attention span (especially on-line).

Read the submissions guidelines before you submit any story. If your story is over their word limit chances are they won't accept it. The same goes for being under their minimum word count. As a rule of thumb I've found that the magazines and ezines want stories of between 2000 to 3000 words and anthologies want slightly longer stories of between 5000 to 7000 words. But seriously, read their submissions guidelines.

I would also suggest taking a long hard look at all the different markets (magazines, ezines, and anthologies) that are looking for short stories before you submit. Who have they published before? How long have they been running? How much do they pay per word? Is it a publication you'd be proud to be in? What do you want out of the deal? Are you just looking for exposure? Or are you only interested in a pay day? Who is the editor? Has the editor been around for a while or are they a "fly by nighter"? If you are happy with the answers to these questions, then go ahead and submit. I'd also suggest having a few stories out doing the submissions rounds. It takes some of the pressure off of having just one out.

Then there's the themed anthology. Just be aware that if you submit to one of these and your story doesn't get picked up, it may be harder to sell somewhere else. A good idea is to have more than one theme to your story so it'll still work for another publication and you're not stuck with a story you can't sell. The nice thing I've found with the themed anthologies is that it does give you a place to start, a jumping off point especially if you're struggling to come up with an idea. Some of them have some really nice ideas and even if I don't submit for it, I file the idea away for a later date.

The great thing about short stories is they don't take long to write. A novel can take years to finish, but a short story can be churned out in a day or a week and be on an editor's desk a couple days later. Talk about instant gratification. Short stories are perfect for the modern age.

Shirley Jackson Award-nominated author Tim Waggoner has published over thirty novels and three short story collections of dark fiction. He teaches creative writing at Sinclair Community College and in Seton Hill University's Master of Fine Arts in Writing Popular Fiction program. Visit him on the web at www.timwaggoner.com.

The Fiction Writing Assessment Form

Tim Waggoner

There's an old saying that the only real way to become a better writer is to read, read, read, and write, write, write. That's true enough, but I'd add another important element: getting feedback on one's work. We write in order to stimulate readers' imaginations and give them the tools to tell themselves a story. But how do we know that we've succeeded – especially when we're just starting out? Often, writers gather together in feedback groups for mutual support and to "test market" their words before taking them public. But writers often have problems identifying specific strengths and weaknesses in a story and then articulating their assessment to other members of the group. That's why I developed the Fiction Writing Assessment form. It's designed to focus a reader's attention on specific elements of fiction writing, so that a reader can rank those elements according to perceived level of mastery, and then provide additional comments. Keep in mind that this form is not an evaluation tool so much as an information-gathering instrument. You're not trying to grade a writer's work, but rather provide feedback to help him or her improve. Also, feel free to adapt it to your own needs as a writer or to the needs of a particular project, changing or adding items as needed.

FICTION WRITING ASSESSMENT FORM

This assessment sheet is based on a simple Likert Scale of 1-4. 1 means little to no evidence, 2 shows some development, 3 means proficiency, and 4 indicates mastery of outcome.

CHARACTERS

Engaging, interesting characters	4	3	2	1
Well-developed characters	4	3	2	1
Clear, believable motivations	4	3	2	1
Clear character goals	4	3	2	1

POINT OF VIEW

Point of view is effective for story	4	3	2	1
Clear, consistent	4	3	2	1
Avoids point-of-view shifts	4	3	2	1

DESCRIPTION

Varied types of description used	4	3	2	1
Types of description well-blended	4	3	2	1

DIALOGUE

Natural–seeming	4	3	2	1
Reveals character	4	3	2	1
Advances story	4	3	2	1
Conventions followed	4	3	2	1

PLOT

Interesting	4	3	2	1
Logical	4	3	2	1
Innovative	4	3	2	1
Surprising	4	3	2	1

CONFLICT

Sharply defined	4	3	2	1
Drives the story	4	3	2	1
Reveals character	4	3	2	1

EXPOSITION

Kept to a minimum	4	3	2	1
Well-blended	4	3	2	1
Used only when needed	4	3	2	1

SCENES

Focused	4	3	2	1
Vivid	4	3	2	1
Effective transitions	4	3	2	1

PACE

Well-controlled	4	3	2	1
Forward-moving	4	3	2	1
Varied	4	3	2	1

LANGUAGE USE

Word choice	4	3	2	1
Precision	4	3	2	1
Effective imagery	4	3	2	1
Effective rhythm	4	3	2	1

GRAMMAR

Rules adhered to	4	3	2	1
Rules "bended" where needed	4	3	2	1

COMMENTS:

Michael Wilson is the Managing Editor and owner of 'This Is Horror' website. He is a life-long horror fan and fiction writer. In addition to his work for This Is Horror he has over ten years of freelance journalism, editorial and digital marketing experience. His freelance journalism includes work for horror magazine Scream and heavy metal magazine Terrorizer.

Michael graduated from The University of Warwick with a degree in English Literature and Creative Writing and is also a qualified ESL Teacher.

Michael is currently working as Digital Publishing Associate for Rebellion where he spends most of his time digitising 2000 AD's back catalogue including Judge Dredd, Slaine and Nikolai Dante.

You can connect with Michael on Twitter @WilsonTheWriter.

A Beginner's Guide to Setting Up and Running a Website

Michael Wilson

My name's Michael Wilson and I'm the Managing Editor and owner of *This Is Horror*. I started the website back in April 2011 and have transformed it from a one-man horror fiction blog to a multi-contributor horror website. We're also a small press and record a regular podcast.

Understandably two questions I'm asked most are, "How do you set up a website?" and "How can I get more visitors to my website?" This article isn't an exhaustive guide but rather a starting point for those dipping their feet into the murky waters of website management and blogging. I've sectioned this article into handy sub-headings so you can drop in and out at your leisure. I hope this gets you thinking and inspires you to create your own website.

Setting up a website

Come up with a great name for your website

Choosing a name can be a daunting task, but it's an important part of the process. Either choose a unique name that will become synonymous with you and your website (think '*Fangoria*' and '*Bloody Disgusting*') or choose something that will leave the reader with no doubt as to what your website is about (think '*Horror Etc*' and '*SciFiNow*').

Potential visitors must be able to find you. You could have the best website in the world but if no one discovers it, what's the point? The easiest way for visitors to find you is through search engines, so it's wise to set yourself up for a high-ranking position. If your website has a unique name everyone will associate the word or phrase with your brand (and a website is a brand). If you're the only website called '*Dread Central*', for example, you'll rise to the top of the search engine rankings like *that*.

However, if you're just starting out, an unambiguous name will help you reach the top of the search engines faster than an original but not wholly obvious name. *Think about the purpose of your website and the key* **terms users will be searching for.** If you're primarily focussed on horror fiction reviews in the UK then it's a good idea to include one or more of the terms 'horror' 'fiction' 'reviews' and 'UK' in your website name. Even if you don't include any of these do make sure your 'about' page includes each of these keywords. Regarding the 'about' page you'll want to make sure this tells readers what your website will do for them. If it's centred on you and not the visitor they may feel unimportant and won't revisit. Let's face it, when browsing a website we're looking for information or entertainment; if it's all self-serving to the creator we're hardly likely to stick around.

Register the domain name
Check the domain name of your website is available. I wholeheartedly recommend registering a domain name for your website. You can pick one up for as little as £10 or less per year and it adds a stamp of professionalism to your website that sets it apart from other less succinct web addresses. Whilst it's possible to register a domain name a few months down the line it is less hassle to do it at the outset. There's also the real possibility someone might have snatched your desired domain – this comes with its own set of complications. No one really wants to append unnecessary words to their domain as a solution to this problem.

Decide on your content management system
A content management system (CMS) is the backend in which you can publish, edit and modify your website content. If you've a lot of money to play with you may even consider employing a professional to set up your own bespoke CMS. However, that is beyond the scope of this article. If you have website hosting, three of the

top CMSs are Wordpress, Drupal and Joomla. You can also consider a self-hosted free blogging platform such as Wordpress.com and Blogger. Personally I would suggest hosting as it's more versatile in the long-term. I'd also recommend Wordpress for its easy-to-use functionality and virtually limitless possibilities for customisation. Wordpress is great for both beginners and professionals working within website design.

Decide on a subject for your website

Find your niche

When setting up a website think about what it is you want to focus on. Try to be as specific as possible in your aim – remember you can always expand later. A poor general aim would be: to write about all things horror around the world. An improved aim: to write about all things horror fiction. A good aim: to interview horror fiction authors within the UK. This is great as it's incredibly focussed. The website has a specific field of interest, a location and a specialised medium of delivery for content. It can be tempting to set up a huge website from the off, but grandiose ideas soon fizzle out when you realise the sheer magnitude of work involved. As a wise man once said, "Success will never be a big step in the future; success is a small step taken just now."

Find your authentic voice and style

Once you've found your niche it's important to find your voice. Is this a one-man blog or a website with multiple authors? If the latter, will these be distinct separate voices or do you want to create a uniform style? For one-man blogs it's important to remain true to yourself and your vision. Don't try and become something you're not or say what you *think* the audience wants to hear. With integrity and authenticity remain true to yourself and your readership will respect you for it. If you're heading up a website with multiple contributors consider creating a style-sheet. Do you write in the first or third person? Is there a certain tone you want to convey? Do you write film titles in italics or quotation marks? Single or double quotation marks? Where do you source images? How do you attribute quotes? How do you display links? Consistency is key for a positive reader experience.

Writing your content

Content is king

I'll say it again: *content is king.* You can apply all the internet marketing techniques you like to your copy, but if the article is bland, irrelevant or of no interest to your reader then it's all for nothing. Similarly if it's stilted or forced, readers will stop reading. Never compromise the quality of your posts for the sake of internet marketing. *Never.* Content that's relevant to your reader's interests will do much of the marketing for you. People will share it and link to it from their own websites; it may even trend on social media within your area of expertise (presumably horror). It is far better to write one high quality post per week than four or five average posts per week. Quality over quantity every single time.

Proofread your articles

Always proofread your articles, or better still, ask

someone else to proofread them. If you're running a large website consider having section editors and/or proofreaders to make the task easier. While your readers will largely forgive you the odd typo here and there, thoroughly proofreading articles will add a further level of professionalism without investing much extra time or money. We're fortunate to live in a time where it's easy to start-up your own website and have your voice heard, but everyone else can start up their own site, too. If your standards slip, so will your readership.

Create a regular writing habit
Just as it can be tempting to cast the net out wide when defining your website's focus, it's also tempting to set the standard high from the off with your writing schedule. Remember whilst you may be able to write five posts per week for the first few months, how sustainable is that over a year or years? Start slow. I recommend a maximum of three posts per week and a minimum of one post every fortnight. Rather than churn out uninspired posts, take your time to craft a well-considered, high quality post. It's said it can take just three weeks to form a habit, so decide what you want your writing routine to look like and stick to it. You may opt to publish posts on Monday, Wednesday and Friday, dividing your writing time between evenings and weekends. There are no hard and fast rules, just keep it consistent and do what works for you.

<u>Social media and email marketing</u>

Use social media wisely
Social media is both an excellent marketing tool and a

huge excuse for procrastination. I recommend setting up a Twitter and Facebook account for your website. The secret here is to engage your audience. Don't simply post links to new content (although *do* post links to new content) but ask questions, stimulate discussion, share images and videos that are relevant to your website and mission statement. If you don't have a mission statement write one and include it in your 'about' section. Refer to it whenever you lose focus and wonder 'why exactly am I doing this?' If you're using a CMS such as Wordpress you can 'link' it to your social media accounts. This means every time a new post goes live it is automatically posted to your social media accounts. The take home point is *a social media platform should become a forum for discussion about your chosen niche*, not just a place to self-promote. Involve your readership and for goodness sake listen to them.

Create an email newsletter

A newsletter is arguably more important than a presence on social media. Unlike social media where algorithms determine just how many people see your post, a newsletter is delivered directly to the reader's inbox. You can either create a bespoke email newsletter using services such as MailChimp, AWeber and Constant Contact, or you can set up a newsletter alert system within your CMS whereby subscribers are notified every time there's a new post on your website. In fact there's no reason why you shouldn't consider implementing both. To add an extra incentive and increase your newsletter subscribers, offer a reward. At This Is Horror we offer subscribers a free *'What is H orror?'* eBook. You could offer an eBook, exclusive content, secret webpages, downloadable videos or a whole host of other goodies to entice readers.

Don't fear failure

So many people don't get started with websites because they're afraid of failing. Do not listen to the voices that tell you to give up or the fear that you may fail. As C.S. Lewis said, "Failures are finger posts on the road to achievement."

I'm conscious this article provides only a small insight into setting up a website. Hopefully it's given you some inspiration and ideas to begin planning your own website today. As I said at the outset I'm happy to answer any specific questions about website management or online marketing. Just drop me a line at *Michael@ThisIsHorror.co.uk*. Good luck!

Blaze McRob has penned many titles under different names. It is time for him to come out and play as Blaze.

In addition to inclusions in numerous anthologies, he has written many novels, short stories, flash fiction pieces, and even poetry. Most of his offerings are Dark. However dark they might be, there is always an underlying message contained within.

Join him as he explores the Dark Side. You know you want to: http://www.blazemcrob.com/

Poetry And Horror

Blaze McRob

One does not usually associate horror and poetry as belonging in the same genre, unless written by the skillful pen of a master such as the great Edgar Allan Poe. But why? Is the great Poe the only author capable of stringing together words in the complex rhyming Trochaic octameter as he did in *The Raven*, and with less complex schemes as he used in *Annabel Lee*? I think not.

Goethe, Robert Frost - yes *that* Robert Frost - A. E. Houseman, Tennyson, Keats, Rudyard Kipling, Clark Ashton Smith, and more all wrote great horror poetry, some using rhyming styles, and some using free-form.

And we cannot limit ourselves to just the great masters from the past. As I am writing this, it is Women In Horror Month, and many contemporary women poets are writing horrific poetry, rivaling that of the men. Nina D'Arcangela, Leslie Moon, E.A. Irwin, Quinn Cullen, Lisa McCourt Hollar, and Lori R. Lopez are only a few.

Their poems are deep and Dark.

Now we get to a rather sticky question. Does poetry sell? That depends. Sometimes an author can mix poetry in with a collection of short stories, adding a unique balance to the tome. A mix of poems by one author can sell rather well, as long as the selection is eclectic and speaks to different readers. Many of these don't run to novel length, many of them being chapbook size. My collaborative Press published an anthology of love poems last week. There are a number of authors in it, none of us having more than three poems in it. Not only has it been ranked at #13 on the Amazon poetry charts for a while, but it is ranked well in the sales of all paid Kindle books and is our Press' top seller. Go figure.

My horror poems are popular. I write in a number of different styles, a couple of my poems using a modified version of the Trochaic style Poe used in *The Raven*. Modified, you ask? Yes, I changed it to my own particular likes, so that it resonated better in my mind. I'm certainly not knocking the great Poe. I'm simply stating that we are different people and appreciate a little variation. For most of my poetry I use a simple eight syllable per line rhyming scheme which sings to me as I read it to myself. Yes, my friends, horror can sing to the soul; sing of evil as well as good. A poet can raise the fever pitch of evil with each line, with each stanza. My favorite St. Patrick's Day poem is one I wrote about an evil Leprechaun who lives in old tunnels behind the walls in a basement in a bar in my town of Cheyenne, Wyoming. The bar exists, as do the tunnels. Why is it my favorite St. Paddy's poem? My ex-wife is Irish, and I was married on St. Paddy' Day. Since I couldn't get divorced on St. Paddy's Day, I did the next best thing:

wholesale slaughter in my charming poem. 'Tis one of the perks of being an author. By the way, I'm going to be holding book signings in this bar.

Poetry, at least for me, takes much longer to write than prose. I can write as much as 9,000 words in a day for a novel, but less than a thousand when writing decent poetry. It is a mind tuner, a tool to sharpen your skills in prose. How many times have you heard where an author writes poetic prose? Many, I'm sure. Does anybody complain about this? Not hardly, except for the fans of pure, blood and guts and gore. Good writing is good writing, period, amen.

I had the good fortune when I was a teenager of going to some of the coffee houses in the Village in New York City, and, every so often, being treated to majestic poetry of the great Allen Ginsberg. Allen always cut quite a figure in the little enclaves of poetry. Yes, a lot of his poetry was raw and riddled with obscenities, but he told it like it was, and was certainly respected by the beat generation as well as the literary poets to the left of center. Whether you agreed with everything in his great work *Howl* or not, his genius could not be denied. Even though I don't hold many of the late great Allen Ginsberg's beliefs, I still enjoyed his poetry and was captivated by his style. Much of what he wrote involved real life horror, and it resonated through everything he did. Anger and terror were expelled from his soul.

Psychological horror rings true in poetry, reaching deep into the heart and soul, extracting memories and thoughts that other forms of storytelling are unable to do. My greatest example of this is the great Friedrich Nietzsche. While not remembered primarily for his poetry, some of the most startling and introspective pieces of horror surrounding the man are present there, far surpassing his prose. One can absorb the horror of his tortured mind while reading his poetry, knowing that the pain inside him was horrendous. I have many of his tomes, and am always saddened when I myself feel his pain as I read his poetry. Rest in peace, my friend.

So yes, poetry can talk to us in many different ways. My favorite, even though it makes me grieve, is Dark poetry.

It is the most honest of writings.

François Bloemhof is the only author in the world to write so extensively and successfully for the adult as well as teenage and youth markets. He has received multiple awards in each category, including the De Kat Prize for his debut novel 'Die nag het net een oog'. His other prizes include several awards bestowed on the winning books by young readers themselves.

His ground-breaking work (on an international and not merely South African level) includes the first novel with an original (self-composed) CD soundtrack, first novel with its own computer game, first flip-over novel, first interactive newspaper serial and first magazine novel. Add to this the first/only Afrikaans comic strip series and the very first eBook in Afrikaans. He has also produced texts for the stage (a cabaret, drama and two teenage plays) and radio (dramas and serials). Film and TV work and song-writing are his latest 'pastimes'.

He is a freelance language practitioner as well as copywriter, reviewer, journalist and compiler. He has also been fiction editor at a South African magazine and book editor for a leading Afrikaans newspaper.

Horror for Kids: Not Child's Play

Francois Bloemhof

Horror is not huge in South Africa, so despite being Afrikaans-speaking I always planned to write in English and publish overseas. However, in 1991, just as I was about to start writing my first book in order to unleash my dark visions on an unsuspecting world, a local

Afrikaans magazine announced a novel-writing competition in which authors could tackle any topic and genre, and manuscripts would be judged anonymously. So I transposed the Gothic horror that would have been set in the English countryside to rural South Africa.

I didn't really think I stood a chance of being a finalist, much less winning the prize for best first novel, but fate was kind. Having received a literary prize even before publication, I figured the book would be bullet-proof, since how could any critic now dare savage it?

With great ease, it turned out! The first reviewer had a lot to say about the clichés of the horror genre having been rolled out yet again, citing Gothic examples which he misspelt, and the tone was derogatory throughout. Later reviews (for which I had to wait three weeks) were all good, but that first one made it clear, if I hadn't known it before, that many South African readers don't have an appreciation for such things and won't take them seriously, and won't have fun with them either (and by the way, *what's wrong with a few clichés?* Activating and then undermining them is one of my favourite writing devices).

After publishing one more book in the horror genre (the first two titles translate as '*The Night Has Only One Eye*' and '*The Devil's Garden*'), I realised that if I wanted a long-lasting career, I'd better become a bit more accessible. Fortunately, I like different genres. My horror roots remain though, and sneaking in supernatural elements almost subliminally has provided me with a great deal of pleasure in the more than two decades during which I have now published over sixty books for different age groups.

I never planned to write for children specifically until

an editor of youth books asked if I would take a stab at writing for them, since it had come to light that they enjoyed reading my work for adults. I found shifting into youth mode fairly simple. Whereas in my adult books I was by now focusing on psychological tension and drama and off-kilter events, for a younger audience I could get back to 'more basic horror stuff'.

For my '*Chiller's* youth horror series I preferred titles that already introduce the villain or central issue, such as '*The Lady With The Purple Eye*', '*The Gotcha Game*', '*The Water Creature*' and '*Old Aunty Claws*'.

While many local adult readers restrict themselves to books that are serious or romantic or autobiographical, youngsters have fewer preconceptions. They don't censor their own interests as readily and will for example give fantasy and sci-fi a sporting chance. And yes, horror too. In fact, their favourite books may fall into these three categories, as they know they can expect a lot of happenings in between the covers and there almost certainly won't be a sickly sweet moral lesson lurking at the end.

Yet in my youth fiction I hit the brakes far harder than I would if I were writing on the same themes for adults. Because when you write for children, you are also writing for their parents. Many children don't have money to spend on books, or choose not to, and so you have to woo those who bear the wallet. While a large number of children would just love to lose themselves in stories awash with gore, you can't and shouldn't expect their parents to buy it for them.

There are a few principles I adhere to. Most of them are common sense and may have been clear at the outset if I had ever made a study of the sort of horror books that had already been written for children in other countries. I made up my own set of rules as I went along, but am pretty sure they have a much wider bearing.

The rules, then:

Little or no blood.
Blood flying all over the place does not heighten the tension, but dissipates it. So curtailing the blood-flow was no sacrifice for me. Being subtle often gets you a lot further anyway; the atmosphere can be much more disturbing if the central issue is not resolved so spectacularly. Besides, when it comes to movies, why are the torture porn and slasher genres even classified as horror? Those are violent suspense films that feature no monster, but often merely a main character with a penchant for cutting off limbs. Quite understandably, parents will not rush out to buy their children books in which kids get hacked to pieces. Again, that quite a few young readers might like to read stories in which that happens is beside the point!

Children don't die.
Or in any event they don't in my youth horror books. One or two adults may come to a sticky end, but then mostly offstage. The threat of death may be there, and in fact in many a story *should* be there, but killing off a child character, especially one the reader has come to like and identify with, is betraying the reader's trust. You are also betraying the trust of the adult who placed that book in a child's hands. Alfred Hitchcock always regretted having a child character get killed in a bomb

blast in *Sabotage,* and even though it remains one of my favourite films of his and that scene has a devastating impact, I see his point.

Children don't kill.

If a child protagonist does kill a monster or villain, it should be by accident and the event must be brought on by the antagonist. It seems to me better from a moral point of view that an evil force brings about its own destruction. The main character can't be a murderer; he or she can't remain a young representative of goodness once they become guilty of the same level of violence as the antagonist – not even if they are defending themselves. Evil must be destroyed by its own evilness.

Monsters are not safe villains ...

Some of my youth horror books do have monsters in them, but this is risky in terms of sales. Many adults may just decide that their child won't read about such things – forgetting that once upon their own childhood they might have wanted to read entertaining stuff like that themselves, and not the mellow type of book they now want to buy their child. If I do make use of monsters I try to work in a playful tone. If these creatures bleed (see the first rule), green or yellow blood is preferable to red.

... but ghosts are.

While many adults may object to monsters putting in an appearance in a children's book, they accept ghost stories more easily. Perhaps the reason is simply that most people enjoy a good ghostly tale? The frisson of fear it may produce is more genteel than the shudder that waits within the pages of a monster story. That the threat seems less overt is rather a contradiction because for many people ghosts are easier to believe in than monsters. My ghost stories have sold in greater numbers than those starring monsters.

No witchcraft.

The *Harry Potter* books have been translated into Afrikaans after their tremendous success overseas and indeed over here, but had they originally been written in Afrikaans or otherwise in English by a South African author, I am not so sure they would ever have been published. They would certainly not have sold as well as the Afrikaans translations did, since those had the weight of "overseas acceptance" behind them. Though Harry Potter and his foes are certainly no horror icons, the element of witchery appears to be taboo in South African youth literature; otherwise it must be a great coincidence that books containing that element almost never see the light of day around here. In the rare cases where witches and wizards do pop up in South African youth literature, they are comic, eccentric characters that can't do any real harm and whose supposed talents usually work against them.

I would suggest that anyone who wants to write horror stories for young readers should first take a good look at what has been done in that field in his or her own country, since no two countries' banks of literature and criteria will be the same. What already exists and what is selling? That knowledge should help you determine the broad boundaries, as well as avoid blind repetition.

One of the greatest compliments on my writing I have ever received was when I was speaking to a reading circle about an adult novel, and one of the women mentioned that her son had wet his bed recently. He'd been reading a book of mine before bedtime and when he woke up in the middle of the night didn't want to get up and go to the bathroom ... She laughed about this unfortunate event – because she understood. Being an avid reader, she realised that a wet mattress, though certainly an inconvenience, was in this case also testament to a vivid imagination, one that had been activated and was being enforced by the power of fiction. She knew that stories, all the good ones, all the effective ones, are *supposed* to grip you.

To charm you.

Transport you.

And, yes, terrify you.

Christopher Edward Lee Welsh was born the son of a soldier and weaned on Japanese television and classic Rock 'n' Roll when it was just Rock 'n' Roll. His first encounter with the fantastic in books was George MacDonald, given a boost by C.S. Lewis, and locked down forever by J.R.R. Tolkien. He knew he was going to be a writer by age 9. He did not know that it would take him twenty years to get there. He writes and publishes books under the name C.E.L. Welsh because if you have four names and you are a writer you are legally obligated to use all of them.

His published works include Graphic Novels, short stories, novellas, and his debut novel 'Clutch: Book One of The Wrecked Earth', published in 2012 by Rockfall Books.

His daily life is spent chasing down the Muse with a rusty crowbar when he is not analyzing software for defects or annoying his wife and children with magic tricks and Kung Fu demonstrations.

Chris is currently writing 'Sunder: Book Two of The Wrecked Earth', for publication in the winter of 2014.

So you Want to Write Comic Books...

C. E. L. Welsh

A FOUR-COLOR FUTURE

A comic chronicling the miss-adventures of a nascent writer who dreams of an epic career writing for the comic industry.

PAGE ONE (6 panels)

NOTE: The look & feel and tone of the comic should start out very noir, black & white with heavy shadows contributing to an over-all sense of dread and difficulty. Then, as our hero learns what he must do and takes action, the art will lighten up, with a few colors introduced where appropriate and indicated by the script: eventually the comic will transform into a classic four-color comic as the writer finishes one quest (to become a writer in the comic industry) and embarks on another (going to work on his first project.)

PANEL 1

A cramped, one room apartment, filled with the clutter of a life lived desperately. The bed is unmade, there are dishes piled in the sink, clothes are hung where there is room for them, and sitting staring wide-eyed at a rejection letter held fast in both hands is BILL, a frazzled young man wearing a geek-themed t-shirt, sporting glasses and a head of hair that hadn't seen a comb in days. The only hint of order is a neat stack of comic books at one elbow, and at the other an open notebook turned to a blank page, a pen waiting for use at the top.

Narrative Caption

It is an old story, and commonly uninteresting to any but the one at its center. But to that person, to the one who suffers through it, there is nothing more important.

BILL
I am so dead.

PANEL 2
Bill is standing now, his chair falling back suddenly. He has his hands on his head, pulling at his hair, and his expression has grown even more crazed as he continues to stare at the blank screen. The rejection letter falls to one side.

BILL
How am I supposed to be a comic book writer if I have no idea what I'm doing?!

PANEL 3
He snatches up the pile of comics, having to twist at the waist to do so.

SFX
SNATCH!

BILL
I've read every comic! I've seen every movie! I have a hundred stories to tell!

PANEL 4 (Inset, Close Up)
Bill is so flustered he's twisted himself up – his legs have crossed at the ankle, his unlaced Chuck Taylors coming loose as one foot catches on the other.

PANEL 5
We see just the upper portion of his body, from the chest up, his arms out, his eyes wide and his body tilted to the

floor.

BILL
CRIKEY!

PANEL 6 (Bird's Eye View)
Looking down we see Bill is sprawled on his back on the floor, one Chuck Taylor near his head, his expression chagrin, his glasses askew, and comics fluttering down around him like massive leaves in autumn.

BILL
I need help.

~~~

Perhaps Bill is you. Or maybe you are not quite so frustrated, but do want to work in comics and haven't the foggiest idea of where to begin. The particulars of where you are on your journey as a writer are as countless as the pages fluttering in a comic-book maelstrom...as are the possible paths you can take to achieving your quest of writing comics; covering them all would be impossible for even the most powerful superhero, but, we can take a look at some of the basics.

For the purposes of this discussion I will use the word *comic* to refer to anything that fits in the medium: a webcomic (any comic that lives primarily online, be it a daily, a serial or a one-shot), a comic book (such as the 22-page monthlies that come out from Marvel and DC) a trade paperback (a collection of comic books that typically cover a story arc and are bound together in one book) or a graphic novel (a much-longer-than-22-page comic book that typically contains a single story).

When a writer thinks about writing comics professionally, five will get you ten that in their mind they are working for either Marvel or DC or one of their esteemed contemporaries. That might be your goal, but it isn't the ONLY goal. Smaller publishers exist and provide excellent opportunities for acolytes and journeymen. There is always self-publishing, too, although never equate "possible" options with "easy" or "guaranteed successful" options, especially in the publishing world.

There is, surprisingly, a simple answer to the question of how to break into comics, but like all simple answers it unravels into quite the mess once cracked open, much like the innards of a golf ball. I will now, for dramatic effect, repeat the question before revealing the answer.

Question: "How does a writer break into writing for comic books?"

Answer: "Any way he can."

Annoying, yes? Yet much like other mantras that seem so trite when examined by the truth-seekers, those four words contain the sum of the truth. There are literally as many ways to break into the comic industry for a writer as there are writers trying to break into the comic industry, and no one person is likely to do so in exactly the same way as another. In my case I was lucky enough to spot an ad from a publisher in India looking for Western writers to pen graphic novel adaptations of classic works for school-age children. Myself and perhaps a dozen other writers (ranging in skill & experience from 'never having written a comic' to 'wrote comics for Marvel') turned out scripts for classics like "King Solomon's Mines" and "The Strange Case of

Dr. Jekyll and Mr. Hyde", and a few original works, too. That was the start of my path, but I am far from done traveling it.

Here are just three paths available for a writer seeking work in the comic world:

Pitch a story
You've got the idea, you've fleshed it out and you may have even written the script. Now you want to pitch this story to an editor at a comics publisher: first step, hit the publisher's website and review their submission guidelines. Not every publisher will accept unsolicited submissions (in fact, many do not) but some will. If they will, be certain to follow their guidelines for submission, paying special attention to type of story (don't pitch a romance to a horror comic publisher unless they state they are looking for moon-eyed zombies), formatting and submission procedure. Fire it off and immediately try another step below or get to work writing something else.

Pitch a comic
A completed comic. You've managed to get the comic made and printed off and now you want to partner up with a publisher that might buy the rights outright or sign you up on a royalty deal. You've got a bigger net to fish with now, as a lot more publishers are going to look at a book that's already done (after all, you've cut their effort and expense down by a large margin, which increases their profit margin).

Self-publish a comic
There are many sub-paths to take on this path, many

choices to make here, but they all lead to one goal: get attention. If you produce a quality comic that gets some traction (i.e. fans) then you increase your profile, you have something to point editors too when you run into them at a con, and you can use your comic as "proof-of-concept" that you know how to write comics, and do it well.

What are your goals? Do you want to write comics for a living, working for one of the big publishers? Do you want to work on established properties, or something more cutting edge and original? Do you want to be a creator-owned sensation, self-publishing and managing all aspects of your creation? Are you less interested in a carrier in comics, and just want to diversify? Maybe all you care about is getting your book turned into a graphic novel? Figure out exactly what you want out of writing for comics before you begin, and it will help you shape the path you need to follow to your goal.

I've learned a lot walking my path (and plenty still to learn) and I'm happy to share it. Hopefully some of this will help you on your own path.

Comics take a lot of effort to create
There are many, many steps to creating a comic. This list is not all-inclusive, and sometimes a step can be skipped. The medium of comics is wonderfully diverse, and the steps you need to take will depend on what you want the finished product to be.

1. *The idea.* Easy enough, right? You figure out the basics of what kind of story you want to tell in comic form.

2. *The story sketch.* Start to rough out the story, the characters, and the plot.
3. *The story form.* By which I mean what the finished product will be, what particular form of medium will you use. Web comic? Print? Serial? How many pages? And so on. This will have a great impact on:
4. *The outline.* Remember you have restrictions based on the story form here: if you are writing the first issue of a limited series, and each issue is 22 pages, and you plan on covering a thousand years of history in this issue...you will have to make some decisions about how you expect the artist to convey your story in the constraints your story form has. Remember this is a visual medium first.
5. *The layout.* Sometimes called roughs. Here is where your artist reads your outline and sketches out basic shapes and layouts to see if your vision will work or if it needs some tweaking (it is probably going to need some tweaking).
6. *The script.* Here you go: you've gone through a few rounds of discussion with the artist and settled on how to proceed: now you write the script. Note that you will have to decide on a format for the script, how and where you will provide artistic direction, visual aids, and the like.
7. *Editing.* This is an oft-overlooked step outside of comics created by a publisher. Yes, proofing is important, but a comic editor does much more than that: he knows the medium, he knows the industry, and he looks for pacing, crowding and

more. The editor's role is to help you tell the best story possible (just like your prose writing editor) and operates as a specialist in the field of comics.

8. *Storyboards.* This is like the Layout/Roughs above, but more detailed and organized.
9. *Pencils.* The artist draws the comic in pencil. Most of the details are done at this stage.
10. *Inks.* Sometimes the same artist, sometimes not, lays inks over the pencils, bringing out definition and adding depth, shadowing and contrasts.
11. *Colors.* Often a different artist, but not always, applies colors to the comic (unless you are going for a Black and White) which can often completely transform the look & feel and tone.
12. *Lettering.* Again, this could be an entirely different person or it could be the same artist – or even the writer if working digitally and the writer has the chops.
13. *Cover.* Almost always a separate artist does the cover, and this task can also be broken down into pencils, inks, colors, and so forth.
14. *Publishing.* Now the comic gets made, digitally or in print or both, and presented to the world.

Comics is not a genre
Keep in mind that comics are a medium, not a genre. Whatever story you can imagine, you can share as a comic as well as prose.

Special challenge for writers
It is more difficult for a writer to catch the eye of an editor than an artist. An artist can display their skills

visually, in a way that is quickly and easily digested and assessed. A writer has to convince an editor to read something they have written, and that simply takes more time. Furthermore, an editor is much less likely to read a script from an unknown, which means your best bet is to have a complete comic to shop around. Yes, that means art, and unless you are one of those enviable dual-classed, special snowflakes known as the Writer-Artist, having art for your comic will mean collaborating with an artist.

Don't shop your Spider-Man Fan-Fic

Yes, I have a script for a complete issue of Spider-Man that I wrote. Yes, I think it is pretty good (it involves Doc Ock and blue cheese). No, it will never see the light of day, unless I want to pay an artist to create it and then give it away as fanfic. The fact is that companies with established properties, like Marvel with Spider-Man, put themselves at risk for legal action when reading your Spider-Man script, on the chance your story is something similar to a story they already have in the works.

Writers write

It is far more important for you to produce new words than to promote the book you've just finished. As a writer you should be familiar with this idea. The same holds true on this topic: if you want to be a comic writer, make comics. Notice that was *make* comics, not *write* comics. Yes, learn how to write a comic script, and keep writing those, keep improving those. At the same time, you will need to get at least one comic made so that you have something to show.

Where to start?

If you want to be in the comic book industry, then get involved in the industry. With tools like Twitter and Facebook available to you, you don't have to wait to make it to get to know the people in the industry. Follow along and you will have access to those who *have* made it, many of whom are very generous with dropping pearls of wisdom regarding the industry and the craft.

Jasper Bark was very late with his bio for this collection. Though he wouldn't like to be known as the late Jasper Bark just yet. He does like to be known as an award winning author of four novels, 12 children's books and countless comics and graphic novels. He recently released a swarm of piranhas into a hot tub full of politicians and the eBook 'Stuck On You', though only one of these crimes has so far been proven. His forthcoming short story collection 'Stuck On You and Other Prime Cuts' is soon to be released by Crystal Lake Publishing along with loads of other great stuff.

Horror Comics – How to Write Gory Scripts for Gruesome Artists

Jasper Bark

In this entry I'd like to look at the craft of writing horror comics. In particular I'd like to concentrate on the relationship between the writer and the artist and my experience of writing scripts for someone else to draw.

From the outset I have to say that an artist is responsible for more than half the story the writer tells. In truth they are often more than just a collaborator. I know many writers will talk of how the poor 'pencil monkey' is just there to "fulfil their vision", but an artist does a hell of a lot more than that. They not only add a huge amount to a writer's vision, they drag it kicking and screaming onto the page. It takes a lot longer to draw a comic than it takes to write it and there are a lot more pictures on a comic page than words (if you're doing it right). So who do you imagine is doing the bulk of the hard work? This is primarily a visual medium so you need to show the right amount of respect to the person handling the visuals.

The other thing I need to say from the outset is that I will probably be dropping a few names over the course of this article. The more cynical among you will no doubt think that I'm trying to bolster my opinions by trading off the reputations of artists far more successful than me - and you'd probably be right. While those of you who don't read many comics will probably just wonder who the f*** I'm talking about. That's the problem with a niche subject like horror comics. Andy Warhol famously said that in the future everyone will be famous for 15 minutes. He reckoned without the world of horror comics however, where you can be famous for as long as you like, but only to 15 people.

Although Walt Simonson (Clang! that's the first of many) once cautioned me about comparing comics too closely to that other visual narrative medium - film, it's a useful analogy with which to consider the roles of the writer and the artist within comics. The comic writer plays the same role as the screenwriter and if they have a really simpatico relationship with the artists they might be considered a co-director. Usually however, the artist is the director, as well as the cinematographer, the scene designer, the special effects expert, the location scout and every single member of the cast. While a good script is crucial to a good comic, a good writer knows where his or her responsibility to the finished strip ends and the artist's begins.

To elaborate on this point we need to look at panel descriptions. Apologies to those who already know this, but comic scripts are generally made up of two components: a short description of what's happening in each panel, including what the characters are doing, where they are and how they feel about it, and the dialogue and captions that will appear in that panel. There are two schools of panel descriptions, the Alan Moore school and the John Wagner school (no this isn't a name drop because I've only briefly met both men).

I, like most writers, started out in the Alan Moore school. This is partly because Alan Moore's work had such an impact on the field of comics, but mainly because more of his scripts are available to read so most of us learned from copying him. I had the good fortune to be mentored early on in my career by Miracleman artist Garry Leach (Clang!) and to a lesser extent Watchmen artist Dave Gibbons (double Clang!), both of whom quickly (and quite brutally) beat the budding Alan Moore out of me.

The difference between the two schools is detail. Alan's panel descriptions are full of detail but give the artist very little room for their own ideas. John's panel descriptions are short and to the point leaving the artist a lot of scope.

Here's an imaginary panel from an Alan Moore Dredd script (he did write one or two):

PANEL 1:   Okay, we focus on DREDD in this panel and it's pretty obvious he's not in a good mood. His face is twisted into a snarl and his body language radiates menace and the threat of physical violence. The streetlights overhead are flickering and cast him in a red light, The lawgiver in his hand is firm and pointing upward suggesting the sort of erection he probably gets just before meting out the type of physical justice of which he is so fond. Just off panel, we can't see it, but there is probably another crime going on and DREDD is torn between arresting the perp in hand and stopping the other crime he can see. Perhaps this sets off memories of other difficult choices he's had to face. Maybe he thinks of his clone brother Rico, I don't know, but suggest some of this dilemma in his form and stature.

DREDD: DROKK!

This is an actual panel description written by John Wagner:

PANEL 1:   DREDD - grim.

DREDD: DROKK!

If you think about it, everything the artist needs is there in John's description. It also gives the artist far more room to bring his or her own ideas to the panel and to creatively engage in the telling of the story. It's also a lot quicker for the writer to write and the artist to read. Garry and Dave told me they used to skim through Alan's scripts with a highlighter and pick out three or four words per description. That's right, all those award winning scripts that changed the medium forever were only quickly scanned by the artists because of their unwieldy length.

I started my professional career as a comic writer, so when I came to write prose I had to learn to put more visual description into my stories, as I was so used to the artist covering that for me. Many authors who write comics for the first time seem to have the opposite problem. Letting go of the control can be difficult for them, and they feel the need to micro-manage the artist quite unnecessarily. Several of my artist friends have shown me scripts from novelists that make the Alan Moore pastiche above look as terse as the John Wagner script. Seriously I kid you not!

If you're reading this and are just about to write your first comic script, might I politely suggest that you don't need to describe every knot and swirl in the bark of every tree in the forest where your characters find themselves. In fact, you don't need to describe the trees at all, or send reference material. The artist has probably seen quite a few trees already.

The last thing I'd like to mention is the difference in the way that writers and artists tell stories. An artist will often begin a story with a seagull hovering over the New York harbour. The seagull will then fly past the Statue of Liberty before wending its way between the sky scrapers of Wall St and catching an updraft that takes it into a seedier part of town where it alights on a window sill. We push through the window beyond the seagull into the office of a PI. The PI spends several panels scratching his head and polishing his gun before putting it in a drawer in his desk. There's a knock at the door. We focus on the beads of sweat on the PI's forehead. He gets up and puts his hand on the door handle, leaves it there for three panels then eventually opens the door. Beyond the door are shadows, out of which a sultry blonde steps, but she takes six panels to do so. She takes another six panels to enter the office and sit down in front of his desk. Finally, the dialogue starts.

A writer will start with this panel description:

PANEL 1:   We open in a PI's office in a seedy part of New York city. There's a knock at the door, the PI gets up from behind his desk and opens the door. A sultry blond saunters in and sits behind his desk.

Upon reading this the artist will despair over the fact that there are nine such panels on the page and each panel contains so much action that it should, in all fairness, be six separate panels. At this point the artist puts down the script and picks up a bottle, pretending for the next two days that they don't need the money so badly they can't get out of drawing the f***ing script.

As you gain more experience writing comics, you learn to strike a happy medium between these two (only slightly exaggerated) approaches. To give the artist a bit of a lead in to the story and to curb your tendency to cram far too much action into one panel.

This is especially important when writing horror comics because the best horror always depends more on the reader's imagination than the writer's powers of description. The horrors they see in their mind's eye will always outweigh anything you put on the page. For this reason you need to have faith in your artist's talent and imagination and let them put just the right amount of detail into every panel.

Showing respect for your artist's talent is the best way of showing respect for your reader's discrimination. It's also the best way of scaring the pants off both of them.

Niall Parkinson
DARK AGE DESIGN
Dark and Conceptual Illustration

"Surreal journeys through landscapes of the angry and abandoned, the lost and lonely and the weak and wounded. These are the realms of the Dead End Collective."

Niall Parkinson is an Irish artist specializing in the origination of dark, surreal, conceptual and spiritual hand drawn illustration from which he explores the darker regions of the human heart and experience. His background is in commercial graphic design and he has spent over 20 years working in this capacity within the printing industry. Niall has also had success in the music industry designing cd covers and booklets primarily for European metal bands.

His real interest now lies in pursuing his illustration service Dark Age Design from which he hopes to concentrate his work within publishable areas which incorporate horror and nightmarish themes and dark, spiritual concepts such as areas of printed/online magazines, book illustration and cover design with perhaps some comic book work etc. A book entitled 'No Sight For the Saved' featuring short story fiction based on his illustration work is currently being compiled.
Niall's work can be seen at the following sites:
www.artwanted.com/parky68
http://neonangelus68.wix.com/dark-age-design
Niall can also be contacted via email
at: neonangelus68@hotmail.com

Some Thoughts on my Meandering within the World of Dark and Horror Art

Niall Parkinson

I guess I was always destined to dabble in dark art. As soon as I could pick up a crayon it was not giraffes, teddies or trucks I was interested in exploring visually... it was little stick men, sort of twisted wicker men with big googly eyes and leering grins. As I got older I used to love to explore the world of epic battle sets, armies pitted against one another, bloody bayonets and conflict. I remember I was particularly nasty to my action men figures. I used to hang them, dismember them, draw blood on them, decapitate them (I am aware this makes me sound like a serial killer in the making, haha, but thankfully my path led me to benign forms of madness).

For it is a madness, in a way, this love of the dark side, the endless curiosity with pain, suffering and fear. But hand in hand with this is a curious empathy, a sense of urgency to be a part of a spiritual understanding of fear, about the nature of good and evil...about its fundamental essence. When I was 15 I started to work in pen and ink (still my preferred medium) and duplicated what I saw on the movie screens, the aliens, the angels of death, the grave lurkers, the ghouls...but I was always more curious about the outsiders, the lurkers in the shadows, the creatures who jump out, devour and disappear. These creatures were lonely and misunderstood, and I tried to reflect that in my art.

When I was 18 I left school and went straight to work as a graphic designer. Over the years I lost touch with my traditional drawing skills. Apple Mac took over. Everything became Quark XPress, Adobe Illustrator, Photoshop. I worked in large print houses, dealt with customers, liaised on factory floors and left my fine art skills behind (they were superfluous to requirements). In the early 2000's I dabbled in cd cover art and became very proficient in Photoshop creating otherworldly landscapes for European metal bands. It was great but...I missed the simplicity (and the ironic complexity) of what I wanted to achieve with the line art.

One important point to mention. I am a recovering alcoholic. I have been sober now for two years and this sobriety has been vital in my resurgence as a horror/dark art illustrator. I plumb the depths of human despair, I sink in the pain and self-loathing experienced in the void of tormented resentment and anger. I explore the spiritual realms inhabited by the lost...and the wounded. I look the devil in the face and count his warts. I sit side by side in the shadows with the ghoul, with the twisted one, with the zombified, with the empty shell...and I draw it all. My work is not strictly horror art, there is a vast surreal element about some of my work. Metaphors abound. But one thing is certain: it is frightening, it is uncomfortable...and it lives within all of us.

I am becoming quite successful these days and have received commissions to produce illustrations for novels, anthologies and magazines. It's going from strength to strength. My advice to artists who wish to explore this realm? Be honest to yourself, do not follow trends, and keep on working, just *keep on working*. The cream rises to the top. Your honesty will shine through. People will know it is a part of "you" that you are showing, and *that*, in my opinion, is vital.

Armand Rosamilia is a New Jersey boy currently living in sunny Florida, where he writes when he's not watching zombie movies, the Boston Red Sox and listening to Heavy Metal music.

The "Dying Days" extreme zombie series is growing all the time, and he currently has over 50 releases on Amazon. His 'Miami Spy Games' series by Hobbes End Publishing and 'Tool Shed' horror novella from Angelic Knight Press are his most recent releases.

You can find him at http://armandrosamilia.com and e-mail him to talk about zombies, baseball and Metal: armandrosamilia@gmail.com

Writing The Series

Armand Rosamilia

First, I'm going to do some quick bragging to (hopefully) show you I know what I'm talking about. And then I'm going to dazzle and amaze you with my knowledge and all that jazz.

I've written several series over the years. *Dying Days* is my biggest, an extreme zombie series. I'm currently working on *Dying Days 4* but there are many other stories that belong in the world itself.

Flagler Beach Fiction Series is a contemporary fiction arc of stories (yeah, I write in many genres and subgenres) that will eventually be 7 books, each comprised of 10 stories in each.

Miami Spy Games:Russian Zombie Gun was originally a series of 6,000 word short stories released like television episodes and eventually put out as one big collection. It puts zombies in a thriller as opposed to traditional horror.

I'm sure before all is said and done I'll have quite a few more. And the books and stories I have out now with only one release will eventually all have a sequel or three if I can help it, because readers love to read more and more about a character.

When I was growing up I read everything I could about Conan the Barbarian, and not just the Robert E. Howard stories. I read the newer authors dipping into the world as well, because Conan was (and still is) my favorite character. I wanted to read more about his adventures.

I think most readers want to get to know a character and feel like they are a friend (or an enemy in the case of your good villains), and reading more and more about them is comforting. And fun, right?

Look at all the movies with sequels, and it isn't a new fad. It's been happening as long as I've been going to the movies. *Friday the 13th Part 2*, anyone? And who can forget *Breakin 2: Electric Bugaloo*.

Why? Because of the familiarity of characters, places and themes. We like to revisit them and see what they're up to now, like an old friend from high school you haven't seen in years and you're walking out of a bar and he's walking in. You turn around and go back inside and suddenly you're in a Bruce Springsteen video, talking about the good ol' days.

A series also sells because readers want to keep revisiting these characters and/or places, and there is a built-in readership which will follow each and every subsequent release. Potential readers will also see it is not a one-shot book and start from the beginning, helping with your backlist sales as well.

Let's go back to my *Flagler Beach Fiction Series*, for instance. When I wrote the first part of *Kokomo's Café*, it was two short stories and about 5,000 words total and sold for 99 cents. It also sold poorly in the beginning.

By the time I released the last two stories and had all ten done, I still had sluggish sales but it had risen, and the first part had sold a few more. I released it all together as *Kokomo's Café Complete*, all ten stories in print and eBook.

The second book is *Golden Lion Café*, and when I put out the first two stories in the arc as Part 1, a funny thing happened: it sold quite well, and by looking at the numbers I saw I'd sold as many of it as I'd sold total on *Kokomo's Café*. The third book, *J and J Fitness* as well as book four, *Flagler Fish Company*, kept it going by holding onto the reader base and adding more as people saw the series and started from book one.

Often, I could look at my Amazon sales page and see the same x number of each being sold over time, leading me to believe a great percentage of readers were beginning with the first stories and continuing to read them as it moves along. This is a good sign. If I'd only put out the first two stories I doubt it would have ever sold as much or had such legs in sales all these months later. As more potential readers see the series they jump in from the beginning and end up reading the entire series. By the time it is done (seven books) the sales of each book and as a whole will more than justify writing them.

But you can't force it. Tell the story and if it happens to be done after the one book, so be it. Although, of course, you can add some characters and ideas that could swing away from the main story as a sequel or a tie-in. Also another good way to keep your readers excited about your newest work.

I did it with the *Dying Days* series. I spun off several characters into other stories, like taking Tosha Shorb from *Dying Days 2* and writing her prequel story in Dying Days: Origins. You can find other characters in the *Still Dying: Select Scenes From Dying Days* short story collection, too. The point is: people want to read more about your world and your characters as long as it interests them and keeps them involved and guessing what comes next.

Now, let's look at it from an author's standpoint.

You've invested way more time than a reader has in this character. You know more about every one of them and every setting in your world. If you've written people and places interesting, not only will the readers want to know more, but so will you.

There is a sequel in every story, waiting to be expanded on and written. The readers will thank you, and so will the characters.

Tonia Brown is a Southern author with a penchant for Victorian dead things. She writes in many genres from horror (Sundowners) to humor (Badass Zombie Road Trip) to erotica (Lucky Stiff) to steampunk (The Cold Beneath). She also tends to a few webserials such as the weird western Railroad! and the humorous Confessions of a Villainess. She recently signed on with Permuted Press to re-release the self published novel Skin Trade, as well as two more new novels in the series. When not writing she raises unicorns and fights crime with her husband under the code names Dr. Weird and his sexy sidekick Butternut.

You can learn more about her at www.thebackseatwriter.com.

Running a Web Serial
or
How to Slowly Lose Your Mind, One Week at a Time

Tonia Brown

One fine evening I was minding my own business when my brain had an idea. Normally I welcome these things, but every so often those ideas turn out to be nothing but trouble. I don't mean stick your tongue in the fan kind of trouble. Or put lube on the toilet seat kind of trouble. I mean keep you up to your neck in work kind of trouble. The idea went something like this:

"Hey there, Tonia!" my brain said.

"Hello, brain," I said.

"You look like you're pretty busy."

"Yeah, I sure am. Between the fulltime night job and the family and the writing, I stay pretty swamped."

"I'll bet." My brain snapped her fingers, if you can believe that. "You know what? I think you can be more busy."

"It's busier, and no thank you. I'm busy enough as it is."

"Nonsense. I think you can be ten times as busy as you are now. In fact, I know just the trick to keep you up nights."

"I'm already up nights. I work nights. Remember?"

"Meh, whatever. You wanna know my idea?"

"No." I tried to ignore her, but she kept prodding me.

"Hey, hey, hey, hey," she said over and over.

"What!" I finally shouted.

"You should start a web serial."

I cringed. "Oh, no. No, no, no, no, no. I don't have time for that. I barely get anything done as it is."

"I know, but I don't care. I want a web serial."

"I don't."

"I do."

"I don't."

"Do you want to keep writing?"

"Yes?"

"Then I suggest you start working on that web serial, because from now on it is all I plan on thinking about."

And that was that. My mind made up itself and I could do little to stop it. A few months after this encounter, I launched *Railroad!*, a weird western adventure featuring a crazy crew of a standalone train. Four years and many, many words later the story is still chugging along, full steam. Four long dedicated years of once a week updates. Even though my web serial isn't horror, I thought I would share my experience, both the good and the bad, in case you decide you want to run a web serial of your own.

There are many benefits as well as a number of drawbacks when it comes to launching a web serial, but before we go over them, let's take a brief look at the history of the serial in general.

How it all started:

Serialized fiction quickly followed the invention of movable type. Because the printing process was so new and challenging, it was cheaper and easier to produce large works featuring many authors, with new installments of individual stories with each massive publication. This process was streamlined and popularized during the Victorian era. Literacy began to spike as more folks learned to read. Meanwhile, the printing process faced new improvements every day. More outlets to read from plus more readers plus cheaper ways to print caused a swell in demand for more fiction. To fill this gap, publishing houses hired writers to pen tales from week to week, keeping the audience hungry for another installment and thus selling more magazines and papers. Lots of authors got their start and fame from serialized fiction, such as Charles Dickens (*The Pickwick Papers*), Alexandre Dumas (*The Three Musketeers*) and Harriet Beecher Stowe (*Uncle Tom's Cabin*).

The process was so popular among the authors of this

era that it was considered the mark of an amateur to publish a novel in its entirety without having appeared in a serialized form beforehand. Serialized fiction was the go to professional outlet. Full length novels became collected works for a particular series, as opposed to single story arcs.

With the advent of radio, followed by television, serialized fiction shifted away from print to a broadcasted form. There came a steady decline in available serialized fiction, and a rise in complete novels and collections. Authors continue to publish serialized fiction to this day, albeit not as often in the printed form. Many turn to the internet as an option for serialized fiction, using the power of the World Wide Web to post timely updates to their particular story. There are many forms of web fiction available to the public: fictional blogs, serialized novels, web comics, and the web serial. The difference is subtle across the board, save for web comics, which are stories told in installments through an illustrated format. Some authors' works are available for a small subscription fee, while others post their work free for all to read.

But enough of that. Onto losing your mind, one week at a time.

Before you begin:
There are three things you must consider before you decide to take on the labor of a web serial.

Do you have the time to dedicate to the project?

Do you have the resources to produce a quality product?

Are you disciplined enough to follow through?

These might seem like obvious questions for any

writing project, but the success of serialized fiction is especially dependent upon these three things. If you can't dedicate the proper amount of time and effort to your web serial, updating it with well edited work in a timely manner, you will lose the interest of your readers faster than you can read this sentence. Do you have what it takes?

Once you decide to take the plunge, the first thing you need to choose is what kind of story you're going to tell. I don't just mean what genre, I am talking about the style of web serial you plan to run. Would you like to tell a different story every week based in the same universe? Or would you prefer to follow particular characters about, telling only their story? Both formats are popular with today's readers, and each possesses their own benefits as well as downfalls.

The vignette allows for a wider variety of styles and stories, allowing you to tell tales from all manner of perspectives, as long as they all tie together in some way. For instance, you might set up a fictional town which is secretly run by a pack of demons in human form. Each week's story would follow a different demon and his evil work, or maybe even told from the perspective of the victims as they suffer at the demons' hands. The downside of this is the need to complete a finished storyline each week, or at the very least every couple of weeks. Short stories are fun to write, but there is an art in telling a tight tale. Turning out a new short story on a weekly basis, without the time to explore character development or intricate plotlines, might wear you out as a writer.

A tighter continuity in which each week continues the story from the last week provides a more controlled process in crafting your tale. You have the freedom to explore backgrounds and side stories, while all the time feeding your audience more and more of the growing plot. The downside of this is figuring out how to keep your plot going without making it feel like you are dragging everything out. Stories need an ending. Serialized fiction encourages the opposite, which can be a danger if you don't watch yourself.

I found the easiest way to incorporate both of these ideas was to follow a loose continuity. This is when you tell a longer story in a common universe, while following different story arcs along the way. *Railroad!* is told from one character's perspective, Rodger Dodger, and follows his adventures aboard the Sleipnir, an eight cab train that lays her own tracks and picks them up again, allowing her to travel anywhere she likes. The story has a grand over arc involving a main villain and a sinister plot, while the tale is told through smaller novella-sized story arcs. Dodger interacts with a variety of characters throughout the novellas, some reoccurring, some one time cameos. This allows for me to keep the ideas fresh and the story moving, while continually developing the characters and atmosphere.

Also, consider why you want to run a web serial. Keep in mind that unless you create a pay per read website, it's a whole lot of work you are essentially giving away for free. Some folks think that it's crazy to give away your work in this manner, but serialized fiction is a great way for a new author to build an audience as well as a brand. Keeping up with your established schedule and meeting your goals creates a trust with your readers, and that familiarity encourages them to check out your other stuff. Besides, just because you posted it online doesn't mean it is out of commission altogether. You can still submit that work as previously released material to publishers, or even self-publish it.

With *Railroad!*, I publish each volume on Amazon for the Kindle the week after the last chapter posts. At the end of each year I gather those three novellas and publish an omnibus on both Kindle and in paperback. The serial does brisk business on Amazon, regardless of the fact that it is available to read for free, in its entirety, online. Some folks find they would rather read the story in larger chunks, and thus prefer the novellas. Others wait all year for the omnibus release. While some of the Kindle readers came straight from the Amazon crowd, many of them started reading the serial online then branched out into the Kindle and print releases for a variety of reasons. Once the story is done, I plan on searching for an agent to represent the completed storyline to a larger publisher.

Time Management:
Now that you have an idea of what type of story you want to set up, we need to go back to the first of our three questions.

Do you have the time to dedicate to this project?

Let's say you post 1,500 to 2,500 words of your serial each Monday. That is 78,000 words minimum every year that you have to produce. We are talking the size of a completed novel. And not only must you produce the work, you should have it professionally edited as well. So that is 1,500 words written, edited and ready for posting every Monday morning. This process takes some time to plot and plan. The easiest way to manage a regularly updated web serial is to write the work as far ahead of time as you can. I wrote almost the entire first year worth of *Railroad!* before I even set up the website. It made for a breezy year of posting, which I completely squandered on other projects instead of setting aside a bit of time to work on the next season. This left me in a panic when the first season finished posting, and I rushed to get ready for the second year. After this, I got used to the groove of working on a full volume until it was done, taking a month or so break to work on other projects, then getting back to work on *Railroad!*. This means every six weeks or so I must stop whatever else I am working on and begin another volume of Railroad! or it won't be ready in time for edits and posting. It sounds like an obsessive agenda but it is the kind of dedication you will need if you want to turn out a regularly scheduled project. Of course, you could choose to update whenever you feel like it, or even post less often, say once a month, but you will find it harder to keep your readers if you don't present a timely and dependable schedule.

Here is an example of a typical process for me: each *Railroad!* volume is about 30,000 words. A finished volume can last me anywhere from twelve to fifteen weeks, depending on the length and appropriate storyline breaks. At any given time I am usually posting one volume while the next is in edits and I'm actively working on the one after that. In the years I have done this, I've only missed one Monday update so far, and it wasn't because I was unprepared. It was due to being sick and missing my posting date because I couldn't make it out of bed! Again this might seem obsessive, but if you want to keep your audience happy, you must meet your deadlines.

Production:
It takes more than just the will to write to produce a great web serial.

Do yourself and your reputation a favor and hire a professional editor to go over your work. Just because you are giving the story away for free doesn't mean you can slack on the quality of it. Treat your web serial as you would any other writing project. Write, edit, proof and only then should you publish. Railroad! has seen several editors in its days, with Joe Mynhardt as the latest talent behind the wheel.

If you have the time and luxury, try to run the sections past a few beta readers too. Ones that are intimately familiar with the story can provide valuable third party insight to your developing plot. It might take a while to gain some beta readers, but once you do, they won't be able to resist the chance to have a peek at your work long before the rest of the world gets a chance to read it.

Aside from an editor, you need to consider the outlet for your work. There are several avenues you can pursue, from setting up your own website dedicated to the task, to using one of several available free websites. An easy and useful solution is using a premade blog site, such as Wordpress or Blogspot. I use Blogspot for *Railroad!* and highly recommend it for its simplicity and ease of use. I was able to set up the site in a matter of minutes, and once I settled into a format, posting became a breeze. I can even schedule chapters to automatically post if I want, though for some reason I prefer the act of manually posting every Monday. Blogspot's layout is fairly adaptable, with lots of little widgets and tools to help you maximize your web serial's navigation. Keep in mind, an easy to navigate website makes for an easy to read web serial, which encourages return readers.

The biggest drawback to Blogspot is the same as its blessings—it's just too simple for some folks. The tools are restricted in what they can do, and there are a limited number of layouts for you to choose from. If you are adventurous and web savvy and crave total control over your end product, then you might want to look into something a little more complicated such as Wordpress. There are far more tools available for Wordpress, allowing you to achieve a more distinctive blog as opposed to the cookie cutter layout of other blog sites.

The best thing about using either of these sites is the built in audience tools. Both Blogspot and Wordpress allow other folks to easily follow your site at the click of a button, with little to no upkeep from your end. And if you prefer to have a standalone web address, as opposed to the tags of the premade blog site, you can always purchase a domain name and set up a forwarding page that send visitors straight to your blog when they type in the original address.

Once you've chosen an outlet, consider hiring an artist to help you design a look for your web serial. Much like cover art for a book, a web serial should have at least a notable header image that folks can associate with the work. You can use this same style to make banners and smaller ads for link exchanges with other blogs and serials. A few extra pieces of art to embellish your site is a good idea too. Try and keep the same artist throughout your serial if you can, employing them to work on your covers for Kindle and print releases if you choose that route. Transferring that same look from the web to your finished collection makes for a memorable branding technique. David R Shires has been with me since the beginning of the *Railroad!* series, providing amazing digital art for both the website and the book releases.

Keeping it Going:
Follow through is the key to successful serialized fiction. Sure it takes time, effort and talent to write the thing, but keeping those wheels moving is the heart of the web serial engine. Posting it in a timely manner and making sure any extra pages you set up stay fresh and relevant are the acts that will bring readers back to your site. Return readers equal a dedicated audience, and a dedicated audience will lead to future sales.

As I said before, while I can set my site to automatically post my entire novella, chapter by chapter, I like the act of manually posting my work every Monday. I gain a sense of accomplishment by taking a bit of time out every Monday morning to cut and paste the work, then proofread it once more before posting it. When I click the publish button and send that chapter out into the world, I feel like I've achieved something. That measurable effect keeps me motivated.

Reader feedback is another great motivator. Make sure you set up a contact page and allow comments on your chapters. Encourage the readers to let you know what they think, or even where they would like to see the story go. Once those comments and emails start rolling in, you will look forward to rewarding your readers with reveals and plotline completions.

Should you find yourself in a scheduling crunch and

unable to make a timely post for whatever reason (a death in the family, sickness, rampaging elephants...) don't panic. There are several ways you can handle a hole in your schedule. If your timeline slips with enough warning—for example, you don't get the work to your editor in time and he can't get to your serial in time—then consider filling the gaps with guest posts. I did just that very thing when it came time for the second season of Railroad! and I was nowhere near ready. I asked four authors I admired if they would each write a short story in the weird western vein. I posted one a week, giving me a month long window to catch up. Since then, this unintended intermission has become part of my serial's format.

If you find yourself short of a post just a few days before it is needed, consider whipping up a character profile and posting that instead. Or maybe a rundown of the location you set your work in. As long as you post something for the readers to enjoy, they should remain satisfied. At the very least, if you are able, post a brief technical difficulty note, explaining the lack of a recent post and the date you plan on resuming.

When it comes to marketing your serial, turn to places like Facebook, Twitter, forums and other social networking sites. Try and stick with online advertising, because after all, your product is just a click away. Connecting with other web serial authors and swapping links to post is a cheap and effective way to gain more readers. You can also employ a pay per click ad site, such as Project Wonderful. These kinds of advertising setups usually have something to fit everyone's budget.

Overall, your web serial should be a labor of love. Yes, it takes tons of time and effort and a bit of money on your part, unless you can barter for your editing and other services. But in the end, the benefits and fun of the project outweigh the insanity that comes with it.

I hope this proves helpful to you out there in writer land. If you decide you want to start a web serial, be sure to let me know! I am always interested in connecting with other authors and especially reading others' serialized fiction. But hands off the demon run town. I got plans for that one.

Jim Mcleod has been a fan of horror for over thirty years. Ever since that fateful day when he happened across a copy of James Herbert's 'The Fog'.

His passion for horror led him to found Ginger Nuts of Horror.com in 2010. Since its birth Ginger Nuts of Horror has grown into one of the most viewed resources for horror fiction. The site regularly gets over 90,000 views a month and is currently ranked number one for Horror Fiction Reviews and Horror Author interviews on Google.

Reviewing

Jim Mcleod

There are millions of guides about writing, publicising and promoting your magnum opus horror novel. Most of these guides are written by other authors, some are written by authors who have paid their dues, who have numerous publishing credits to their name. Others are written by "authors" who claim to be bestselling authors, whose lack of basic language skills, means they don't know the difference between 'bestselling' and loads of free downloads of their eBook on Amazon. These are my favourite guides, how can an author who hasn't actually sold a book write a guide on selling your book. And by sold I mean have someone part with their hard earned cash for the book.

However both of these types of author guides lack one important factor, a factor that I like to call Reviewer Etiquette. Reviewers are an odd bunch, we tend to get looked upon as a necessary evil, loved by authors when we give their book a good review, and despised like a mass murdering pervert when we give a book a negative review. Which is fine by me, you as a writer are entitled to get upset at a bad review. Hell I get upset when the wife criticises my attempt at housework. I spent the best part of a day doing it, how dare she, and like a lot of the books I receive it does seem as though the author spent the same amount of time writing their book as I did doing the laundry. But this isn't about author meltdown, that's for another day. This is about getting your book in the reviewer's review pile, and what you as a writer should do in the run up to the review being published.

First up, the majority of reviewers don't get paid; we do this out of a love of the genre. If you are lucky enough to work for a publication that can afford to pay you as a staff writer, then good for you, I hate your guts, but good for you. Yes there are "reviewers" that will take payment for writing a "review", those are not reviewers, they are scum, and they do more damage than good. The rest of us reviewers do this for fun, we all have a life, and we have work, family commitments and other stuff to do.

Now some authors I have dealt with seem to think that giving a reviewer a free copy of their 99p eBook is payment with an unmentioned contract to review that book. I'm sorry to say that this isn't the case. If you pretend that reviewing is my job, and my pay was the minimum wage of £6.31, then your 99p eBook is only worth around ten minutes of my time. When you look at it this way, this doesn't give you the author any right to get all uppity when I decide not to review your book.

I'm getting ahead of myself. To put things into perspective, when I was on holiday the other week, I came home to around 300 emails all demanding my attention, yes some were for hair replacement therapy, and investment opportunities in Zimbabwe, this still left hundreds of emails all wanting either an interview, a review, or news item or even all three on my website The Ginger Nuts of Horror. I'm sorry to say this is a depressing sight to behold. So how did I tackle it? Firstly I scanned the emails for authors whose work I was familiar with, these went straight into my holding folder. Or the deleted bin, depending on my past interactions with the author concerned. I then checked for anything in the subject line that sounded like a red flag.

The sort of thing I was looking for were phrases such as 'ZOMBIE', 'ROMANCE', 'SEX', and my personal most hated phrase 'THE NEXT BIG THING IN HORROR FICTION'.

These emails were all deleted without a second thought. The next filter was another simple one, any email that used colourful or stupid childish unprofessional   fonts, was again deleted without reading. Annoying as hell, isn't it? If you want to be taken seriously as a writer, then act serious, comic sans is a font that should never be used outside of a child's Birthday Part invitation.

This still left rather a lot of emails that required proper attention, and this is where it gets interesting. The emails deleted previously were all down to schoolboy errors, you could have gotten past these stages if you just read my review criteria, or taken your inner child and told them to fucking stop using fonts and colours that are just plain stupid. This is where we get to the real crux of this article, *etiquette* and *politeness,* two words that so many authors are not aware off.

When you send an email to a reviewer, I know you think sending a mass email will save you time, you know the sort headed with phrases such as 'Dear Sir / Madam'. We reviewers are people too, we like to feel special. So yes, use copy and paste for the main body of your email, but go on, at least try and find out what my name is.

Please don't say you love my site, and think your book would be a good fit, when your book clearly isn't a good fit. That just makes me think that you have just sent the same email to every review site going. Again we want to feel special.

Don't ever, and I mean EVER send out a review request, and then expect the book reviewer to actually have to pay money to buy the book. That's just cheap. I don't like cheap. I got an email like this where the author wanted £9.99 for their eBook. To use a famous Scottish saying, Aye right!

Actually ask for a review, interview, or a news article. Don't just send an email with the book's synopsis, and a link to download it or the book as an attachment. That's just lazy, and if you are too lazy to write a simple email it suggests that your writing will also be lazy.

Sell me the book, your email is probably the only way I will hear about your book. If your synopsis of the book is dull, and your email itself is poorly worded, then I won't want to read your book. However don't go too far, selling yourself as the greatest new writer I have never heard of just smacks of arrogance, and will get your email, can you guess? That's right. Deleted.

Congratulations, you have managed to get your book into my review pile. But don't get cocky, kid! This still doesn't guarantee a review. It is clearly stated in my review policy that I won't guarantee that I will actually review your book even if I accept it. This may sound unfair, and I'll be honest, I review 99% of all physical books that get sent my way. I used to feel obligated to review everything; it has only been in the last few months that I realised that I don't owe anyone anything for a 99p eBook.

Like most review sites Ginger Nuts of Horror is run by one person and as I have said before I have a life outside of this site. So if I take a bit of time in posting your review, please, please don't send me a nasty email saying "WHY ISN'T MY REVIEW UP?". That will just get my back up, and yes, you guessed it, the review deleted.

I can't promise that if you follow these points your book will get picked up by every review site going. I do think, though, that your chances will be increased.

Just remember we reviewers don't need your book, most of us have a book buying addiction and have more books to read than we have time left on this plane of existence. So please treat us nice, make us feel special, and we might just let you get to second base, hell you may even get a home run.

And once you get friendly with a review site, please don't just forget about us once your review has been posted. There is so much more we can do for you, interviews, guest posts, blog tours and giveaways. If you are on social sites talk to us, share our posts, like our Facebook posts, retweet. Remember the more you share a review site, the bigger the audience, which means the bigger the audience for your book. It's a hard game, but if you get a handful of reviewers on your side, you might just make the big leagues

"There are worse crimes than burning books. One of them is not reading them."
— Ray Bradbury

On Weird Fiction:
READ, damn it. Fill your brain to the bursting point with the good stuff, starting with writers that you truly enjoy, and then work your way backward and outward, reading those writers who inspired the writers you love best. That was my path as far as Weird/Horror Fiction, starting with Lovecraft, and then working my way backward/outward on the Weird Fiction spiderweb. And don't limit your reading. Read it all, especially non-fiction and various news outlets. You'd be surprised by how many of my story ideas were born while listening to NPR, perusing a blog, or paging through Vanity Fair. Once you have your fuel squared away, just write what you love, in whatever style and genre. You'll never have fun being someone you're not, so be yourself. When a singer opens their mouth, what comes out is what comes out.
Also, don't be afraid to fail, and don't be afraid to walk away. Writing isn't for everyone, and that's totally fine. One doesn't need to be a writer to enjoy being a reader and overall fan of genre or wider fiction."
— T.E. Grau

"There comes a time in a man's life when to get where he has to – if there are no doors or windows – he walks through a wall."
— Bernard Malamud

Dirty Deeds
(Being a Writer)

The Oxford Companion to English Literature describes Ramsey Campbell as "Britain's most respected living horror writer". He has been given more awards than any other writer in the field, including the Grand Master Award of the World Horror Convention, the Lifetime Achievement Award of the Horror Writers Association and the Living Legend Award of the International Horror Guild. Among his novels are 'The Face That Must Die', 'Incarnate', 'Midnight Sun', 'The Count of Eleven', 'Silent Children', 'The Darkest Part of the Woods', 'The Overnight', 'Secret Story', 'The Grin of the Dark', 'Thieving Fear', 'Creatures of the Pool', 'The Seven Days of Cain', 'Ghosts Know', 'The Kind Folk', 'Think Yourself Lucky', 'Thirteen Days at Sunset Beach', 'The Last Revelation of Gla'aki' and 'The Pretence' are novellas. His collections include 'Waking Nightmares', 'Alone with the Horrors', 'Ghosts and Grisly Things', 'Told by the Dead', 'Just Behind You' 'Holes for Faces', along with his non-fiction are all collected as Ramsey Campbell, Probably. His novels 'The Nameless' and 'Pact of the Fathers' have been filmed in Spain. His regular columns appear in Dead Reckonings and Video Watchdog. He is the President of the Society of Fantastic Films.

Ramsey Campbell lives on Merseyside with his wife Jenny. His pleasures include classical music, good food, wine, and whatever's in that pipe. His web site is at www.ramseycampbell.com.

Avoiding What's Been Done to Death

Ramsey Campbell

You can't avoid anything unless you know what it is. This idea alone would be sufficient reason for me to recommend that anyone who wants to write worthwhile horror fiction have a working knowledge of the tradition of the field. The finest single introduction to it is *Great Tales of Terror and the Supernatural,* edited by Wise and Fraser, and still, I believe, readily available. If you find nothing to enjoy and be awestruck by in that book, then it seems unlikely that you have any real feeling for horror fiction. On the other hand, you may be taken aback by how many of the themes in the book have recently been bloated into best sellers. I would hope that realisation may make you deeply dissatisfied, because that kind of dissatisfaction is the first step in creating something new.

Some people (generally critics with no fiction to their name and writers near the end of their careers) claim that there's nothing new in horror. In a sense that may be true. Most of sixty years ago, H. P. Lovecraft drew up a list of the basic themes of weird fiction, and I can think of very little that the field has added to that list. But that's by no means as defeatist as it sounds, because the truth is surely that many of the themes we're dealing with are so large and powerful as to be essentially timeless.

For instance, the folk tale of the wish that comes true more fully and more terribly than the wisher could have dreamed is the basis not only of "The Monkey's Paw" but of Steve King's *Pet Sematary* and of my own novel *Obsession,* yet the three stories have otherwise far more to do with their writers than with one another. That suggests, if I may be forgiven for emitting a homily now and then in the course of this essay, that one way to avoid what has already been done is to be true to yourself.

That isn't to say that imitation never has its uses. Here, as in any other of the arts, it's a legitimate and useful way to serve your apprenticeship. Though it may not be obvious to readers who know only my recent work, I began my career by imitating Lovecraft. No writer has orchestrated terror in prose more carefully than Lovecraft, but you won't learn how to write dialogue or deal with character from him. Such skills are best learned by reading writers outside the field (in my case, Nabokov and Graham Greene, among others). If you're writing in a genre, it's all the more important to read widely outside it in order to be aware what fiction is capable of. It's less a matter of importing techniques into the field than of seeing the field as part of a larger art. Depending wholly on genre techniques can lead too easily to the second-hand and the second-rate. There's only one Stephen King, but there are far too many writers trying to sound like him.

It's no bad thing to follow the example of writers you admire, then, but only as a means to finding your own voice. You won't find that, of course, unless you have something of your own to say. I did, once I stopped writing about Lovecraft's horrors and began to deal with what disturbed me personally. I began to write about how things seemed to me, which was more important and, at first, more difficult than it may sound. I tried and still try to take nothing on trust, to describe things as they really are or would be.

I'm sure I don't need to tell you that the horror field is riddled with clichés. The house that's for sale too cheaply, the guy who must be working nights because he sleeps during the day (must be a handyman, too, to judge by that big box he keeps in his cellar), the attic room the landlady keeps locked, the place none of the topers in the village inn will visit after dark – we can all have fun recognising these and many others, which is by no means to say that they haven't been used effectively by masters of the craft. But I think there are more fundamental clichés in the field, and I think today's writers may be the ones to overturn them.

Take the theme of evil, as the horror story often does. Writing about evil is a moral act, and it won't do to recycle definitions of evil, to take them on trust. Horror fiction frequently presents the idea of evil in such a shorthand form as to be essentially meaningless – something vague out there that causes folk to commit terrible acts, something other than ourselves, nothing to do with us. That sounds to me more like an excuse than a definition, and I hope it's had its day. If we're going to write about evil, then let's define it and how it relates to ourselves.

All good fiction consists of looking at things afresh, but horror fiction seems to have a built-in tendency to do the opposite. Ten years or so ago, many books had nothing more to say than "the devil made me do it"; now, thanks to the influence of films like *Friday the 13th,* it seems enough for some writers to say that a character is psychotic; no further explanation is necessary. But it's the job of writers to imagine how it would feel to be all their characters, however painful that may sometimes be. It may be a lack of that compassion that has led some writers to create children who are evil simply because they're children, surely the most deplorable cliché of the field.

Some clichés are simply products of lazy writing. Tradition shouldn't be used as an excuse to repeat what earlier writers have done; if you feel the need to write about the stock figures of the horror story, that's all the more reason to imagine them anew.

For instance, we might have believed there was nothing new to be written about vampirism until Karl Wagner wrote "Beyond Any Measure", whose stunningly original idea was always implicit in the vampire tradition and waiting for Karl to notice. Again, generations might have thought that the definitive haunted house tale had been written, but it hadn't been until Shirley Jackson wrote *The Haunting of Hill House* (a statement guaranteed to make some of you try to improve on that novel, perhaps). Put it another way: one reason some folk recoil from my own novel *The Face That Must Die* seems to be that it confronts you with what I imagine it might be like to be a psychotic killer, rather than keeping a Halloween face or ski mask between him and the audience, and depicting him as a bogeyman we could dismiss as being nothing like ourselves. It's only fair to warn you that many readers and publishers would rather see imitations of whatever they liked last year than give new ideas a chance. But I've always tried to write what rings true to *me,* whether or not it makes the till ring. If you don't feel involved with what you're writing, it's unlikely that anyone else will.

There's another side to the field that is overdue for attack by a new generation – its reactionary quality. A horror writer I otherwise admire argued recently that "it has been a time-honoured tradition in literature and film that you have a weak or helpless heroine" – implying, I assume, that we should go on doing so. Well, tradition is a pretty poor excuse for perpetrating stereotypes (not that the author in question necessarily does); time-honoured it may be, but that doesn't make it honourable. In fact, these days, so many horror stories (and especially films) gloat over the suffering of women that it seems clear the authors are getting their own back, consciously or not, on aspects of real life that they can't cope with. Of course, that isn't new in horror fiction, nor is using horror fiction to define as evil or diabolical whatever threatens the writer or the writer's lifestyle; but at the very least, one should be aware as soon as possible that this is what one is doing, so as to be able to move on. I have my suspicions, too, about the argument that horror fiction defines what is normal by showing us what isn't. I think it's time for more of the field to acknowledge that, when we come face to face with the monsters, we may find ourselves looking not at a mask but at a mirror.

Now all this may sound as if it requires some discipline and dedication, and my experience is that it does. After all, the best way for a writer to compete is with oneself, to do better than one did last time. I'm not the first to say that the most important thing for a writer to do is to write, but I'll add that you should work on whatever you're writing every day until it's finished; to do otherwise is to court writer's block, every blank day adding to the hurdle that prevents you from getting back into the story and making the task seem more impossible. When I was writing my story "Litter", six months elapsed between the first day's work and my return to the story, which I took up by writing the line "That's how he enters the story, or this is." I should have rewritten the story to improve its shape, of course.

Now I rewrite more and more severely, and I take great pleasure in cutting thousands of words out of first drafts; I think that's a pleasure worth learning as early as possible in one's career, not least because realising that one can do it helps one relax into writing the first draft, in which it's better to have too much material for later shaping than not enough. Learning to relax enough with the technique of writing novels comes easier to some than others; you may feel you need to plot a novel in advance (maybe all the way to breaking it down into chapter synopses) before you begin the first chapter, but it's worth trying to regard the synopsis merely as a safety net once you begin writing, trying to let the novel develop itself as it takes on more life. I did that first in *Incarnate,* and since then I've avoided plotting or constructing too far ahead, trying to know only as much as I need to know to start writing and head in the right direction. It can be fearsome to find yourself losing your way halfway through a novel, all by yourself in the unknown, but I find that the solutions are usually somewhere in what you've already written, and I can tell you that the bad days are worth the days when you feel the novel come to life.

I'm still stressing the arduousness, but let me see if I can pass on some tricks I've learned. We all have an optimum period of creativity each day, and it's worth beginning work then if you possibly can. Mine is from about six in the morning until noon or so. It's easy to get distracted from your desk, but music may help; my desk is between the speakers of the hi-fi, on which I play compact discs (which last longer than records and keep me there longer) of all sorts of music from Monteverdi onwards. (Steve King uses rock; Peter Straub, jazz.) Don't be too eager to feel you've exhausted your creative energy for the day, but if you sense you're close to doing so, then don't squeeze yourself dry: better to know what the next paragraph is going to be and start with that next time. Scribble down a rough version of it rather than risk forgetting it. Always have a rough idea of your first paragraph before you sit down to write, and then you won't be trapped into fearing the blank page.

If you must take a day or more out from writing a story, break off before the end of a scene or a chapter, to give yourself some impetus when you return. Always carry a notebook for ideas, glimpses, overheard dialogue, details of what you're about to write, developments of work in progress. If an idea or something larger refuses to be developed, try altering the viewpoint or even the form: if it won't grow as a short story, it may be a poem. Sometimes, two apparently unproductive ideas may be cross-fertilised to give you a story. Then again, you may not be ready technically or emotionally to deal with an idea, and it can improve with waiting.

What else can I tell you? Surprise us; show us things we haven't seen before or didn't admit that we knew. Write the stories that only you can write. Some of the best horror stories have yet to be written. I have no idea what they'll be about, but maybe you will have.

Kevin Lucia is an Associate Fiction Editor for The Horror Channel. His short fiction has appeared in several anthologies.

He's currently finishing his Creative Writing Masters Degree at Binghamton University, he teaches high school English and lives in Castle Creek, New York with his wife and children.

He is the author of 'Hiram Grange & The Chosen One (Book Four of The Hiram Grange Chronicles). His first short story collection, 'Things Slip Through' was published November 2013, and his next collection of novellas, 'Devourer of Souls', is due June 30th, 2014. He's currently working on his first novel.

What Are You Reading?

Kevin Lucia

I've been a voracious reader since childhood. I can thank my parents for that. From the very beginning, reading held an important place in our home. My dad was (and still is) a voracious reader of nonfiction. My mother diligently read to both my sister and I. By sixth grade, I was given the honored privilege of walking across the big parking lot to the high school to take books out of their library, because I'd exhausted all my options in the elementary library.

So when I first started taking my writing seriously, Stephen King's admonition "*If you don't have time to read, you don't have the time (or the tools) to write*" was music to my ears. This was advice I'd have *no* problem following. Indeed, my desire to write had sprung from a childhood spent reading, so this was a no-brainer to me.

However, like many young readers, I'm sure I didn't show much discrimination in my reading. I simply read what I liked, and that was all. In many ways, this is very natural. William Faulkner's advice expresses it best:

> *"Read, read, read. Read everything – trash, classics, good and bad, and see how they do it. Just like a carpenter who works as an apprentice and studies the master. Read! You'll absorb it. Then write. If it's good, you'll find out. If it's not, throw it out of the window."*

Of course at the time, I didn't have a wide enough frame of reference to make the distinction between *"trash, classics, good and bad"*. I just obsessively read what I liked, one book after another. Because of this, my diet wasn't very diverse. I read all of Stephen King and Dean Koontz's novels, a few of Peter Straub's, and that was it. When I began actively reviewing in the horror community, I read all the latest titles Leisure had to offer, too.

The problem was, I was missing out on *so much.* I had very little sense of the horror genre's history. I had no idea what stories had already been told, and my reading palate didn't offer me nearly enough variety. Three years ago, I discovered just how much I was missing, and it's fair to say the experience changed me forever.

tom Monteleone and F. Paul Wilson were visiting my high school, conducting a fiction workshop with my Creative Writing students. The second night here, Paul called me at home, asking if I wanted to spend the evening with Tom, him, and a "friend" of theirs that lived in my area. Of course, I jumped at the chance. Turned out, this "friend" was Stuart David Schiff, former editor of the *Whispers* magazine and speculative anthology series.

Until about midnight, Tom, Paul and Stuart regaled each other with stories of the genre's history, their own beginnings, influences, and just about everything and anything to do with speculative fiction. Stuart's basement was like the Smithsonian of Genre Fiction, a literal museum of the weird and fantastic. I had a front row seat to three legends waxing about the genre and its history. As they talked about one writer after another, it struck me right between the eyes: *I had no idea who these writers were.*

Fritz Leiber. Manley Wade Wellman. Hugh B. Cave. James Herbert. Ramsey Campbell. T. M. Wright. Charles Grant. Karl Edward Wagner. And *so* many more. The very first thing I did after getting home (much to my wife's chagrin) was order all the *Whispers* anthologies off Amazon. Then, several months later, I followed that up with the *Shadows* anthology series, edited by Charles Grant. This, of course, introduced me to Charles and his wonderful brand of quiet horror. Through *Whispers,* I discovered Manley Wade Wellman, Russell Kirk and Karl Edward Wagner. This, of course, led me to Karl's run as editor of *The Year's Best Horror Stories*, which opened the floodgates wide. Of course, I'd be remiss if I didn't explore Tom's *Borderlands* series, as well as J. N. Williamson's *Masques.*

This changed my outlook, completely. Now, I lament all the years I drove by used bookstores, thinking, "They won't have anything by anyone I know, anyway." Today, I *know* what to look for. I have a hit list in my head. The local library's used book sale has become a monthly treasure hunt. I've spent the last three years scouring used bookstores wherever I go, looking for books by Charles Grant, T. M. Wright, Kathryn Ptacek, Ramsey Campbell, Chelsea Quinn Yarbro, Manley Wade Wellman, Nina Kiriki Hoffman, Melanie Tem, Alan Ryan... the list goes on. I'm always on the lookout for horror anthologies edited by any of these fine fellows, too.

You'd think such a heady infusion of so many different voices would double my output as a writer. Initially, the result was the opposite. Reading so many of these stories made me realize how many of my ideas – clever, original, AWESOME ideas, I'd thought – simply weren't original at all. They'd been done before by folks much better than me. All this reading actually slowed my output for quite some time, because my increasing awareness of the genre's history (still so shallow, in my opinion), was pushing me *away* from those ideas I'd thought so original, into territory more my *own.*

There are many *contemporary* writers all young horror writers should be reading: Ronald Malfi, Rio Youers, Mary Sangiovanni, Gary McMahon, Norman Prentiss, Kealan Patrick Burke, and more. There are also the "greats" whom I still love and adore: Stephen King, Dean Koontz, Robert McCammon, and Peter Straub. But I've come to believe through personal experience that exploring the history of the genre is essential. And (even though this feels like an injustice) these writers, their novels and anthologies are often available at very affordable prices on the secondary market. If you're like

I was three years ago, then I suggest you scour Amazon for the following, right now:

Whispers, edited by Stuart David Schiff (searching Stuart's name alone on Amazon seems to Bring up better results, for some reason)

Shadows, edited by Charles L. Grant (and ANYTHING edited by Charles L. Grant)

Borderlands, edited by Tom Monteleone

Masques, edited by J. N. Williamson (copies of these seem tough to find)

The Year's Best Horror Stories, edited by Karl Edward Wagner

Also, search for novels written by any of the authors I mentioned above. You can't go wrong.

This, of course, is by no means a definitive list of horror that everyone should be reading. For example, I've yet to read any of the Pan Books of Horror, or Ellen Datlow's Best in Horror collections. But if you've not read any of those anthologies mentioned above, several editions of these alone will expose you to a whole new world of horror and speculative fiction, which you will only be the better for.

The 7 Signs that make Agents and Editors say, "Yes!"

Anonymous

As a former acquisition editor, agents knew what would interest me. And they also knew what wasted time. If your work didn't display any of the following, you saw rejection. Because, if what the agent sent lacked the Seven, those agents saw rejection too.

So what are the 7 Signs to Success?

Sign #1: Credentials.

It's the first item some agents seek. And it may be the only one you need. If a famous author recommends you, agents listen. Your work winning or placing in contests also achieves attention. Previous publications and praise show you're serious about writing. Prove you're not some wannabe with Daiquiri dreams, but Top Ramen talent. And, yes, celebrity still sells. But, if you're a celebrity, you won't read this. Though, your future ghostwriter might.

Sign #2: Setting that Shows Something New.

Setting must not only be unique, but it must also show us something new. Something we, as readers, would never experience otherwise. It doesn't just mean fantasy. It also means the exotic. It means places on Earth, with cultures from the foreign to the familiar, we'll never see.

If setting teaches the reader something new, it stands out. And agents and editors take notice.

Sign #3: Voice and Style.

These are the golden tickets that make every agent and editor unwrap your writing. If they find them, they sign you. Simple. But what is it? Not so simple. We call it the ingredient that everyone knows when they see it, but few can state what it is. So what is it? You. It's your charisma and the way you share a story. It's the difference between a child playing Chopsticks and a champion playing Chopin. It's how your sentences sing. Like music, each style is different. Each voice special. But, as with singers, the audience knows talent when they hear it. The same must be true with your writing as well. And, as with all art, it takes time to develop. So take your time. The writer you are today shouldn't be the writer you are tomorrow.

Sign #4: Devilish Dialogue.

If your dialogue turns a phrase, becomes the new cliché, and makes writers wish they wrote it, it's devilish. It demands attention. The best sounds like poetry, and the worst sounds like cheese. Perfect, English sentences don't smell sweet. They light up a room like Limburger. When everyone sounds the same, there's a problem. Devilish dialogue beats drums and creates anxiety within readers through denials. It demands you read more. Confrontation is key. Don't confuse dialogue, much less devilish dialogue, with conversation. Devilish dialogue makes you rubberneck and eavesdrop. The test is, if you hear it on the street, would you stop and listen? If not, it's a dud. Not devilish. Make your dialogue demand attention. Because your readers will too.

Sign #5: Charismatic Characters.

Do you wish you could befriend your characters? No? Then why would your readers? Your writing requests your readers, "Care about my characters. Stick around and listen to their plight. Their pilgrimage. Like them. Love them. And live with them in their world." Your characters need charm. Because agents and editors must not only like, love, and live with your characters, we must also sympathize. Sympathy is a novel's soul. Without soul, your writing reads lifeless. Worthless. We call characters without charisma cardboard. And agents and editors recycle that.

Sign #6: Humor that Hooks.

It sounds simple, but it's not. In fact, it's a well-kept secret. If you can make an agent or editor laugh, no matter the genre, you're sold. Because it's rare. Think about it. When was the last time a novel, outside humor, made you laugh because of witty wordplay? Yes, that rare. Even the darkest novel should show some sunshine. And that light is laughter. Don't underestimate this sign. Why? When you make an agent or editor laugh, they'll remember your work. And that goes a long way into getting your work to readers. Laughter makes you and your writing memorable.

Sign #7: A Powerful Premise.

This is the biggest selling point. It overcomes everything else that creates rejection. And yes, this is the reason you'll read bad writing on the bestseller list. Premise, or a new perspective, creates buzz or controversy. Either is good because it also births word-of-mouth. And that is a writer's most powerful ally. Jesus married Mary of Magdalene and sired a daughter. Superheroes once existed, but supervillains erased them from memory. A husband retells the romance that won his wife, now affected with Alzheimer's, so she can remember why they fell in love. Again, premise overcomes everything if it entices agents, editors, and readers alike. So make yours count.

Agents and editors want to say, "Yes!" But most submissions force them to say, "No." The seven signs make them pause and consider your writing. Have two or more, and they'll ask to see your work. Have all seven, and they'll send you a contract.

Because the seven signs always signal success.

Shirley Jackson Award-nominated author Tim Waggoner has published over thirty novels and three short story collections of dark fiction. He teaches creative writing at Sinclair Community College and in Seton Hill University's Master of Fine Arts in Writing Popular Fiction program. Visit him on the web at www.timwaggoner.com.

The (extremely) Short Guide to Writing Horror

Tim Waggoner

- Horror comes from a fear of the unknown. Keep a sense of mystery going in your story. What's happening? Why is it happening? What's going to happen next? How much worse is it going to get?
- Horror comes from a violation of what your characters consider to be normal reality. This violation shakes them to their very core because it raises the possibility that everything they thought they knew is wrong and that anything could happen. The Universe isn't orderly or benign. It's chaotic and malicious.
- **Dread** is the mounting anticipation of a threat drawing ever closer. **Terror** is a deep emotional and intellectual reaction to a threat, a profound realization that reality isn't what we thought it was. **Horror** is an immediate reaction to a threat – disbelief, denial, turning away. **Shock** is a surprise, an adrenaline rush, while **Disgust** is a queasy

visceral reaction. Dread and Terror are the most effective weapons in a horror writer's arsenal – they have a much greater impact on readers – but all the techniques have their strengths.

- The horror equivalent of the *Hero's Journey*: some Poor Bastard's Descent into Hell. Horror works best when it focuses on normal people (hence the "Poor Bastard"), and the characters' situation steadily and nightmarishly worsens (the "Descent"). "Hell" can be physical, spiritual, mental, emotional, internal, external – or better yet, a combination of them all. Possible Story Outcomes with this pattern: the Poor Bastard Escapes Hell, the Poor Bastard is Eternally Damned, the Poor Bastard Escapes with Severe Wounds and Scars, the Poor Bastard is Transformed by Hell, the Poor Bastard Carries Hell With Him, the Poor Bastard Drags Other to Hell or Brings Hell to Them, and the Poor Bastard Becomes the Devil.

- Horror is internal more than external. In the movie *Alien*, the crew of the *Nostromo* aren't trained to deal with monsters, so they're terrified. In the sequel *Aliens*, the space marines are trained soldiers and while they might be frightened by the monsters they face, it's not to the same degree as the characters in the first movie. *Alien* is a horror film because of the characters' internal reaction to events. *Aliens* is an action movie because of how the characters in that film react. Write with a close point of view to show your characters' emotional reaction to events in order to create effective horror.

- Give readers characters they care about. Horror stories aren't about the monster. They're about how people *react* to the monster (or in some cases, react to *becoming* monsters). If readers care about your characters, if they empathize with them, then the threats these characters face will be meaningful to readers. If your characters are the equivalent of video game avatars with no personality, the threats they face will be meaningless to readers.

- Respect your characters – all of them. In horror, sometimes a character's only function is to die in order to establish how serious the threat is and build suspense. Even if these characters only have a short time on stage, give them their dignity. For the brief time that they appear, try to present them as full, rich characters as much as possible. This will increase your reader's emotional involvement in the story and make the threat seem even worse.

- Avoid clichés. Horror is about the unknown, and once a specific type of character, threat, or story structure becomes too familiar, it loses its power to engage and affect readers – especially in horror.

- Make your horror personal. Draw from your own experience, observations, and fears to create horror only you can write – horror that's yours and no one else's.

- Take new approaches to old archetypes. Instead of writing about a classic vampire, rework that trope. Put a new spin on it. For example, vampires drain life-force from their victims. So what if there was a creature that injected life-force into its victims? Perhaps the souls of people that have died, souls that eventually try to gain control of their new hosts. Instead of people spending the night in a haunted house, what if the house was broken into hundreds of pieces, and each piece was given to a different person? This way, the haunting comes to them.

- There are no limits, but horror elements should serve the story and the characters' journey. You don't want your stories to be the equivalent of a simple walk through a carnival spook house, no matter how grotesque and bizarre the attractions inside may be. Character and story come first. After that, your tale can be as weird and extreme as you want to make it.

- Physical pain is easy – too easy. In horror, characters are often under the threat of physical violence, injury, and ultimately death. But the mental, emotional, and spiritual wounds characters suffer can be far worse than mere physical pain. Make sure that death isn't the worst thing that can happen in your horror – not by a long shot.

- Don't save the best for last. In *'The Body Politic'* Clive Barker takes the old horror trope of the living severed hand that's out for revenge and puts a new spin on it. Normally, stories using this trope end with the hand of a dead person returning to enact revenge on its murderer. "Oh my God, the hand is alive!" In *'The Body Politic'*, Barker begins with the premise that our hands – all of them – have separate lives and personalities, and they wish to be free from "the tyranny of the body." Barker didn't save his best idea for last. He *began* with his best idea and kept going from there. You should do the same.

- **How** you write is just as important as **What** you write. Example Version 1: *There was a monster outside the front door. A man opened the door and* *the monster ate him.* Example Version 2: *Bob had his hand on the knob, was just about to turn it, open the door, and walk outside to check the mail, when he felt the metal vibrate beneath his flesh. Not much, just a little. But it made him think that someone on the other side had put* their *hand on the outside knob, making it jiggle the tiniest bit. And was the metal starting to feel colder, as if a silent arctic wind caressed the knob outside? It was a ridiculous thought, but he removed his hand from the knob all the same and, without realizing it, took two steps backward.* The way you tell your story is just as important, if not more so, than the kind of story you're trying to tell. This is true with any type of fiction, but it's especially true in horror.

- Horror shouldn't be safe – in any way, shape, or form. Horror should take risks with characters, story elements, and narrative techniques. Readers shouldn't be able to guess what's going to happen next, and once they think they have your story figured out, that's when it should take a shocking left turn. Keep your readers off balance the entire time, and they'll experience something of what your characters are going through in the story. They won't feel safe – and they'll love your stories all the more for it.

Resources for Further Reading:

- Horror Writers Association, www.horror.org

- International Thriller Writers Association. www.thrillerwriters.org

- *'Supernatural Horror in Literature',* H.P. Lovecraft

- *'On Writing',* Stephen King
- *'Danse Macabre',* Stephen King
- *'On Writing Horror'*, Mort Castle, ed.
- *'Writers Workshop of Horror'*, Michael Knost, ed.
- *'How to Write Horror Fiction',* William Nolan.
- *'To Each Their Darkness',* Gary Braunbeck
- *'Writing the Paranormal Novel',* Steven Harper
- *'Dark Dreamers: Conversations with the Masters of Horror',* Stanley Wiater
- *'Dark Thoughts on Writing',* Stanley Wiater
- *'How to Write Tales of Horror, Fantasy, and Science Fiction',* J.N. Williamson
- *'Now Write: Science Fiction, Fantasy, and Horror',* Laurie Lamsen

Gary McMahon's short fiction has been reprinted in both 'The Mammoth Book of Best New Horror and The Year's Best Fantasy & Horror'. He is the acclaimed author of the novels 'Rain Dogs', 'Hungry Hearts', 'Pretty Little Dead Things', 'Dead Bad Things' and the 'Concrete Grove' trilogy. He lives with his family in Yorkshire, trains in Shotokan karate, and likes running in the rain.

Website: www.garymcmahon.com

Growing Ideas

Gary McMahon

An idea, an idea…ah, what price an idea?

Ideas are often hard to come by, but sometimes they jump on you like Kato, Inspector Clouseau's frenzied manservant. And it's strange how an idea can slowly grow and mutate and eventually take on a life of its own, leading to all sorts of interesting problems.

A couple of years ago I woke up in the middle of the night and went to stare out of the bedroom window. It's what I do: I'm a hopeless paranoid insomniac. Along the street, outside one of my neighbours' houses, there was a battered old 1970s style dining chair set out at the kerb. I haven't a clue what it was doing there – the next day wasn't bin day – and the following morning when I checked again the chair was gone.

Obviously this meaningless little event gave me an idea for a story, and over the following week I wrote a tale called "The Chair", which I then managed to sell to

Black Static magazine. A nice result all round.

Then the idea began to grow…

I had a stray thought about a linked story, called "The Table". Getting out a notebook, I scribbled down a few images and sensations; then I developed a rough outline involving a man seeing silent, possibly mouthless people sitting and staring at his dining room table. At some point during those few minutes of frantic scribbling, I got an idea for – yes, you've guessed it – another story, this one called "The Drawer".

Finally I wrote the outline for the final story in the sequence, "The Room", where all these threads come together and form a statement about the way modern living has turned us into willing prisoners in the comfortable little cells of our own homes.

So, from a single late-night glimpse of a battered old dining chair in the street, I now have a proposed four-story series of linked tales that I'm calling "The Domestic Sequence".

It's strange how an idea can slowly grow and mutate and eventually take on a life of its own: a chair, a table, a drawer, a room…a short sequence of stories hopefully amounting to about 16,000 words.

It's almost as if an image can act like a trigger, setting off a series of detonations in your subconscious, releasing things that have been buried for a long time. These things snuffle around for a while, looking for a direction, and when they finally find one, they begin to mass and gather together to form the germ of an idea. Then that germ grows and bloats and takes on a form of its own – if you're lucky, you can catch it and pin it down and write it. If not, it escapes to fight another day.

I think it was Stephen King who once said there are

two kinds of writers, those who add and those who take away. Some people are like artists sculpting granite: they take a hammer and a chisel and delicately tap, tap away at the thing, gradually revealing the shape of the story beneath.

Others, like me, do it the opposite way around. If the first lot are like sculptors, then we are like potters: we grab a small lump of clay, throw it down, and then add the layers, all the time throwing more and more lies at it in the hope of creating a representation of the truth.

This is how ideas come together for me: in small stages, with each new day bringing along another layer to add to the core, and at the end of an unspecified length of time I hope to have a finished story. Like the potter at his wheel, I press and I mould and I add more clay, looking for that which I must find, I *need* to find, within.

In this way, my first draft is usually not much more than an outline and I add the bulk of the piece in phases. I usually have to write a first draft in a single sitting – or at least in a single day – because I'm scared that I'll lose the original fire that inspired it. Then, after that initial white-heat frenzy, I can settle down and start repairing whatever damage I made to the original idea, adding those layers, and shaping the tale. The hard work, though, is always done in that first draft. The central idea rarely changes, and the theme usually presents itself to me during the opening salvo of writing. Everything afterwards is refinement.

All of this means, of course, that I always have a lot of first drafts on my computer hard drive; stories that never got to have their layers added and their wounds dressed. Like immobile rows of the undead, they rot away quietly, never complaining, but hoping to be noticed again. Perhaps I should open the door and take a peek, see if any of them twitches in the darkness and catches my eye. I'm sure some of them are worth saving from the Hell of Unrealised Ideas.

Jasper Bark was very late with his bio for this collection. Though he wouldn't like to be known as the late Jasper Bark just yet. He does like to be known as an award winning author of four novels, twelve children's books and countless comics and graphic novels. He recently released a swarm of piranhas into a hot tub full of politicians and the Ebook 'Stuck On You', though only one of these crimes has so far been proven. His forthcoming short story collection 'Stuck On You and Other Prime Cuts' is soon to be released by Crystal Lake Publishing along with loads of other great stuff.

Filthy Habits – Writing and Routine

Jasper Bark

I once heard a fantastic piece of advice at a reading I did. It came from Ramsey Campbell who, in my opinion, is the greatest living British horror writer. In spite of drunkenly heckling me from the stage, we were sharing and graphically demonstrating how to anally rape a Lovecraftian entity (I'm lying about that last bit). Ramsey did share some amazing bits of writerly wisdom.

One thing in particular sticks in my mind. Ramsey told us that he always composes the next sentence of whatever he's writing, before he sits down to work for the day. That way he's already overcome the first hurdle before he even begins to type. This probably saves him hours of angst and indecision over the course of a working week and allows him to coast along on the compositional momentum he's already built up before he even gets to his desk.

This is one of those sage pieces of advice that has me marveling at its wisdom even as I realise I'm sadly never going to follow it. Along with all those other great pieces of advice that I ignore such as 'write what you know'. Yeah right, I'm a comic writer and horror novelist. I don't have superpowers (other than my ability to spout heroic amounts of bullshit) and I live in a small Wiltshire town. The most horrific thing I face all day is emptying the litter tray (although given the nature of the local wildlife, my cats' litter tray often resembles the highlights of a Shaun Hutson novel). Along with other pearls like: 'never end a sentence with a preposition', something I was never very good at.

What Ramsey's point highlights is the extreme importance of habit and routine to the working life of any writer. The poet W. H. Auden put the prolificity of his output down to one thing, a strict daily routine. Writers as diverse as Ernest Hemingway, Kurt Vonnegut and Haruki Murakami would rise early in the morning, to get in a good four hours before the rest of the world woke up. Other writers such as Neil Gaiman, Pablo Neruda and Charles Dickens preferred writing into the wee hours of the night. Given the chance, that's how I like to write myself (probably because it's easier to buy hard drugs at that time; drug dealers are not known for being up with the lark).

Jack Kerouac would light a candle, say a prayer, then type continuously on an endless roll of paper until the candle guttered and went out. While writing Fahrenheit 451, Ray Bradbury would visit a basement typing room at the UCLA every evening, drop a dime into one of the unclaimed typewriters and type furiously for the thirty minutes that his ten cents bought him. When the allotted time was up he would scrabble around for another dime and begin the process all over again, teasing out his first real masterpiece in these thirty minute increments.

As to my own schedule, I tend to wake fairly early when the blunt object my wife has thrown connects with my head. Usually because the kids are driving her psychotic. When the kids are safely delivered to school or, if it's the weekend, safely locked in the basement with power tools and matches, I'll settle down in my office to work. I tend to begin my day by writing a list. Lists are great ways of pretending to work without actually doing anything and they bring a completely unearned sense of achievement. I'll start with a 'to do' list that I'll pay about as much attention to as the great advice I'm always being given by other writers. Then, if I'm about to embark on a new endeavor, like a short story, a script or another of these columns, I'll write an ideas list like this one:

LIST OF IDEAS...

1) Erm....

2) Err....

3) How about....no that's a bit obvious...

4) Well I could always...no I couldn't - God what was I thinking!

5) There's always the old one about....no, everyone's

used that...

6) Does an inappropriate thought about the Creature from the Black Lagoon actually count as an idea???

Once that's successfully accomplished I may even write another list as a direct consequence of the last list. Such as this one:

LIST OF POSSIBLE REASONS WHY I'M GOING TO MISS THE DEADLINE:

1) I'm on the run from the CIA - again (this has possibilities)!

2) Look, it's women's problems alright! You wouldn't understand (not sure if I can pull this one off - fnarr, pull this off, snerk).

3) I've just suffered a rectal prolapse due to a civil war between the microscopic alien races inhabiting my lower colon (might need to work on this one, fnarr - work on this ... oh wait that's not an innuendo).

Once the serious business of list making is out of the way, along with other important admin tasks such as 'liking' every lame picture of a cat that I can find on Facebook, it's time to settle down to some serious writing. First I open a new document. Next I spend two or three hours staring alternately out of the window and at the blank screen of my laptop. At some point during this vital stage in the process my wife will walk in and say something devastatingly witty like: "Working hard are we?" I'll then spend half an hour contemplating whether I should draw up a list of snappy comebacks for the next time she cracks this particular howler, but failing to come up with anything in the least bit 'snappy' or 'comebackable' (yes that is a word) I'll abandon the idea.

After eating a light lunch I'll return to my desk for a concerted hour of weeping tears of bitter frustration, interspersed with kicking my desk and weeping tears of pain from the injury I've done to my foot. Then I'll lie on the floor, stare at the ceiling and bemoan the fact that I was stupid enough to enter a profession for which I obviously have no talent and my children will undoubtedly starve as a consequence.

Remembering that my children will soon have to be picked up from school (or released from the basement) finally spurs me into action and, fueled by sheer panic, I manage to rattle off a thousand words or more before I have to down tools and resume my role as a parent. In the 30s and 40s at the Disney Studios, the sixty minutes before the animators would clock off for the day at 5pm was known as the 'golden hour'. This was the time when all the guys in the studio would stop giving each other hot foots, or drawing penises on each other's cells when they weren't looking, and knuckle down and do some serious work. It was estimated that the majority of work that you see on the screen from that period was drawn in this single hour.

That's how it is for me too. I'd like to say that all the preamble leading up to this hour or so is an integral part of the process, but even I'm not that self deluding. In fact one of the main reasons for having a routine is not so much to encourage yourself to write, but rather to avoid all those things that stop you writing (namely just about everything). Don DeLillo said: "A writer takes earnest measures to ensure his solitude and then finds endless ways to squander it." Which effectively says in seventeen words what I've taken over a thousand words to say. But I don't think my editor would have been very pleased with a seventeen word entry that has none of the trade mark knob jokes.

And while I'm quoting writers who are far more respectable than me, Haruki Murakami said: "I keep to this routine every day without variation. The repetition itself becomes the important thing, it's a form of mesmerism. I mesmerize myself to reach a deeper state of mind." I think Murakami has hit on the nub of the matter here. Writing for long periods of time is like falling into a trance and letting your consciousness travel to another place. This other place is the location of your fiction and as you conjure it up for the reader, it has to be more real for you than the physical space you're inhabiting as you write. There are times when I'm writing that I'm so immersed in what I'm working on that my children could run into my office in flames and I'd simply open the window to cool the room.

In this respect writing shares certain features with shamanism (by which I mean falling into a trance like state, not letting your children burn). Routine and ritual are important tools in the Shaman's armory and it is the same with the writer. That's why a good working routine is so important to us. It's also why the first thing you should look at, if you're not working to full capacity, is your working routine. Changing the way you work and scrutinising the working habits you've developed is often the best way of overcoming a creative block and maximising your productivity. The key to realising your potential as a writer is improving your working routine.

Trust me, this is the best bit of advice that you'll ignore all month.

V. H. Leslie's stories have appeared in *Black Static*, *Interzone*, *Weird Fiction Review* and *Strange Tales IV*. She has also had fiction and non-fiction published in *Shadows and Tall Trees* and writes a monthly column for *This is Horror*. She was recently awarded a Hawthornden Fellowship and the Lightship First Chapter Prize. Her work is due to appear in *Best British Horror* and *Best British Fantasy* available later this year. More information on the author can be found at *www.vhleslie.wordpress.com*

A Room of One's Own - the lonely path of a writer

V. H. Leslie

"We must reserve a little back-shop, all of our own, entirely free, wherein to establish our true liberty and principle retreat and solitude", wrote the Renaissance writer Michel Eyquem de Montaigne, considering the subject of solitude and a life of imagination. For writers, a space within the mind is incredibly important for the creative process, providing a fertile environment for the imagination to conjure ideas. But how many writers have an actual "back-shop" in real life, a place that they can retreat to, where they can contemplate and study and construct their narratives? In an age where living costs and financial pressures seem to be ever increasing, I wonder how many writers do have access to a private writing space. A space that isn't shared with a partner or kids, that doesn't double up as a dining room or lounge, a room that is solely and uncompromisingly for the business of writing.

In Virginia Woolf's famous 1929 extended essay based on a succession of lectures she delivered at Girton College and Newnham College, Cambridge, she declared that if women want to write fiction they need two things – money and a room of their own. Though Woolf was addressing the difficulty for women at the time to support themselves independently in order to pursue a career in writing, I think the sentiment still holds true, for both men and women writers today. But it is not so much the money (how many writers are sustained rightly or wrongly by a *for-the-love-of-it* mentality than an actual wage?) but the room that interests me. For those who take their art seriously, how integral is it to possess a little space where you can lock yourself away from the rest of the world? Dr Anthony Storr in his book *Solitude* speaks of the importance of his own space: "My study, lined with books, reflects my interests, confirms my identity as a writer, and reinforces my sense of what kind of person I consider myself to be." If identity is bound up in what we read, a place that exhibits your preferences strengthens your connection with yourself and therefore your ability to be in your own company. Dr Storr's book challenges the idea that interpersonal relationships are the only basis for happiness. It is the capacity for solitude and the introspection it allows, that for creative individuals in particular, provides greater fulfilment.

Dr Storr lists a whole host of writers and thinkers who elected to live predominantly solitary lives and even considers those who had, for various reasons, isolation forced upon them. It is quite interesting to consider how many great works were written in conditions of enforced solitude, such as in prison. Sir Thomas Moore, Sir Walter Raleigh, John Bunyan, Dostoevsky and Oscar Wilde began or completed some of the work they are best known for in captivity. Though they had their personal liberties restricted or curtailed, they had a room, and to varying degrees, freedom to write. Dostoevsky on the one hand kept a surreptitious notebook, whereas conditions were sufficiently liberal for Sir Walter Raleigh in the Tower of London to write *The History of the World* and have it published whilst serving his sentence. What is fascinating though, is the attainment of the mind when it is the only source of solace.

Other writers, recognising this need for solitude, imposed their own restrictions and boundaries on their lifestyles and with regard to their relationships with others. Famously Kafka preferred an epistolary relationship with his girlfriend of five years, Felice Bauer, only meeting in person a handful of times. When she said she would like to sit beside him while he wrote, he replied that "[he] could not write at all." He believed writing to be "that utmost of self-revelation and surrender, in which a human being, when involved with others, would feel he was losing himself". And Kafka is not alone is seeking complete isolation. For many writers, a room of their own wasn't sufficient; they needed a complete departure from society. Wilkie Collins, Ann Radcliffe, H.G. Wells and George Orwell all sought island spaces, needing to be cut off topographically from the hustle and bustle of civilisation.

For speculative writers especially, perhaps the need

for solitude is more pressing, with themes such as isolation and segregation such a genre staple. It could be argued that George Orwell could only have written *Nineteen-Eighty-Four* from the remoteness of Jura, a tiny island in the Inner Hebrides, the bleakness and hostility of the landscape crucial for reinforcing these themes in the text. The connection between the world of the imagination and the world the writer inhabits has all kinds of implications and may account for the rise of urban horror in recent years.

My own quest for isolation was governed not so much by a desire to be on my own, but for research purposes. I've spent a month in a cabin in a forest in the Scottish highlands and most recently, a month in a croft house on a small Shetland island. In both instances I was without the Internet and separated from commercial centres by the landscape (the forest in the first instance and the sea in the second) and I came to appreciate this barrier between the outside and myself, like a little moat protecting my inner writing world. As well as allowing more concentrated writing time with my days undisturbed by visitors or obligations, it provided opportunities for introspection and self-reflection, which though taking a little getting used to, was extremely rewarding.

I suppose you could say that I am an isolation junkie now, as I write this from a Writer's Retreat in Scotland. There are a surprising amount of retreats out there, which a quick Internet search will reveal, and I would certainly recommend them to any writer keen to make space literally and psychologically for their work. As Kafka wrote in his reply to Felice Bauer "one can never be alone enough when one writes ... there can never be enough silence around one when one writes, why even night is not night enough." It might seem a little extreme but the business of writing is after all a solitary act. But being a writer doesn't mean being condemned to a life of isolation and loneliness. As with many other retreats, though silence is encouraged in the day, in the evening I can gather with my fellow writers to share ideas, to discuss our progress and to enjoy each other's company. For there are some benefits to belonging to a crowd, particularly one that shares similar interests, and especially when you have a little "back-shop" that is all your own.

Eric S Brown is the author of numerous series including the 'Bigfoot War' series, the 'A Pack of Wolves' series, the 'Crypto-Squad' series (with Jason Brannon), and the 'Jack Bunny Bam Bam' series. Some of his stand alone books include 'Homeworld' (with Tony Faville), 'The Weaponer', 'World War of the Dead', and 'War of the Worlds Plus Blood Guts and Zombies'. The movie rights to the first book of the 'Bigfoot War' series were picked up by Origin Releasing and the film will be released in 2014 (staring C. Thomas Howell and Judd Nelson).

Do You Need an Agent?

Eric S Brown

I've been a writer for around twelve years. I pay the bills by writing scary stories and tales of futuristic warfare. One of the questions I get asked the most by new writers who are just starting out is "Do I need an agent to make it as a writer?" This is a tough one to answer as many of my friends and fellow authors who do make a living by writing are somewhat divided on this topic. My hero, David Drake, would likely tell you that you need to skip the small press entirely and aim straight out for getting an agent to pitch your work to the big publishing houses while others that I know, like a certain successful and bestselling screenwriter who publishes her books via KDP, would argue completely the opposite.

In my own personal experience, I didn't have an agent when I first picked up the pen. I started by submitting to small press magazines and literary journals as well as writing for local newspapers. The first story I ever sent out was accepted by two different publications. I gave that story to the larger of the two indie magazines and wrote a second tale for the other. Neither of these paid "pro" rates by any means but they were a start. By the end of my first year, I had placed around fifteen tales with small press publishers, both print and online, earning out a total of five dollars and a stack of contributor copies. I kept right on writing though. By the end of the second year of my career, I had over eighty five stories accepted by various publications in the Horror/SF world and was making at least some side/hobby money for my efforts. This was all back before the "Kindle Revolution" took place. As my name became somewhat more known in the genres I wrote in, I landed a book deal to have many of my initial stories collected into a book like my hero, David Drake, had with his Hammer Slammers tales. That first collection was by no means a hit like Drake's was but it was a starting point again of a different kind. As much as I, and folks like H.P. Lovecraft before me, prefer the short form, books are where the money is at. No one, not even Stephen King, can make a living off just short fiction.

That first collection of my work led to several more and by 2005, I landed my first novel contract and the sales on it were far better than anything I had experienced in the past. By 2009, I had made enough of a name for myself, through sheer prayer, force of will, and prolific, hard work, that I had books with publishers like Permuted Press and titles that were actually carried in store by chains like Borders. I was being featured in mass market books about the genre I worked in like Zombie CSU: The Forensics of the Living Dead (by

New York Times bestselling author Jonathan Maberry) and more academic nonfiction books like Halloween: The Secrets of America's Fright Night (written by a Harvard affiliated author). I did all of that without an agent and my career was really beginning to take off in the indie world.

By 2010, I was making a living (if not a great one) from writing. Simon and Schuster came to me about the reprint rights for my book War of the Worlds Plus Blood Guts and Zombies. It was my first sale to one of the really big publishers. Simon and Schuster likely would have bought the book without an agent anyway as they came to me asking for the rights, but at that point, with a mass market deal in hand, I did finally get an agent. The agent did very well for me, getting Simon and Schuster to increase that first ever five figure advance for me by a whooping fifty percent. However, after that deal, said agent never really did anything else for me. I was far from one of his top clients and seemed to merely sit in limbo as he handled deals for the more established authors signed with him.

My career kept right on growing though despite the lack of involvement from my agent. My Bigfoot War series took off like crazy. I begged my agent to see if he could take it mass market but due to the length of the books in the series, he wasn't interested in even trying regardless of their success. However, the attention the Bigfoot War series garnered landed me my first novelization deal. A producer at Studio 3 Entertainment, who had just completed the 2011 remake of Boggy Creek, hired me to turn the script into a book for them and they also optioned the first book of the Bigfoot War saga for film as well during that process. This led to many more novelization deals from smaller, indie film companies and by this time, the "Kindle Revolution" and self-publishing via Amazon was occurring. I had always been taught that self-publishing was "bad" and not the way to go. I held off from trying it for a long time. I created my first Kindle Direct Publishing account in Sept, 2012. Every month since, I have always gotten a check from it like clockwork. The idea was for it to be a supplemental source of income to my publisher sales. It became much more than that though. By early 2013, KDP was paying the bills all by itself and my publisher work had become the supplemental income.

Today though, with the market flooded by self-published titles and the entire writing industry in a state of turmoil from it, I make my living from publishers and KDP combined. And that film option I got on my own, by the grace of God, got the green light. The first movie based on one of my books was shot in the fall of 2013 and is expected to have a limited release in theaters in early 2014 before hitting Walmart stores etc. across the country later in the year on DVD. The upfront money from it gave me a cushion to fall back on and help me feel more secure as a full time writer. Again, it was another "big time" deal that I didn't use an agent for at all and I even scored a decent cut of the movie's backend residuals.

Now one has to ask, would I have been even more successful if I had an agent that whole time, pitching things to the big publishers for me? Well, maybe. The big publishers usually won't even look at your work without an agent repping it for you and with the movie deal under my belt, one of the first things I did was get a new agent who seems to really be out there working on my behalf. At this point, our relationship is too new to really tell if his pitches will make a difference in my career, but I continue to write full time and pay the bills while I wait for him to shop my latest, full length Military SF novel around in the hope of another large advance.

So in my personal opinion, the answer is this: you do not need an agent to become successful or write full time, especially with higher royalty paying options like KDP out there, but an agent can make the difference in some deals happening for you and possibly take your work to being reached by a far wider audience than the indie world can offer, even if it is paying the bills. Hard work, being prolific, and determination to make it are far more essential elements to any writer's career than having an agent, but if you *need* to be with the big publishers to feel like a success then you will eventually truly need an agent to reach that point.

William Meikle is a Scottish writer with twenty novels published in the genre press and over 250 short story credits in thirteen countries. His work appears in many professional anthologies and he has recent short story sales to 'Nature Futures', 'Penumbra' and 'Daily Science Fiction' among others. His ebook 'The Invasion' has been as high as #2 in the Kindle SF charts. He now lives in a remote corner of Newfoundland with icebergs, whales and bald eagles for company. In the winters he gets warm vicariously through the lives of others in cyberspace, so please check him out at www.williammeikle.com/

Ten Short Story Endings to Avoid

William Meikle

A logical, satisfying ending is always required in a short story, but how do you ensure that yours is fresh and new? One of the ways is to avoid the obvious. Here are some common endings seen by editors: use them at your peril.

And then I woke up.
The *'Dallas'* gambit. This approach is nothing more than a cop-out for people with no imagination. Stories should reach a logical conclusion that satisfies the reader and resolves any conflicts. This method does neither.

And then I died.
The *'Weird Tales'* gambit. This one turned up regularly

in horror tales during the early part of last century, until it was overplayed by HP Lovecraft, among others. A diary which ends in a string of nonsense words as a crawling terror from beyond comes for the author was fine the first time out, but most editors have seen it too many times.

And I found out I'd been dead all along.

The *'Sixth Sense'* gambit. This is an old one, which is why people who were well read in the genre spotted the twist very early in M Night Shyamalan's film. An overused variation is to have someone breaking out of a coffin after a supposedly premature burial. Don't do it; the editor will see it coming from a mile away.

And they called them Adam and Eve.

The *'Bible'* gambit or, as Michael Moorcock puts it, Shaggy God stories. If you start with a nuclear holocaust or human colonists on a new planet, make sure you don't use this ending or the story will be bounced back to you straight away. The other trap to avoid is having a computer become a god. That avenue was new in the '40s, but these days an editor will laugh himself out of his chair.

And then I saw the fangs, just before he bit me

The *'singles bar pick-up'* gambit. With this worn-out ending, a person visits a bar and is seduced by a pale, interesting stranger who turns out to be a vampire, a ghost, a werewolf or an alien. There are several variations seen nowadays, such as same-gender meetings and graphic sex scenes before the revelation, but the stories are all the same and editors know it.

And then I caught up with the '@!* who'd done me wrong and shot the @'!** out of them.
The *'Death Wish'* gambit is the beloved technique of Michael Winner fanatics and gun-nuts. It makes for a very dull story unless you can bring style, energy and a unique vision to it, in which case you'd probably be better off trying to sell it as a film treatment. There's a long tradition of revenge movies, but in the written word they all come across as being very similar. A variant on this handling is the Charles Atlas gambit, where the weedy nerd becomes a kung-fu expert to wreak revenge on his tormentors. Don't be tempted to use this angle. Editors will know what's coming.

And the next day I read in the paper that he'd died.
The *'I talked to a ghost'* gambit. This practice turned up frequently in Victorian literature. It's usually no more than an anecdote turned into a story. Variations include talking to someone who is later discovered to be the victim of a plane crash, an automobile wreck or a major catastrophe. Editors see a slew of these after a natural disaster, but whatever caused the person's death, the stories are all the same.

And it was a man in a mask all along.
The *'Scooby-Doo'* gambit. Pretend spooks are a cliché. The whole story builds up a sense of supernatural menace, only to reveal a human agency behind it all. It won't usually get past an editor but if it does, readers will feel disappointed and let down.

And it was my evil twin; we were separated at birth.
The *'doppelganger'* gambit. Stephen King got away with

this in The Dark Half and Dean Koontz pulled off a variation by making both twins evil in Shivers, but unless you have their style and wit, you shouldn't attempt it. Another variation, beloved of the romantics among us, is to have the protagonist find out they're really the son, daughter or sibling of a rich family. This mode is really just wishful thinking on behalf of the writer. You shouldn't be sharing your daydreams with editors.

I'm really a dog/cat/demon/alien.
The *'non-human storyteller'* gambit is tried and tested. That's the problem. If you don't leave any clues to the fact, the reader will feel the ending is a cop-out. If you do leave clues, the reader and your editor will spot the ending coming unless you're very good at disguising the fact.

Remember, people have been writing stories for a very long time. If you've read a similar ending in a story or seen it in a film, you can bet the editor will be aware of it, too. There are only so many original endings to go around; *make sure yours is one of them.*

John Kenny is a freelance writer, editor and creative writing tutor. His short stories have appeared in The World SF Blog, Jupiter, First Contact, Woman's Way, Fear the Reaper, Emerald Eye (an anthology of the Best of Irish Imaginative Fiction), Transtories and many other venues. John has been co-editor of Albedo One since its inception in 1993. Prior to that, he wrote extensively for Stargate, the magazine of the Irish Science Fiction Association, and was editor of FTL, the successor to Stargate. He is editor of original horror anthology Box of Delights for Aeon Press and is currently hawking his mainstream novel Down and Out to publishers. John lives in Dublin, Ireland, with his wife, two daughters and neurotic cat.

Submitting Your Work: Read the F*****g Guidelines!

John Kenny

I thought long and hard before including the word 'F*****g' in the title of this second part of my occasional series on submitting work to publishers; reason being I didn't want to be seen as potentially disparaging towards the vast majority of writers who do go the trouble of checking out the guidelines to a specific market before sending something their way. But, unfortunately, a sizeable minority don't and the inclusion of the 'F' word is to demonstrate the level of frustration, and indeed occasional anger, that this lack of basic manners and cop-on induces in editors everywhere.

It may seem obvious to most writers that the first thing you do when you're thinking of submitting to a particular market is visit their website and check out their guidelines. But a surprising number of writers don't do this. After all, if you've written a science fiction story, why not just send it to a science fiction magazine? That literary opus you've completed surely belongs in the New Yorker, so just send it on in. So why should you bother reading guidelines before submitting? And why do writers who flout this prerequisite often bring editors to the very brink of apoplexy?

Different magazines, webzines, anthologies and book publishers have different requirements. These requirements have been arrived at for a variety of reasons, which range from specific market factors to the personal whim of the editor and/or publisher. Some markets will specify a particular sub-genre or cross-genre, such as SF horror, that is science fiction that has a large element of horror to it (a la the movie Alien). Other markets, such as anthologies, may be themed, such as the impending Steampunk Cthulhu, edited by Brian M Sammons and Glynn Owen Barrass, which will be publishing stories that do what it says on the tin. No point sending this particular anthology a straight Cthulhu story. Or a general horror piece. Other markets, such as the New Yorker or the Stinging Fly allow only a limited number of submissions from an author in a given year, or are only open to submissions at specific times of the year.

Guidelines also include information on the required format of submissions, font, font size, spacing, margins, minimum and/or maximum word counts, etc. They specify payment rates, or lack of, rights bought or secured, and whether or not they accept simultaneous submissions. Writers who don't make the effort to review guidelines risk wasting both their own time and the editors'. Outlined below are a number of particular examples of this time-wasting phenomenon.

As co-editor of Albedo One for many years now, I've lost count of the number of times I've read a story that is plainly not the kind of thing we publish. On several occasions I've read a story that turns out to be a mainstream literary piece with no genre elements whatsoever. It may be beautifully written, with great character development, but I end up reading right to the end in search of the science fiction-, fantasy- or horror-related denouement and discover there is none.

More often, it's clear the author hasn't read a sample copy of the magazine to get a flavour of the kind of stuff we go for. Now I fully understand that writers, including myself, by the way, can't be buying copies of every magazine they want to submit to. But most magazines will have sample stories posted to their websites or cheap pdfs or other e-versions of back issues available and writers should make the effort to review these. You mightn't even have to go that far; many magazines, webzines and anthologies will include an extensive list on their guidelines webpage of what they don't want to see.

Just because you've written a masterpiece doesn't mean any magazine at all, randomly plucked from a hat, will publish it. Do the homework. Otherwise you risk tying up your story for three or four months or more with an unsuitable market, only to hear back that they don't publish that sort of thing. Better to have your story considered on its merits by a market that might actually publish it.

We often receive submissions that don't adhere to our guidelines on format. Albedo One isn't too fussy on font or font size (within reason!), but it is on line spacing. Other markets are very particular on font, font size, the type of paragraphing and width of margins. Until recently, Albedo One didn't accept email submissions as attachments. Now we do, but we have listed the file formats we take. For example, we don't accept docx files, reason being we can't open them. One submitter emailed us, a short while ago, with a link to where we could download her story, rather than simply attaching the story to the email. Needless to say, we couldn't risk clicking on the link.

We still get hard copy submissions in the post, which is all well and good, but many arrive with no SASE (self-addressed stamped envelope) or email address on the cover letter. These submissions go straight in the bin because we have no way of replying to the author unless we spend money on postage, which we don't have to spare. Any writer who thinks we'll read the story anyway and be so overwhelmed by its brilliance that we'll be willing to spend money on tracking him or her down in order to beg to publish it is sadly deluding themselves.

A corollary to this is the SASE included with the manuscript that is adorned with US or UK stamps. Unfortunately, these are useless to us and a waste of the writer's money, as we are based in Ireland and are subject to the Irish postal system when it comes to posting out rejections and acceptances. If you are including a SASE, it must have stamps relevant to the country you expect to hear back from. Ireland opted out of the IRC (International Reply Coupon) scheme that would be a viable alternative to having to source stamps, so this is not an option for someone posting stories to us from outside Ireland. There is also a difficulty for writers posting to US markets from outside the US, in that the US Postal Service won't sell stamps to anywhere outside the North American continent. In these cases, it's best to rely on email communications. It's quicker and easier for a magazine to reply by email, so include your email address on your cover letter and the first page of your manuscript. Most markets that insist on everything being done in hard copy form only will listen to reason if you contact them to say you can't include a SASE with a relevant stamp on it; under those circumstances, they will likely accept an email submission or a hard copy submission with your email address included.

Check payment rates and rights purchased to make sure you're happy before submitting. Albedo One is a semi-pro level magazine that regretfully pays very little (we hope in the future to improve the rate, but for the moment, it is what it is). If you are not happy with this, don't submit to us. We had a submission recently, which we went to the trouble of reading, withdrawn when the writer belatedly realised we didn't pay professional level rates. He wasted his time and ours, and for all his talk of professionalism, didn't demonstrate much of that from his end, i.e. he didn't read the f*****g guidelines.

A lot of the above dovetails into a strategy many, many writers employ when trying to get work published; that of the scattergun approach. I speak of simultaneous submissions, the bane of many an editor. Unless a magazine, webzine or anthology specifically states that they accept simultaneous submissions, you can assume that they don't. In fact, most markets will categorically state in no uncertain terms that they don't want to see submissions that are currently being considered by other markets. A writer may think it's great to have his or her story considered by 17 magazines all at the one time, but there is nothing worse for an editor than to have to spend precious time reading a submission, only to have it withdrawn by the author because it's been accepted somewhere else. A writer may not care, once the story gets published somewhere, but he or she risks burning bridges instead of building them.

A while back, a writer emailed us a story for consideration and one of the editorial team discovered, quite by accident, that it had been copied to about 50 other magazines simultaneously. This explained the 'Dear Editor' at the beginning and the 'your magazine' in the body of the email. I guess he was inviting us to fill in our own name in the relevant places. The sheer arrogance of it was breathtaking, not to say anything of the laziness demonstrated (he couldn't even make the effort to bcc it) or the plain evidence that he hadn't bothered to check our guidelines, which state very clearly that we don't accept simultaneous submissions.

I'm not, by the way, trying to make out that an editor's time is more precious than a writer's. But writers who think that it's only one little story, sure what's the harm, are missing a vital piece of information about the life of an editor: that editors have to wade through vast quantities of submissions in order to select what they wish to publish. And I mean vast; Albedo One typically receives several thousand submissions a year. And that pales into insignificance beside what the pro-rate genre magazines get, which, in turn, pales beside what the likes of the New Yorker gets.

Any writer who thinks they'll impress Editor X by having managed to sell their story to Editor Y while it was under consideration by Editor X's magazine, that this will engender in the Editor X a deep regret that they didn't read the story quicker and snap it up, or that this will instil in Editor X a sense of urgency with the writer's next submission, is again, sadly deluding themselves.

So why does this all drive editors nuts? It should be pretty obvious from the specific examples above, but it all boils down to the fact that editors are generally dealing with huge levels of submissions, and guidelines are there to make an editor's life a little more manageable. Adhering to them, even if they may seem a little inconvenient to you, will at least demonstrate to the editor a minimum quotient of professionalism, even if some editors themselves may not always be very professional.

Jasper Bark was very late with his bio for this collection. Though he wouldn't like to be known as the late Jasper Bark just yet. He does like to be known as an award winning author of four novels, 12 children's books and countless comics and graphic novels. He recently released a swarm of piranhas into a hot tub full of politicians and the Ebook 'Stuck On You', though only one of these crimes has so far been proven. His forthcoming short story collection 'Stuck On You and Other Prime Cuts' is soon to be released by Crystal Lake Publishing along with loads of other great stuff.

Rejection Letters – How to Write and Respond to Them

Jasper Bark

Greetings gentle reader. Before we get down to the business of this essay, I'd like to tell you a horror story. A real life horror story.

A good friend of mine, with an especially bad history of boyfriends, once told me a tale about her worst date. The guy in question actually picked her up from a friend's house to take her to the restaurant. This might have scored him some brownie points had it not led her to wonder which he had last cleaned – the car or his armpits? So great was the throat stopping odour of un-scrubbed body parts that she was actually glad when he filled the car with cigar smoke and cranked Barry Manilow to the max on his stereo.

Through the haze of cigar smoke she noticed he was perched on the sort of cushion favoured by those stricken with haemorrhoids. On route to the restaurant he stopped to fill up his car. As he went to pay she glanced over at the cushion and a saw a huge, sticky puddle of blood and other liquids on it. She then glanced out the window at the seat of his pants and the large wet stain that glistened in the forecourt lights. It seemed that his haemorrhoids had just burst.

Choking back the vomit, my friend slipped off her heels, scrawled a hasty note and then ran for her sweet life. The note read, "So sorry, changed my mind. Please DON'T phone me. Xxx". Brutal perhaps, but she had to do something. There are worse ways of breaking up with someone. One of my sister's ex-boyfriends once ended their relationship by throwing a flaming bag of dogshit at her head (which probably tells you all you need to know about my family background). My friend chose to end this brief encounter with a rejection letter.

Which brings us rather neatly to the subject of this entry – Rejection Letters. If you have a writing career that lasts any length of time, then you're going to amass a lot of these, from agents, editors and just about anyone to whom you send your work. They're an unfortunate, but unavoidable part of our careers. Every writer gets them. Stephen King used to have a huge spike on his wall where he'd impale his rejection letters. James Lee Burke kept his in a shoebox and told himself one day he was going to autograph every one of them and auction them off. Every major publishing success of the last hundred years from Gone With the Wind and The Wizard of Oz through to Harry Potter and the Philosopher's Stone has racked up an impressive pile of rejection letters.

Like all jobbing writers I've learned to cope with rejection letters and the disappointment they bring. What seems most ironic to me however, is that considering these letters are written by people whose job it is to spot good writing, they're often not at all well written themselves. It's not that they're misspelled or riddled with the sort of mistakes that send grammar Nazis reaching for their Lugers, it's just that I'm not sure enough thought was put into how they're received.

I have to admit from the off that while I've had a career that's included just about every form of professional writing, from journalism and copywriting to novels and scripts, I've never actually written a rejection letter myself. Not even to a guy whose piles had just burst. So while I'm aware of what a difficult and delicate matter it is, it's a dreaded deed I've never had to do (unlike excessive alliteration, which I can't seem to get enough of).

George Bernard Shaw (a leading proponent of beards and plays that never seemed to end) once said something along the lines of: "The right to criticise is attained by the ability to do better". As I can't claim I would do a better job myself, I decided instead to devote a good part of this entry to helping those who are forced to shatter the hopes and trample on the dreams of budding writers everywhere. Think of it as a public service.

The best way I can think of to go about this is to write a composite rejection letter based on those that I, and my many colleagues, have received, showing what your average editor/agent says. Then below each line, in italics, I'll show you what the budding author actually hears.

So here goes:

Dear Author

And I use the term Author in its loosest possible sense.

Thank you for sending us your manuscript.

No honestly, we really appreciate it. Our Mailboy's been wanting a break for ages and thanks to the hernia you gave him lugging the blasted thing upstairs he can now take all the time he wants.

Unfortunately I'm afraid we can't take it any further.

Any further than the incinerator that is, which is where the cliché ridden, turgid pile of unreadable crap I referred to, even more loosely, as your 'manuscript' actually belongs.

While we took every care to consider your work ...

Yeah right! I removed it from the envelope like it was an anthrax coated dog turd and flung it instantly into the slush pile. A toxic mound of manuscripts that have been festering in the corner of my office for so long that some of them are written in languages nobody speaks anymore. Then, to punish a junior employee for letting yet another bestselling author slip through our fingers I commanded her to read it. She immediately stapled her eyelids shut to avoid doing this, so I was forced to hand it over to the chimp I hired as a teaboy, in our latest cost cutting program, who had great fun using it as a target for his own faeces.

... we really don't think there's a market for it at the moment.

Outside of the seventh level of HELL that is! Where my rival colleagues should be forced to listen to you read it aloud for all eternity as a punishment for their insufferable smugness.

You must understand that we are a very small company and we receive a lot of submissions.

Me! Me! It's all about MEEEEE! Never mind that I just wiped my butt with your dreams I'm now going to complain that I just burst a haemorrhoid while doing so!!! Do you have any idea how tough it is out there at the moment? Do you know how many kidneys my junior employees had to sell just to keep this place afloat?! And now to top it all off you want me to interrupt my nervous breakdown to read your unpublished work. I mean it's not like it's my job to read manuscripts or anything... oh wait...

But I'd like to take this opportunity to wish you lots of luck finding a home for your work elsewhere.

Cos let's face it Buddy, You Are Going To NEED IT!
yours & Etc ...

A. S. S. Hole (D.Lit.)

If I'm honest, I don't think there is an ideal way to write a rejection letter. No matter how you go about it, or how tactfully you choose your words, you're still going to be dashing someone's hopes. If you are landed with the unenviable task of writing one, might I politely suggest that you take the time to really consider how the person to whom you're writing might take your words. Sometimes the most innocuous comment can turn out to be amazingly crass or insensitive.

From my own experience the worst rejection letter I ever received was from a children's publisher who'd actually solicited a contribution from me then sent me a standard rejection letter that informed me that they were only a small imprint (owned by a multi-national publisher) so they had to: "... really, really love everything we publish." A phrase which has the unspoken corollary: "... and we fucking HATED your work."

If you do receive a rejection letter yourself, the single best bit of advice I can give you is to make sure you always respond as politely and graciously as possible. I owe my entire career to the fact that I binned the excoriating rants I first dashed off to the ignoramuses who rejected my work, took a deep breath and instead wrote a polite and humble letter thanking them for the time and the trouble they took to consider my work. In many instances this opened up a correspondence that led to my first professional sales.

If I'd sent that first letter I'd probably be toiling as teaboy for some two bit publisher right now and flinging my own faeces at the slush pile.

Gary Fry lives in Dracula's Whitby, literally around the corner from where Bram Stoker was staying while thinking about that legendary character. Gary has a PhD is psychology, but his first love is literature. He was the first author in PS Publishing's Showcase series, and none other than Ramsey Campbell has described him as "a master." He is the author of more than 15 books, and his latest are the Lovecraftian novel Conjure House (DarkFuse, 2013); the short story collection Shades of Nothingness (PS Publishing, 2013); the highly original zombie novel Severed and novellas Menace, Savage and Mutator (DarkFuse, 2014). Gary warmly welcomes all to his web presence: www.gary-fry.com

Buttoning Up Before Dinner

Gary Fry

The key piece of advice I'd offer aspiring writer can be reduced to a single phrase and covers every aspect of the process: keep it simple. Editors do not want to read an introductory letter as lengthy as the tale you're submitting, so be short, punchy and polite. Do not use fancy fonts for your story – just a clear one, with headers kept direct and pagination attended to. Make sure all indents are the same depth. Be consistent in your use of dashes; there is a difference between an n-dash and an m-dash, so be sure to know when to use both. Do not include speech-marks curled the wrong way. Use the ellipsis correctly. Don't overuse italics – they're more powerful when deployed sparingly. The prose itself should be clean and pared down. New writers tend to use too many words. Make it a daily exercise to go through your stuff and omit as many words as possible without marring the meaning; that's a good habit to develop. By all means, be suggestive and abstruse in your storytelling, but be sure to keep the surface of the text as clear as possible. Read the great short story masters – for instance, Richard Matheson. Complex, sinuous fiction, but delivered in an unfussy style. Consider all the senses of your characters; we live in a world governed by the visual and the audible, but also consider touch, taste and smell. Let your readers experience your fictional world through your character's sensations. Focus on three fundamental elements of all successful fiction: character, story, theme. Do not let any one of them bully the others into submission; consider the process of writing a tale as one of juggling these three elements. And most importantly of all, if you want to stir your reader, write about what stirs you. It ain't quantum mechanics.

Diane Parkin has been writing since 1985, having stories and articles published in magazines and newspapers, and features and stories broadcast on BBC radio. She is a qualified broadcast journalist who has also edited books, novels, classroom resources, newspapers and magazines since 1998. She currently edits and proofreads novels and non fiction books for Pen & Sword in Yorkshire, England, and for private clients. For ten years Diane wrote Market Index for Writers' News and she taught several of their creative writing courses for the best part of fifteen years. In 2010 Diane self-published her first book, Night Crawler, which was later taken on by a traditional publisher. She also has a collection of short stories, Twee Tales, and an almanac of the first year of her blog, Baggins Bottom Best Bits Book One.

More about Diane Parkin:

Website: http://dianeparkin.wix.com/dianeparkin

WordPress: http://bagginsbottom.wordpress.com/

Facebook: www.facebook.com/diane.parkin

Twitter: @DianeParkin

LinkedIn: www.linkedin.com/in/dianeparkin

Editing and Proofreading

Diane Parkin

Editing and proofreading are very different but necessary functions in the writing world. We can do it ourselves, or we can hire a professional, or we can call a friend. What we don't want to do is send our first unpolished draft out for consideration. As an editor I woe every time a first draft is sent to me for work. It's lazy and many publishers simply don't have the staff to do a lot of the work a writer can do for him or herself. I've often sent a submission back for completion too. I just don't have the time to write the piece for them.

Editing is usually carried out after the initial writing stage, after the author has polished and scrubbed his or her prose until it's gleaming – or to the best of their ability. Editing is rewriting, revising, rejigging, deleting, relocating, adding, shaping, adhering to house-style. It's a necessary part of the process.

When the work has been written and polished and scrubbed and edited and polished and scrubbed again, then it can be proofread. Proofreading is checking for consistency in spellings (American English, British English, Australian English, etc). It's checking for consistency and accuracy in grammar and punctuation – are the colons in the right place, does the publishing house use asterisks or dots for bullets, do you really need semi-colons when commas or full stops (periods) would work just as well? It's checking for repetitions (and taking them out), for rogue punctuation (did a sly hyphen sneak in?).

Make your work stand out from the crowd. Ensure it is presented in the way preferred by the publishing house. Show the commissioning editor that it doesn't need any work, that you've read the style guide and taken note, that you're familiar with the content, the length, the style.

If you hire an editor or a proofreader, don't necessarily go for the cheapest. Think about how long it would take you to read 1,000 words, 50,000 words,

100,000 words. Then think about how long it would take if you were writing all over it, proofreading it, editing it. Then think about your own hourly or daily rate if you have/had one, or if you'd like one. If someone comes in with a quote of $20 US to edit your 300,000-word tome within three days, you're not getting a quality job. And the chances are you'll need to hire someone else to put it right. Don't skimp, value your own writer's worth and then apply that to a proofreader or an editor too. I can proofread 5,000 good words an hour; I can edit 2,500 good words an hour. Poor words take longer, and my hourly rate is more than $20 US. So just bear that in mind.

An excellent piece of writing will stand out; a poor piece of writing will too, but for the wrong reasons. If a publisher doesn't have the time – or the cash – to do this extra work, then you need to do it yourself, to give your submission a fighting chance. Be the favourite freelance/contributor/author. Make it as easy as possible for them to accept your work.

One of my own editors once said he liked commissioning me to write for him as my work never needed anything doing to it once it arrived. When an editor says that about you it feels good – almost as good as the acceptance itself.

Let your own work sparkle and shine through, do as much of the work yourself before sending it off – to a contractor, a beta reader or a publisher. Don't let the editor have to send it back for more work. Be your editor's best contributor. They'll remember your name next time, and for all the right reasons, if you do.

Rick Carufel has been a commercial and fine artist for over 40 years. During that time he has lived in Rhode Island, California, Hawaii, Arizona and Minnesota. Always an avid reader since the 1950s he finally tried his hand when recovering from knee surgery in 2002. He had plenty of time while recovering and wrote his first full length novel, The Chronicles of Underhill at that time. One of the first self-publishers, he published the book as a POD on Lulu.com in 2004. Since then he has written several books in the horror genre and also publishes and formats books for others as well as doing cover design. His books are available on Amazon and Smashwords.

Rick lives in rural Minnesota along the Mississippi River.
Author Blog: http://rickcarufel.blogspot.com
Publishing Blog: http://indie-publishing.blogspot.com/
Amazon Author page: http://www.amazon.com/Rick-Carufel/e/B004LCK4P4/
Publisher website:
http://richterpublishing.wix.com/richter-indy-publish

On Formatting: A Concise Guide to the Most Frequently Encountered Issues

Rick Carufel

I have been self-publishing since 2006, fully three years before the self-publishing movement is supposed to have started. But long before eBooks there was Lulu.com where an author could publish POD books. That's where

I published my first book, *"The Chronicles of Underhill"*.

Over time the self-publishing movement has evolved and taken off with the advent of the ebook. The methods used to publish eBooks and PODs differ and I will try to write a short guide here for my friend, Joe Mynhardt, owner of Crystal Lake Publishing.

When writing a book for eBook or POD publication it is best to set up the pages and paragraphs to the size of the finished product. Many authors fail to do this. The reality is no matter how well you think your book is formatted, it is pointless if the formatting is set at 8.50" by 11.00" when the finished product will be a 5" by 8" POD paperback.

So know what the target finished size will be and work with that size. The next biggest problem with self-publishing seems to be meeting the requirements for inclusion in the Smashwords premium catalog. This has mystified many authors, and if you know a few simple rules there will be no problem.

The biggest problem is extraneous spaces. Many authors, including myself, automatically double space at the end of a paragraph and then hit the return. Smashwords hates that. The same goes for using a tab or spaces to indent. Won't fly. The indent has to be set in the formatting tab. This is good formatting for all eBooks and PODs, not only Smashwords. So here is my concise guide to Smashwords premium catalog:

Use standard fonts and nothing larger than 16 font size.
No more than 4 returns between lines.
No more than two consecutive spaces anywhere and no extraneous spaces in the document.

The extra spaces can easily be found by clicking the view tab in Word or Open Office and clicking the non-printing characters option. You will be amazed how many extra spaces can creep into your work.

I know Mr. Coker gets a little wordy and technical in his guide to formatting for the premium catalog but that's basically what you need to know.

When formatting for an eBook include a TOC that is linked to the chapters using target tags in HTML.

Most word processing programs will easily add links in a document including target links within the document. This adds another level of professionalism to the product.

In eBooks, always add links to your Amazon author page, your blog, your website and other books you have available through different sites. Also if you have a book trailer link to that.

When formatting for a POD you also need to have a TOC. This just is how it's done professionally.

Page breaks are important as one should always have chapters start on the right-hand page. This can be tricky. First you want to set up your manuscript like a book. This mean using the mirrored option with an inside and an outside margin as opposed to left and right. I usually set the inside at .75" and the outside at .5" as well as for the top and bottom.

Next you have to realize that adding a page break anywhere in the book is going to affect all the formatting after that page break. So it is very important to start at the front of your book and work your way back from there. If you have to add a page break anywhere in the book all the page breaks after that may need to be adjusted.

Another thing that seems to be a problem is getting the page numbers to start on the correct page, usually page one being the same page that says "Chapter One."

This is done by using section breaks. All the pages before the chapter one page must be in one section and from chapter one on need to be a separate section.

I would also suggest using a header and a footer in the formatting. The header will have the book title on the left and the author name on the right typically. This will only work if you are using the mirrored pages layout. Use the footer for the page numbers.

I hope this is helpful. These aspects of formatting seem to be the most frequent issues when preparing a book for publication. If you get stumped with any formatting problems I can be found on Facebook to answer your questions. Keep writing!!!

Jasper Bark was very late with his bio for this collection. Though he wouldn't like to be known as the late Jasper Bark just yet. He does like to be known as an award winning author of four novels, 12 children's books and countless comics and graphic novels. He recently released a swarm of piranhas into a hot tub full of politicians and the Ebook 'Stuck On You', though only one of these crimes has so far been proven. His forthcoming short story collection 'Stuck On You and Other Prime Cuts' is soon to be released by Crystal Lake Publishing along with loads of other great stuff.

How to Dismember Your Darlings – Editing Your Own Work

Jasper Bark

Sir Arthur Quiller Couch, the patron saint of modern grammar Nazis and bedroom blog critiques, famously said: "Writing is murdering your darlings." While this quote might suggest that it probably is a good idea to keep most writers locked in their studies for days on end without a change of underwear, it's not actually because they have homicidal tendencies.

I'll quite happily admit it's not a good idea to marry a writer, not because you'll fear for your life every time they dig a big hole in the back garden (it probably is just for that triffid they've always wanted to grow). It's simply because they're not legendary for the size of their pay packets. I'll also agree that you shouldn't leave them in charge of a room full of school children, but only because of their irregular underwear habits.

What the Edwardian uber-critic Sir Arthur was actually getting at was the ruthlessness with which all writers should approach their work, especially when it comes to editing. I'm quite aware of what a painful chore editing can be. So much thought, so much effort and so many beautiful words went into your story and now you have to throw some of them away forever. It's like clearing out your bookshelves and deciding which of your six copies of Fahrenheit 451 you're going to get rid of. The old battered edition was the copy you read in school, whereas this one has a really cool Kelly Freas cover, oh - and you bought this one cos the gorgeous book seller recommended it and that eventually got you laid. I mean how often does a book purchase get you LAID, you can't part with this one ...

In all seriousness though, you really only need one copy. Just as you really only need one adverb in a sentence like: "Slowly, tenderly, assiduously I reached into the cot and picked up the newborn." In fact personally, I agree with Stephen King, Ernest Hemingway and many other writers, that you should probably avoid adverbs altogether whenever you can.

The ancient Egyptians used to believe that when you died, before you were allowed to enter the afterlife, you'd have to face the god Horus who would tear out your heart and weigh it against a single feather. If your heart was not pure it would be heavier than the feather and you'd be thrown to a monster called Ammit who was like an escapee from Dr Moreau's island, with the head of a crocodile, the body of a lion and the back legs of a Hippopotamus. It's my belief that writers are a special case though. When we enter the afterlife we have to face Thoth, the god of magic and writing. He doesn't weigh our hearts next to a feather, he weighs every single adverb we've ever published. If the scales overbalance then we're thrown to a creature made up of the backsides of every critic who's ever lived, most probably with Sir Arthur Quiller Couch's asshole at its head screaming: "Time to murder your darlingsssssss!"

So you see why editing is such a serious and important business. Perhaps the single most important facet of writing in fact.

It's not only a matter of knowing what to cut from your first draft it's also a matter of knowing how much. In his excellent book On Writing (required reading for any writer) Stephen King (yes him again) speaks of a note he got from a now forgotten editor, back in 1966, that gave him the magic formula: "2nd draft = 1st draft minus 10%. Good luck." While this is quite a prescriptive formula it isn't a bad rule of thumb.

It would seem then, that editing isn't so much murdering your darlings as dismembering them. Try to imagine the target market for your story as the coffin you've brought to a remote rural shack in order to bury the body of the darling you've just murdered. As is always the case in these matters (and please don't ask me why I'm so knowledgeable) the coffin is ironically 10% too small for the deceased. So you have to decide whether to saw off the head or the feet first, and then pick the arm that has to go.

Without wanting to sound too bloodthirsty, hacking up your darlings may be a gruesome business, but the longer I've written, the more it's become the part of the process that I enjoy the most. Maybe it's the mad professor in me, but I see editing as the act of perfecting my work. Like Dr Frankenstein I see myself stitching together the body parts of my murdered darlings to create the 'perfect adonis' of a story.

Before I became a full time writer I was a stand-up comic, traveling up and down the country performing gigs night after night to pay the rent. Like most stand ups, once the gig was done I would replay the performance over and over again in my mind, dissecting it to find which bits worked and which didn't. There would always be parts of my performance I wished I'd done differently. A pause I should have extended to get twice the laugh, a new quip I ought to have dropped into a routine to make it funnier. The only problem was, that gig was over and done with. It was a moment in time to which I could never return and no matter how much better I thought it could have been, the gig would never be more than what it was in that moment. I could not go back and extend that pause, or drop that quip into the routine.

With writing however, that is exactly what I can do. Once the first draft is written I can revisit it as many times as I like (within the given deadline), until it's as close to perfect as I can get it. If a certain passage needs an extended pause I put one in, if it needs a new quip I drop it in at exactly the right place and no one will ever know. As far as they're concerned it was this good from the word go.

Editing isn't just a matter of shedding unnecessary words and sentences. It's also about shedding unnecessary concepts and plot strands if need be. This is the part of writing that demands the most ruthlessness from the writer. Sometimes the concepts or plot lines that need be cut are utterly priceless. They may be the single most ingenious and original thing in your story, but if they don't serve the overall needs of the story itself, if they're a square concept in a round plot hole, they just have to go.

This doesn't need to be murder though. The pulp sci-fi doyen Robert Heinlein always insisted that nothing you write is ever wasted. It will always find a home some place, even if it's not the first story into which you put your concept. If the idea is good, it will eventually find a home, and that home will most likely be the place it was always supposed to be. In this instance, writing isn't so much murdering your darlings as cryogenically freezing them until medical science, or your imagination, is sufficiently advanced to resuscitate them.

I had a personal experience of 'freezing my darlings' when I wrote the story 'How the Dark Bleeds' for the anthology *'For the Night Is Dark'* (also from *Crystal Lake Publishing*). Now if you're one of those terribly cynical individuals who imagine that the only reason I've written this entry is to plug a book, you'd be perfectly right. This is the very laboured equivalent of one of those interminable Facebook postings that run along the lines of: "Hey everybody, there's 20% off my latest eBook all this week at Amazon". But you have to admit it's been a great ride so far, so you may as well stick around for the sales pitch.

The idea for the story originally manifested in a graphic novel I was pitching to an American publisher. One of the subplots contained a concept that increasingly unnerved and disturbed me. It grabbed hold of the darker side of my imagination and tortured it incessantly, until I was both in love with and terrified of the concept all at once. I had never seen this idea anywhere before and I knew I had to write about it. The only problem was, as amazing as this concept was, the graphic novel I was pitching was better off without it. So it was with great reluctance that I took it out.

At around the same time I was stuck for an idea for the short story I was contracted to write for Crystal Lake's upcoming anthology. Well not so much stuck, I had plenty of ideas, it's just that none of them were as good as I thought they ought to be. The pay for writing short stories is frankly lousy, so I always figure that, if I'm going to go to the trouble of writing one, it better be something I really want to write.

Then I remembered the concept that enthralled and unsettled me, the one I'd put in the bottom drawer. If anything, it had grown stronger since I'd dropped it into fictional suspended animation. I found it had been waiting for me and it wanted to take me to places far darker than my fiction had ever been before. It forced me to confront and record the taboos I'd previously shied away from and to enter those territories I'd always thought of as 'off limits' - even as a horror writer.

The experience of writing this story was both exhilarating and excruciating. There were several moments during its composition when I wondered not only if I wanted to finish it, but whether or not I wanted to write another piece of horror fiction as long as I lived. Ultimately, I did live to tell this tale and I will certainly tell others.

With hindsight, I'm glad that I did. The story turned out really well. It scared my publisher and made my editor queasy. None of this would have been possible if I hadn't been prepared to hack the concept off the corpse of my graphic novel and pop it into a petri-dish to grow a darker and more disturbing story from it. All of which supports my earlier claim that editing is perhaps the single most important facet of writing.

Emma Audsley was born for horror fiction. With a burning desire to help the horror genre evolve & expand, she helps in her own little ways namely reviewing, editing & mentoring.

Born in the UK in 1977 she's had a long time to study the field & adores this eerie genre of ours. She's proud & honoured to be working alongside Joe Mynhardt as Publishing & Editing Consultant. Having already worked with many notable names in Horror, she is ready to assist Crystal Lake Publishing in their blazing trail across the plains of the genre.

Emma also has a review site over at The Horrifically Horrifying Horror Blog, she's a member of the British Fantasy Society & The Horror Writers Association where she hosted 2014's Women in Horror Month & is currently assisting in the lead up to The Bram Stoker Awards alongside Douglas Murano.

From Reader to Writer: Finding Inspiration

Emma Audsley

You've been reading horror fiction for as long as you can remember.

You know which authors to read and which you'd personally prefer to avoid, you've pushed your limits by going to the dark places these scary writerly folk can lead you.

You know each and every trope used within the horror fiction genre, especially the ones flogged to within an inch of their lives and twisted and warped so much resulting in the average reader barely being able to see them for what they are anymore.

You've pondered on the high and low points of each plot(s) within each book you've absorbed more readily than the oxygen surrounding you...you're also sure you could match this, or even better out-do it. Surely it can't be *that* hard...can it?

So, what next?

Maybe you choose to Google 'How to write horror fiction', aim to remember to read the bookmarked pages you've just amassed, you might even decide to buy a few guide books for your new terrain, raid a stationary store for some luxurious notebooks that only a real *writer* would use!

So now you've covered what you think are the essentials to starting on your journey to fame & fortune. You've set up a nice writing space just like the guidebooks say, now all you have to do is begin. The blank page (or screen) is waiting. What's it waiting for? Oh yes. The. First. Line.

You start off with a scene, an element of a character, a situation that causes conflict...but still, you falter. You've looked at what sells, but maybe (hopefully) you're not interested in what sells. You know there's something there, something intangible and just out of reach. You scribble that first line, then, perhaps after some more coffee, you scratch that one and begin again. *No, not good enough...that isn't it.*

Your life. They say 'write what you know'. What can you use? Sure, there's been some stuff that you could use, moments of intense sadness, a trauma, but what if you don't feel ready to delve there alone. That's what your reading is for...exorcising those ghosts, the demons.

What you really need to do is to get to the very roots of Horror, what creates fear and what causes us to cling to it, be haunted by it, even be consumed by it. Horror, such a broad sweeping word, is the essence. We know that...but what *is* it? Is it a thing? A person? An event? An ancient entity blood-bound to ensure the destruction of the Soul itself? No. It's not that simple.

Horror is what makes us get up in the morning, it's what makes us fear sleeping while those dark shadows loom around us threatening to swallow us whole leaving no trace of our existence behind. Horror is the *Thing* behind every loss we suffer. It's every hit, kick or slap that pushes us further into the ground. It's the bullies in the school yard. It's the parent that hits you. It's that strange person that always seems to be hovering near a school. It's the accident that seems to have been waiting to happen, just waiting for you to get close enough to grasp. It's getting ill. It's dying, knowing that the end is coming and there's not one goddamn thing you can do about it. It's being born. To put it bluntly: it's being alive and still kicking. As long as you still fight to go on...it will follow. It will haunt you. It will hunt you down.

Let me interrupt my incessant ramblings to mention who I am. Or rather, what I do. As some of you know, I'm the Publishing & Editing Consultant for Crystal Lake Publishing. I'm also an avid reader of Horror Fiction, a reviewer, a freelance editor and a writing mentor. I'm also a writer, yes, I'm proud to say that I write. I sit and write, I can't finish my own work (heck, even my good friend Erik Smith had to help by reading this and giving me a title!) yet I aid others to finish theirs. I've taken writers with complete block, resigned to having quit, and then after talking through what they think has stopped the muse from calling, I start doing what I do. I'm ready and waiting with files, books and masses of photographs. Lists of recommended reading and quotes (some of the ones included between the articles in this very collection) and friendly wake-up reminders with a pic prompt for the day, asking them how they've been feeling about writing again, maybe even a first line – yes, THAT First Line – to get the blood moving.

As a reviewer and reader, or absorber, of horror fiction I aim to look at what lies 'beneath the veil' of what's being written. A former psychology student, I look at what's happening in the world and compare that to what I've found in new fiction. Just open the paper, or turn on the news, you'll see it all right there. The things that are once seen can never be 'unseen'. War, Politics, Famine, Rape, Murder, Mass Movement, Prejudice; the repeating of history. That eternal circle of life. The things that shape us, mould us, cage us, fill us with frustration, or worse…apathy. Remember, while the form of apathy is not feeling or, well, caring, the form of *empathy* – also the key to reading or writing damn good horror – is not sympathy, it's the understanding of another person's situation. Quick quote:

'Could a greater miracle take place than for us to look through each other's eyes for an instant?' – David Henry Thoreau

What does Horror Fiction do if not give that to us? How else can we get that horrible feeling out? Exorcise our demons and release the empathy.

Now, where were we? Oh yes, I remember now. What to write about? Any ideas?

How about that *First Line*?

My work has been featured in various magazines such as Shroud Magazine, Black Petals and The Ashen Eye. I also have a short story appearing in the horror anthology Between The Lines edited by Bram Stoker award winning editor Michael Knost, which will be published spring of 2014. My website is www.beneadsfiction.com and my blog's address is www.beneadsfiction.com/blog.

Writing Exercises

Ben Eads

Let's be honest, shall we? Writing is a tough gig. Creating worlds and characters readers can experience should not be approached lightly. Do not fret, my friends. I have a few simple things to share with you that I'm sure you'll love. They're called exercises!

After writing, beta-reading and editing horror fiction for four years, I've found the two biggest complaints in creating realistic fiction: dialogue and description. What I have to share will be most beneficial to writers who are just starting down their dark paths.

We'll tackle dialogue first. You may be able to avoid dialogue in flash fiction, or even a short story, but you can't avoid description no matter the size. That's why we will cover description and how it coalesces with dialogue at the end.

So you're weak in dialogue. No worries! Imagine Al Pacino in your mind telling you to "Fuggettaboutit!"

You know your characters better than anyone. You created them. So, when creating your tales, use dialogue that fits your characters better than their clothes.

Dialogue will *show* your readers who your characters are, where they live, their gender, where they work—hell, it will even show them their mood! If your protagonist is visiting Egypt, I doubt he or she will find much help at first. It will probably take some time before they find someone who can even speak broken English. Which brings us to separation.

Whether it's a character traveling to Egypt, or three teens traveling to California, there must be a separation. Notice how each of your characters speaks. It will kill a lot of speech tags and, my dear friends, will make it much easier for the reader to believe these are actual people and not an *attempt* at people.

Ever read anything by John Steinbeck, Elmore Leonard or Douglas Adams? Have you ever seen a Quentin Tarantino film? They are masters at dialogue. *Of Mice and Men* by John Steinbeck was the first example that came to my mind. If you haven't read it, please do. When was the last time you watched Pulp Fiction? Watch it again and pay close attention.

Here is a great example of dialogue from John Steinbeck's *Of Mice and Men*:

"I forgot," Lennie said softly. "I tried not to forget. Honest to God I did, George."

"O.K.—O.K. I'll tell ya again. I ain't got nothing to do. Might jus' as well spen' all my time tell'n you things and then you forget 'em, and I tell you again."

"Tried and tried," said Lennie, "but it didn't do no good. I remember about the rabbits, George."

"The hell with the rabbits. That's all you ever can

remember is them rabbits. O.K.! Now you listen and this time you got to remember so we don't get in no trouble. You remember settin' in that gutter on Howard street and watchin' that blackboard?"

Lennies's face broke into a delighted smile. "Why sure, George, I remember that...but...what'd we do then? I remember some girls come by and you says...you say..."

"The hell with what I says. You remember about us goin' into Murray and Ready's, and they give us work cards and bus tickets?"

"Oh, sure, George, I remember that now." His hands went quickly into his side coat pockets. He said gently, "George...I ain't got mine. I musta lost it." He looked down at the ground in despair.

"You never had none, you crazy bastard. I got both of 'em here. Think I'd let you carry your own work card?"

This is your first writing exercise for dialogue. And feel free to create your own exercises. That's the real magic of it. Here's the prompt: Your protagonist is a police detective walking up to a house in a poor area of town. He's there to ask the old woman who lives there a lot of questions about the whereabouts of her sixteen-year-old grandson. Remember the police detective from the TV show *Dragnet*? His famous catch phrase was: "Just the facts, ma'am." Just the facts, indeed. Remember, the detective is your protagonist and the grandmother won't be happy he's there. No matter how many words it takes you, write it. Just a simple exchange. However, you cannot say or tell he is a cop in narration. It must be in speech. Again, we're *showing* the reader.

Here's another writing exercise for dialogue: Your

protagonist is a five-year-old girl out with her mother trick-or-treating on Halloween for the first time. It starts with the mother urging your little protagonist to knock on the door and say those famous words. The exchange will be between your protagonist and the person who answers the door, while the mother is coaching her along. This exercise is easy because of the stark contrast between the three characters.

Once you have finished one of these exercises, or both, read it out loud to yourself. Does it sound real to you? If it does, move forward to the next step.

Find a family member, a friend, or better yet, a writer or editor that knows how to beta-read constructively. Make them aware of your concern and to focus on the dialogue. Follow up on the feedback you receive.

This is where the magic comes in. You will walk through a wall you once thought impenetrable. Keep doing this and making variations thereof until your heart's content. Besides, writing is just practice, anyway. Once you have nailed these, implement what you've learned in your own fiction. You may have characters that are very much alike; their backgrounds, neighborhood, etc... But this time you'll have a new tool in your toolbox. And the wall won't be there.

Now let's tackle one of the horror genre's hardest parts: description. Simply put, description begins with the writer and ends with the reader. You have Stephen King and a lot of other amazing and successful writers to thank for that gem. Let's pause right here before we get into what description is, because this is powerful. What is too much? What is too little? Let's take this example of bad description:

"Larry walked up to his BMW 500 series that housed

a 400 horsepower motor under that candy-red hood. He pressed a button and the car unlocked. He slid into the plush, white leather seat that was made in Italy by a guy named Anthony Rapino two years ago whose wife had called Naples home for over three hundred years."

Wow! Who farted, right? Do we really need to know all that? Of course not. It takes the reader *out* of the story. However:

"Larry got into his BMW 500 series. He cranked the beast to life and turned out of the parking lot, heading for the highway."

OK, better, but aren't we missing something here? The reader needs to be connected as to *why* Larry is driving like a madman on the highway. And where is he headed? Perhaps we can do a bit better.

"Larry swung the door of his BMW open and slid inside. Four hundred horses came to life and roared under the hood. He turned out of the parking lot, heading for the highway. His thumb massaged the face of his wife and her new boyfriend in the picture all the way to her house."

OK, it won't win a Pulitzer, but we're starting to get there.

Here is an excellent example of description from Stephen King's, *Pet Cemetery*, where we find Jud leading Louis to the Micmac burial ground to bury his cat:

"Come on," Jud said and led him twenty-five yards toward the trees. The wind blew hard up here, but if felt clean. Louis saw a number of shapes just under the gloom cast by the trees—trees which were the oldest, tallest firs he had ever seen. The whole effect of this high, lonely place was emptiness—but an emptiness which vibrated."

Stephen King does an amazing job of interacting with the reader's imagination in the above example. The supernatural force is only hinted at; it could be Louis himself. This is what gives this scene the suspense and power it has. And note the excellent word selection for what lies below: vibration. Myriad words come to mind: power, knowledge, etc...

So, what is description? If dialogue defines a character, then description is what frames the character, the world he or she lives in. Notice in the above example how King keeps it short and sweet. He only describes what he has to describe. Again, the rest is left to the reader's imagination, like a carrot in front of a donkey.

Think of description as a skeleton key that can elicit emotions from your reader. Description can shock, scare and make the reader feel in lock-step with the character. The latter is vital. The entire world your characters exist in should, in some way, either echo or reflect your character's inner struggle. It could be weather. It could be winter. It could be the dead of winter during a storm. And this external struggle must be just as real as the internal struggle. Both coming to a resolution at the ending due to them being connected in some way.

It can also be the people around your characters. How do they act? How is the family influenced by this? What do they *show* the protagonist that he or she did not see before due to their preoccupation with their inner struggles?

In reality, if you're depressed you won't see the vibrant colors of nature. You'll see what your limited perspective will allow. So, like characters in a Lovecraft story, if they see something that is literally another world, or beings from that world, their sanity is forever lost. Their minds become one with the chaos that they fail to comprehend as they slide down that dark drain.

Here is your first description writing exercise: Your protagonist is a young woman, or man, meeting a long lost friend at his or her favorite restaurant. You must use all of the human senses to describe the inside of this establishment. What does the protagonist see, smell, taste and touch? And what does his or her friend add to the surroundings that your protagonist missed? What do they point out? The catch? You must find some emotional inner-struggle for the protagonist that is echoed by the external environment in as many senses you can get. Keep going at it until you hit all of them.

When you are pleased with the results send it off to a beta-reader, or a writer or editor capable of constructive criticism. Follow up on the feedback. Here, you will find more magical moments occurring. You will see pathways that you didn't see before. The pool you were swimming in just got bigger. You will have a much more profound understanding of weaving the outside world with that of the protagonist. After all, perception is everything, my friends.

Here is your second description writing exercise— and this one is a doozy: Your protagonist is delivering a meal to an elderly man who has been blind since birth. During a conversation, your protagonist is asked by this elderly blind man to describe what a TV is to him. Again, the elderly gent has been blind since birth. Once he has done that, he is urged by the elderly man to go deeper; what does the TV display? Yes, a doozy, but that's the point of the exercise. Will your protagonist ask the elderly man if he can see any color at all as a reference point? Again, it's just an exercise designed to broaden your creative horizons. Nothing more. Nothing less.

Once you are finished, send it off to beta-readers. If you know a writer or editor willing and capable of constructive criticism, send it to them and follow up on their input.

Now we will coalesce dialogue and description with this example from the opening line of a short story I wrote:

"We're here to fuckin' work, son. We get in, paint that damned house, get paid and get the fuck out," Scott said and flicked his cigarette into the ashtray.

Little Andy flinched and brought his hands together in his lap, massaging the burn scars between his knuckles."

Did I have to tell you that Scott is not a good father? Look at the language he uses with his little son! And most importantly, did I have to tell you that his father is abusive? Did I have to tell you who gave little Andy those burn scars? Action, reaction. All of this is shown, not told.

Here is the final writing exercise: You have five hundred words to describe a verbal fight—borderline physical altercation—between two brothers over the inheritance money from their father's death. Here's the catch: you must have one brother do something—an action—which will force a reaction in the other brother *telling* us what it is. What did one brother do to the other that has brought them to this emotional intensity? And can this brother—which one is left up to you—be healed by this experience? Or will it blow up in to a full-on fight?

Once you expose the vulnerability of the brother from action-reaction, you must find a way for the brother to heal this past trauma right there. You must fix the external conflict by fixing the internal conflict first.

There are a ton of exercises you will come up with on your own while working on these. Write them down and exercise, my dear friends! Again, this is to open your imagination to possibilities you did not see before.

I would love to hear about your experiences with these exercises and the ones you will create on your own. Please, drop me a line @ *beneadsfiction@gmail.com* with your results.

"Insanity is relative. It depends on who has who locked in what cage."
– Ray Bradbury

"Perseverance is a great element of success. If you only knock long enough and loud enough at the gate, you are sure to wake up somebody."
– Henry Wadsworth Longfellow

"Books are companions, teachers, magicians, bankers of the treasures of the mind. Books are humanity in print."
– Barbara W. Tuchman

"Those who dream by day are cognizant of many things that escape those who dream only at night."
– Edgar Allan Poe

"The most durable thing in writing is style, and style is the most valuable investment a writer can make with his time. It pays off slowly, your agent will sneer at it, your publisher will misunderstand it, and it will take people you have never heard of to convince them by slow degrees that the writer who puts his individual mark on the way he writes will always pay off."
– Raymond Chandler

"We make up horrors to help us cope with the real ones."
– Stephen King

Hiding the Body
(Career Advice)

Rena Mason is a Sin City writer and a longtime fan of horror, sci-fi, science, history, historical fiction, mysteries, and thrillers, who began writing to mash up those genres in stories revolving around everyday life. She is a member of the Pacific Northwest Writers Association, a member of the Horror Writers Association, an active member of the International Thriller Writers, and is a literary committee member representing the Horror genre for the annual Vegas Valley Book Festival. She is a two-time Bram Stoker Award® Finalist and the author of The Evolutionist, East End Girls, and a handful of short stories. To learn more about Rena and her upcoming projects, visit www.renamasonwrites.com/
and www.renamasonwrites.blogspot.com/

The Year After Publication...

Rena Mason

Congratulations! Your first novel has been published. Open up that box, arrange the book covers to look great, and take an obligatory "Look What Just Arrived!" photo. Post it on Facebook, Google+, Linked In, Pinterest, and don't forget to Tweet it, then blog about it. Dance around the books, howl, and sing your favorite happy song. Reach in and take one out, flip through the pages, and let them blow your hair back. Take in that new book scent, inhale deeply. Check out your dedication and acknowledgement pages. It's a high like no other. Enjoy it. You're going to have a busy year ahead.

If you're prepared, you've already been working on that second novel. You've made connections via social media and/or by attending writers conventions. Hopefully, some of those people you met are book reviewers/bloggers. It's time to send them that friendly, *"Remember me?"* email. If you have no connections, make some. Do interviews and podcasts when the opportunities arise. With all the competition out there, take advantage of using "Debut Novel" to promote your work. Many readers are looking for new authors to try out, and that could be you.

You can hold social media events, and book giveaways. There are many ezines, traditional magazines, and websites that offer advertising, and some at a reduced cost for members of certain organizations such as the (HWA) Horror Writers Association, (SFWA) Science Fiction & Fantasy Writers of America, and (ITW) International Thriller Writers, to name a few. Visit your local bookstores and ask about doing author signings. Get involved with the annual book festival in your area and others that might be close enough for you to travel to. Go to your local library, and do what's necessary in order for them to get your books circulating throughout your county and into others within your state. Many libraries have events promoting local authors, check their calendar and sign up for all the ones you're able to attend. Promote your events on your websites or with organizations you might be involved with or are a member of. You can find an author friend who also has a new release and do a cross-promotion. And oh yeah, don't forget to keep working on that second novel.

A couple things to avoid, and as difficult as they may be, try not to obsess over rankings and reviews. Don't

SPAM blast everything and everyone you know at once, and never on a weekly basis. There's a fine line between promoting and annoying. You'll figure it out when your work receives less and less attention. This is not a particularly good situation to be in for a first-time author.

Be prepared to get requests for anthology stories. Some of them might be for charities such as cancer, cystic fibrosis, or mental illness. These are usually non-paying markets. Others might be non-paying and simply for exposure (to get your name out there), and others are for token payments like a copy of the book and/or ten dollars or more. Anything that is five cents a word or above is considered pro-rate in the Horror genre. These requests are both flattering and time-consuming. You've got to pick and choose. If you're one of those people who can whip something up in a few hours (I envy you), or you've got an idea already outlined, or have one in a trunk, that's great. If not, think long and hard about whether or not the charity really speaks to you, or if the exposure is worth your time (and whether or not the publisher has a good reputation). If it's an advance payment, or pro-rate request, drop whatever you're doing and give it a shot. But don't forget to keep working on your second novel.

Say one of the stories you were requested to and decided to write caught someone's attention, and that person who's respected in the industry asks you to co-write a movie screenplay for that work? It wasn't something you'd originally planned on ever doing, you know nothing about it, but are curious. You do a lot of research, are encouraged by your prospective co-writer, and decide to take on the task. It'll be fun! *Right?*

Oh, and remember that second novel you were supposed to be working on since your first novel got published? Go ahead and put it on the backburner for now, and be thankful your first novel wasn't part of a series and your publisher is chomping at the bit for the second one.

A year later, you've finished the screenplay and after some reviews are told it is a high concept and could possibly not only sell but might actually get made into a movie. It's being "shopped" around. You're both excited and relieved the process is over. You've also written a few short stories that will be published within the next year. You haven't opened the file to your second novel but talk and think about it often.

It is also awards season, and you've received some positive feedback. Even though you're exhausted, you go through the promotional process again to rekindle interest. The whirlwind year will soon be over. It was an emotional roller coaster. You loved and hated it.

You're at a crossroads. That first story you wrote to get out of your head wasn't the only one there. What do you do now? Which path do you choose? Or do you just give it all up for some peace, and go back to the life you had before?

That's just it—you can't. You realize life has changed. The stories must be told, no matter the form, no matter the success or lack thereof. They don't stop coming. It is what keeps you going. You must write, you want to hone your craft, and do the best you can. You took your ideas, spliced, pieced, and shaped them into something more tangible. The feeling of accomplishment is addictive.

So you write.

Steve Rasnic Tem's latest novel is Blood Kin from Solaris Books—a novel of ghosts, witchcraft, snake-handling, and the Great Depression.

His latest short story collections are Here with the Shadows from Swan River Press–a volume of supernatural impressions and quiet vacancies, http://www.swanriverpress.ie/titles.html, and Celestial Inventories from ChiZine–difficult-to-pigeonhole works of the fantastic crossing conventional boundaries between science fiction, fantasy, horror, & literary fiction.

http://chizinepub.com/books/celestial-inventories.php

You may visit the Tem home on the web at www.m-s-tem.com.

Writing Horror: 12 Tips on Making a Career of It

Steve Rasnic Tem

One: Create a Repertoire of Story Strategies

In order to produce a strong body of work, whether it be short stories or novels, you will need a wide range of story structures and approaches for beginnings, middles, and endings in your tool kit. This means reading and analyzing a great deal of fiction, and not just horror fiction. You should read popular and literary fiction of all kinds, both the classics and new work, and make some exploratory journeys into the world of university and small press magazines as well. Look at experimental fiction, look at types of fiction you'd normally never consider reading. The goal here isn't to change your reading likes and dislikes, but to broaden your ideas about the options you have for grabbing a reader's attention, building a narrative, and ending it in a satisfying way. You're likely to discover that there are dozens of techniques you've never thought to apply to horror.

Two: Preserve Your Resources & What Exposure Really Means

Creating fiction isn't easy, and each project you complete is potentially a valuable resource for your career—it's intellectual property, it's copyright. Maybe it pays your electrical bill this month, maybe it's a down payment on a car. Maybe another editor will read it and offer you a slot in an anthology. Hold on to as many rights as possible and limit your publisher's exclusivity as best you can. Potentially you'll be able to resell and repurpose it a number of times. I'm not saying there aren't times you may decide to sell it cheaply or even give it away, but those times should be chosen carefully according to the non-monetary advantages your career might receive.

And one thing about exposure: appearing on a web site or in a book alongside writers few have ever heard of isn't really exposure. Exposure is having your work appear with that of authors whose names sell books and having readers read your work because of that proximity.

Three: Become Your Own Editor & Best Critic

Your progress as a writer will be severely hampered if you never learn how to self-edit and self-critique.

Ultimately, you are the best expert in your own work. You have the best view of what you're trying to accomplish in a story and you're the one the characters are attempting to speak to—they're trying to tell you what should happen to them and what it all means. When an editor or a critic reviews your story they're trying to make sense of it, but they don't really know what the story is "meant" to be, so the sense they make may not be the same as yours and their suggestions therefore may not always be fully applicable. Learn grammar and punctuation and sentence structure. Learn to use a spell checker. But more importantly learn how to take your stories apart so that you'll know how to fix them. Any time you join a workshop or hire an editor your goal should not be just to fix a particular story, but to learn how to be a better editor of your own work.

Four: Don't Despair When There Are Writers Better Than You

The truth is, no matter how good you are there will always be writers better than you. But another truth is that there is no one else out there who will tell *your* stories. If you don't tell your stories no one else will. So your task is to become as good a writer as you can in order to be able to tell those stories as effectively as possible.

Five: Be Patient, but Don't Save Your Best for Last

It's hard to wait. It's not uncommon that as soon as a writer publishes 8 or 10 stories they want to bring out their first collection. Or if you're a novelist and your novel has been rejected a few times during the first year of submission you may want to withdraw it and just publish it yourself as a print-on-demand title or eBook. That ease of self-publication is not an option I had to consider earlier in my career and I have to say I'm glad because I would have been sorely tempted.

For various reasons my first collection (*City Fishing*) came out 2 decades into my career. And my last two novels (*Deadfall Hotel* & *Blood Kin*) were both many years in the making. Although I'm certainly not suggesting that you wait that long, I will say these were much better books because of the wait. For my first collection I had over 200 stories to choose from in order to make this the best representation of my work possible. Readers' first extended exposure to your work is crucial—you only have one chance to present a first collection. Make it a stellar one.

On the other hand, I know writers who have held on to their best ideas until that "ideal" point in their career to bring them out. The problem with that strategy is opportunity is unpredictable and—dare I say it?—none of us live forever. Wait if you don't have the skills yet to pull it off, but as far as I'm concerned that's the only valid reason. And even then, one of the best ways to improve as a writer is to set your goals beyond what you've normally been capable of doing, and then rise to the challenge—writers have been known to make miraculous leaps in skill level that way.

Six: Come Up With Your Own Definition of What Having "A Career" Means
Sometimes writers obsess over whether they're professional or not, whether they make enough money or not—they seem to want some sort of scorecard about how they're "doing." It's the kind of mind-numbing

definition making that only writers seem to care about. Sometimes it drives them into doing projects they don't really want to do simply because they want to quit the day job—and end up writing something every bit as dissatisfying as that day job.

But in the final analysis, readers don't care—they only care about what finally gets to the page, not the details of "how" it got there. So make a career that makes sense to you in terms of getting the work done and still getting rent paid and food on the table. Subsidize it with a day job, write every day or only write on weekends, call yourself a "pro" or call yourself a "passionate amateur"—it doesn't matter. All that matters is getting the work done. Or you can call yourself a writer but never write. Whatever floats your boat. But if nothing ever gets to the page the readers will never know.

Seven: Remember That the Genre World Is a Small One

It's amazing how many people in this field know each other, either through actual contact or through reputation. There's a nice little hometown coziness to it all, isn't there? But the flip side of that is that if you're rude to someone in the field—whether it be an editor, another writer, or a fan, other people hear about it. If you have a serious falling out with an editor you may find that you'll encounter that editor again down the line. You might insult a fan and then five years later find that that fan has become your editor. This is not to say that you should never complain, stand up for yourself, or speak your mind. But consequences can be amplified. It's generally good advice to avoid burning bridges. And well, generally speaking, there's nothing wrong with being nice to people. And that fellow's rudeness that seems so insulting? It might just be because he's awkward and nervous and behind in his social skills. Sometimes it's good to give people the benefit of the doubt.

Eight: Learn To Ride Out the Cycles

Publishing has cycles, as do genres, as do careers. You may sell four novels in a row, and then you may have a five or ten year span when you don't sell any. Suddenly your editors don't seem to love you any more—they're too busy with newer, younger writers. Maybe your agent doesn't seem to "get" you anymore. He used to call you back instantly. Now it takes weeks to get even an email out of him. Or maybe you've lost interest in what you're writing and you want to write something different for a change.

Unless you're very lucky, these events may occur several times during your career. And they can be career-ending, if you let them be. You may feel you haven't any choice—you may feel you've simply stopped selling, for whatever reason, and that's the end of it. You didn't leave publishing, you think—publishing left you.

But if you want a long career you need to learn how to ride out those cycles. There are a number of standard ways of doing this—switching genres, for example, or concentrating on short stories versus novels for a while, or switching to YA, or moving into an editorial role, pitching anthologies, or maybe you'd like to try nonfiction or teaching for a while. The key is to stay flexible and keep moving.

But another strategy is to view this as an opportunity.

Get back in touch with the hunger you may have experienced at the beginning of your career; reacquaint yourself with why you decided to write in the first place, the desire for it before it became a paying enterprise. Take a gamble. Write something more ambitious than anything else you've done. Push your abilities to the limits. Create an inventory of books you can sell when the market changes or, if you're so inclined, embark on a program of self-publication. The important thing is to keep doing it, to recognize this activity as one of the ways you practice your humanity and make sense of the world.

Nine: Don't Lose Your Head over Promotion

Few writers seem to understand how to promote themselves effectively. They're not comfortable with it. Perhaps, if they're the kind of introverted individuals the writing craft tends to attract, it feels completely unnatural to them.

Promotion is a frustrating activity for many writers, in part, I believe, because it rarely seems to work. You can spend a ton of money on giveaways—bookmarks, postcards, notepads and the like, you can take out ads, you can spend countless hours doing small book signings at local bookstores, and none of it seems to make the smallest blip in sales.

But Kris Rusch and Dean Wesley Smith (whose blogs on the business of writing are a great investment of your time) have pointed out something very interesting, and I think reassuring—the best thing you can do to promote a book is to write and publish more books. If readers like one of your books, they know they might like another, and they tell their friends.

Traditionally that's how careers have been built, and it's nice to see that it still works, because writing, frankly, is what writers do best.

Educate yourself about book promotion, make yourself aware of what other authors are doing—educated choices are important here. But don't let it interfere with your production, because writing is what sells.

Ten: Awards Should Be Happy Accidents

Awards are nifty—they look good on the shelf, and they're a nice reminder that people admire what you do, which can be an important incentive in an occupation so lonely and solipsistic. If you receive one you should feel honored, and appreciative of the fact that people cared to read and vote for your work. But keep them in perspective. They aren't likely to increase your sales significantly, unless you've won so many that readers are naturally curious about you. A Pulitzer Prize would help, or a National Book Award, but genre awards tend not to have that sales affect except perhaps for the Hugo or the Edgar, and even those aren't always reliable.

So winning an award is an ego boost, but not a magic bean for your career. Another thing they can be, however, is an enormous time sink—the worrying over them, the campaigning for them—time which could be better spent writing new work.

Eleven: Handle Your Ego Issues

This naturally brings us to ego issues in general. Writing is extremely hard on the ego. Sometimes it feels like "being rejected" is what you do for a living. And yet you have to have some ego just to write at all—after all, you're toiling at the same profession as Faulkner, Shakespeare, and Austen. But remember what I said earlier—luckily for you no one else can tell "your" stories.

Some writers, of course, compensate for this state of affairs by developing formidable egos, and that ego can become a huge stumbling block. It makes it more difficult to work with other people or to see your work objectively. I don't have a magic solution for this, just a gentle suggestion to let your work do most of the talking.

Twelve: Keep Yourself Free

Trying to stay free, flexible, and creative as a writer is essential for producing good work, but becoming a professional actually seems to work against that at times. You spend so much time translating your first, raw attempts into stories that work, that editors will buy, that you often program yourself into one genre, and even one story making approach within that genre. You effectively take that wild, rushing stream of the imagination and funnel it down into a manageable trickle.

But if you're going to grow as a writer you need to revisit that process from time to time, open the imagination up, and discover new ways of telling stories. This will feel counter-intuitive at times. Maybe this is the first time in a long time that you've felt comfortable in your process and satisfied with your writing. That's fine—enjoy it while you can. Just don't lull yourself into believing it's the best you can do.

Michael Arnzen has won four Bram Stoker Awards over the past twenty years he has been publishing. He's created everything from prize-winning novels (Grave Markings) to poetry books (The Gorelets Omnibus) to refrigerator magnets (The Fridge of the Damned) and audio CDs (Audiovile). Arnzen is also a Professor of English at Seton Hill University, home of the MFA in Writing Popular Fiction, near Pittsburgh, where he has taught since 1999.

"The Five Laws of Arnzen" is an expanded version of a piece that first appeared in Instigation: Creative Prompts on the Dark Side (Mastication Publications, 2013). Catch up with him at http://gorelets.com and sign up to his popular e-mail missive, The Goreletter, to keep in touch.

The Five Laws of Arnzen

Michael A. Arnzen

I'm about to megalomaniacally present to you "The Five Laws of Arnzen," but truth be told, like most horror writers, I'm actually kind of "lawless." Even so, we outlaws sometimes share trade secrets.

What follows are essentially versions of the things I say often to writers who are trying to navigate the profession. They're actually more like traffic signs than laws. Treat them like abstract ideas, defined by whatever the context might be – as you read these, think broadly about how they might pertain (if at all) to your career, your daily routine, your present manuscript, your education, your approach to editors, or even just your latest journal entry. I can't promise you that if you "obey" these laws you'll succeed, but they might help you survive if not thrive in your work on the dark side.

1. Persist

Writing, like most arts, is the anti-thesis of immediate gratification. You begin with an idea and it is not until you've written it down that you have a completed manuscript. You write something now and – after many appeals to publishers that take an inordinate amount of time – people might read it later...and then, maybe much, much later, in a galaxy far, far away, you get some kind of reward in the form of royalties or fan mail or literary awards. The book or story will probably be dead to you by then, as you've already started the next project, and are immersed in that instead.

The lack of immediately present reward is the primary reason why so many people talk about writing a book but never follow-through on it. Others take a first stab but never see it through to the kill. The fire goes out. Or they give up after they successfully publish, when they don't become instantly famous or the reality doesn't match the dream.

Get used to it. Your expectations will always be wrong. What happens after you complete a story or a book is ALWAYS out of your hands. Beyond whatever literary rights you retain, by seeking publication you are transferring your text from being a private document to a public document. It becomes a "social" text. It's forever in the hands of readers, publishers, sales teams, reviewers, critics, teachers, and librarians. The cultureat-large will decide your writing's value and determine its fate.

But that is not necessarily YOUR fate. Your books are not you. Your fate is to forever be enslaved to your computer, and to keep producing words. It's a masochistic life, but if you're doing it right you are addicted to the whiplash of your muse.

Though I do believe that writing is its own reward, so many of the payoffs and pleasures of writing – from acceptance in the market to the adoration of fans to royalty checks from publishers – are on time delay, and it takes persistence to stick with something on blind faith that you will succeed. You have to trust that you are going to get what you deserve later and learn how to enjoy the process you are engaged in now, in the immediate present. Trust that you are always learning, always improving, just by doing it. I write to get into the zone and to cackle alone in the darkness of my office at the crazy ideas that spill out of my head. I write to feel the thrill of chasing after my own characters, tormenting them along the way and seeing where they'll end up. I write to sport in the darkness and see what ungodly things I can discover.

I'm always surprised with what I find. And it makes me want to do it all over again, every time.

If you're struggling early on, imagine that you are like a person learning to swim. It takes time but you will eventually do more than just keep your head above water. Soon you'll be racing in laps, or diving in the deep sea. Believe me when I say every word you write brings you one step closer to success, because swimming in the word well makes your muscles stronger. Don't let rejection or ambivalence or negative feedback get you down. Persist.

Don't even listen to the accolades – they can be just as distracting, and can tempt you to think you are superhuman and don't have to swim. You might float on past glory for a little while, but gravity always beats the buoy.

Persistently work to improve for its own sake, because there is no such thing as "perfect" in this trade. Even your published work could be improved, believe me. The more you write, the more lessons you learn (so remember this too: there are no wasted words). And once you're established, don't rest on your laurels. Others will swim right past you. You have to continually be your own best marketer, agent, and librarian. Persist at improving. Persist at staking your claim in the genre. Persistently knock on doors and read new books and go on book tours. Stay in it for the long haul. Your clout and your residuals will only grow over time (aka "the long tail") and you will develop the frame of mind that all life-long learners (aka "readers") have. Persistently challenge yourself to try new things and to question your assumptions. Persist at growing yourself and your readership and your genre.

Don't turn around. Keep looking ahead. And swim.

2. Stay Out of It

When you're just getting started or if you're really trying to become a part of a community, the natural tendency is to imitate, or to follow everyone else's lead until you "fit in." Nothing wrong with doing this – it's called "affiliating" and it's really an important step in joining a genre community. Success is always modeled on others.

You should emulate the best people, and the ones you admire the most. Writers succeed when they establish and give back to a community of peers.

But you also should constantly be attentive to what makes you distinctive. We all want to be known as "horror writers" but we also want to be known by our byline first and foremost. Our name is our brand, and we are each capable of becoming a genre unto ourselves, once we grow a following.

So be an outsider and maintain a healthy skepticism of popular appeals. Don't hop aboard the trend train – because if it's moving slow enough for you to climb aboard, chances are quite good that it is getting bloated and sluggish and ready to come to a full stop.

While following a trend might land you a quick sale, any attempt to ride on the coattails of a surge in the market immediately makes you derivative and exploitative. Your artistic soul will feel betrayed by reducing the pleasure of your artistic process into a mere machine for profit. You will not feel good about your own books. Your brand will feel like a false mask – and you might end up with it stuck upon your face forever. Your success in one slim area might actually force you to quit the whole caboodle. This is avoidable, by being diversified in your interests and topics.

That is not to say you should be oblivious to the marketplace of ideas. If vampires are rising in popularity and you are a long-time fan of Bram Stoker and genuinely want to delve into blood-sucking fiends as a way to explore your dark side, then by all means: write a vampire story. But figure out where everyone is "instinctively" going with that trend, and stay as far away from the obvious choices as you can. Combat predictability. Keep them guessing. Genres fool us into thinking that we should write conventionally – but readers and editors prefer it when we push the boundaries of CONvention and INvent new ways of thinking within the context of our genre. Indeed, this is the dance of creative genre writing: playing to and playing against reader expectations.

This pertains to your writing process as much as your marketing and promotion. Make a list of your first ideas. Push yourself to do better than those initial gut reactions. Surprise your reader! Writing correctly and having a sense of basic story structure is the lowest common denominator. Everyone – from the assistant editor to the die-hard fan – wants their expectations exceeded and to feel that curiosity we ask of the best writers: "What's he got up his sleeve now?" Strive to surprise yourself and to turn around the expectations of others and you will be on your way toward making your own mark.

It is easy to fall for the crass commercial impulses of a business, or to glom on to the bubbles of a trend. But crass commercialism soon becomes phony and bubbles always burst. Never forget that no matter how much money matters in the publishing trade, it has always been the truth that our business is fueled by passion for good storytelling and publishers want to discover uniqueness that can stand out from the pack. Editors represent your potential readership and publishers tap into your potential audience – and your audience is expecting the unexpected. Publishers and readers are looking for original voices and fresh takes on genres. You will never be recognized if you are but one sheep among the flock. Go in the opposite direction, take a side track, color outside the lines and bah like the black sheep you really are (yes, you! Take a look around: all writers on the dark side are black sheep!).

So if you see a pattern, don't presume it is the magic formula. Keep your distance. Deviate from the norm and transcend the trend. Be skeptical of "common sense." Better to be a lone wolf than a face in the crowd. The outsider is the one that is distinctive by contrast. The outsider is the one who stands out from the herd and gets more attention BECAUSE they are not settling for the easy flow of the mainstream. Do the same as those you respect, but really emphasize what makes you different.

Or think of it this way: be a mutant, not a clone. Be the mutated version of your literary heroes: same genetic make-up, only distorted. Look for the books nobody else is writing and write that book. Because THAT book belongs on the shelves. The clones are just recycling trees with inkstains on them to turn a buck, and they will have the shelf-life of a greeting card, at best.

3. Use Focus Words

Writers take complex things and make them simple, digestible and understandable. But writers' lives are complicated and hectic. And sometimes writers' stories unravel into messes because of that.

You need to respect simplicity, minimalism, and brevity. Whether as a motto for your life, or a slogan for your current novel, it helps if you carefully choose just a few keywords to keep you grounded. I call them "focus words." Let these words "focus" your work and help you navigate the chaos.

I try to do this at the beginning of each year, settling on two focus words instead of making new year's "resolutions."

My focus words one year, for instance, were simple ones: "consolidate" and "listen." I tend to choose verbs, but I know others who have used character names or popular phrases for their own choices. I turn to these words for answers when I feel overwhelmed or off-track. For instance, the term "consolidate" motivated me to organize my office documents, refocus my independent publishing campaign, recommend changes in my workplace and backup files on my computer that were cluttering my life. "Consolidate" even helped me bring my book, Instigation: Creative Prompts on the Dark Side together, as I assembled prompts I'd published in different contexts, and contemplated unifying clusters of them into chapters. Likewise, the focus word "listen" guided me to attend a concert, solve a personal conflict with a colleague, attend a speech I otherwise might not have bothered to sit through, recognize the symptoms of my cat's ailing health, learn new things about people I had been taking for granted (since listening encourages others to speak), analyze a character's voice, take advice from a reader in revising part of my website, rework an audiobook recording I'd made and improve my concentration in general. Now I am always on the lookout for new opportunities to organize through consolidation and to learn through listening.

Focus words can focus a scene, a novel outline, a website, or your brand. Focus words can set up boundary lines for a journal entry or underpin your lifelong goals. The job of a word is to contain meaning, so use focus words to control and shape the meaning of things. You'll begin to see that the meanings a word holds are deep ones, and over time more meanings will "unfold" for you. Inquire into these deeper meanings: look them up, study the word's origin, think about its synonyms and near rhymes and muse deeply over its significance.

Some people use focus words like a mantra or chant. They can keep you centered or oriented. Use them to focus your next novel. You'll be happy you did when you have to come up with an "elevator pitch" or synopsis afterward.

Some people use them to brainstorm associations. They can be the center point of a "mind map" or a categorical term above a long list of other words. Work the words as you will. But look for unifying principles. We writers are always working with themes – so practice what you preach and think thematically about your life's work.

4. Be Contrarian

Contrarians can be real jerks, always arguing for argument's sake and simply saying "no" to every request. They refuse to play along. But that's not what I mean by this law. Similar to being an "outsider," in my view to be contrarian means to always consider the opposite point of view. To think against the grain. The world is on the "light" side – the dark side, our side, is on the contrarian side. The side of the alternative, the negative and the occult.

So use opposition as a way to generate fresh looks or unexpected takes on things that others take for granted. To impede the rush to judgment and be skeptical of hasty generalizations. To recognize differences and value diversity.

Evil witches are all the rage in your genre? Then

write a story about a good witch, tormented by the evil behaviors of "normal" people. Everyone likes stories about the bloodthirsty zombie horde? Write about an alienated zombie who is pitiable all alone. No one writes about the occult anymore, and you enjoy those kinds of books? Write a satanic thriller. Every hero in your subgenre is a white guy? Make your protagonist a kick-ass black woman. It's no guarantee that you'll sell or even produce a workable plot, but you may find energy to tell the untold story this way. Your approach will stand out in contrast to the pack. Being a genre writer means taking an original approach to a conventional idea – to bring the "new" into conflict with the "old" in a way that "renews" the genre in some way. So avoid the easy way: push yourself to think in opposition to ways in which the world would like you to think. It can really ground you by giving you something new to say, and ultimately the novelty of your vision will help you stand out.

Contrarianism is not just a worldview, it's actually a business strategy. In the stock market, most people invest in stocks that are on the rise – conservatively going along with what is most likely to rise in value as more and more people buy it up. Contrarians do the opposite: they buy the cheap stocks that no one is paying attention to, or even those tending down, down, down, in hopes that some day it will later bounce back and take off. They are banking on the fact that in a fluctuating market, the pendulum always swings back in the opposite direction some day. Apple's hot today and Microsoft is bottoming out? Invest in Microsoft, because Microsoft will compete to become the next new trend while Apple will eventually rest on its laurels or lose fans by being too popular, too big, too unmanageable.

This approach to investing is considered quite a risky venture, but when contrarians invest routinely in this way, across their portfolio, the stocks that "surge" after the trend wanes will generate enough profit to make up for the other risks they took that failed.

So don't worry if you're writing about werewolves and nobody in New York is buying werewolf stories. They might be back in fashion some day. In genre fiction, the pendulum always swings away and back again. Be ready to see it coming. But don't fixate on just one product as if all your eggs were invested in just one basket. Keep weaving the next one.

5. Never Doubt the Power of Clout

Writers always debate about whether you should write for money or write for love. I don't play that game, because these are not mutually exclusive acts. In other words, you can do both. You should be savvy enough to market what you love to write – and even if you write a poem just to write a poem and later place it in a humble little magazine that doesn't pay more than a contributor's copy for your efforts, you can always later reprint that poem in a collection that you sell, or land a paying gig where you can recite it before an audience, or resell it as a song. Anything is possible, because everything you write has myriad formats in which it could be packaged and sold, reprinted and renewed. The release of a title is just one license among many that you have punched on your contractual dance card. The work still has many other dances it can swing to.

Paychecks and publication credits come and go over

time. This is why I always recommend writers buy something concrete (even mundane; something like a kitchen appliance) with their royalty checks, instead of celebrating success with a champagne-fueled night on the town.

Money doesn't last. Hell, neither do books, which go out of print or get forgotten in a dusty library somewhere.

No, your achievements as a writer will be short-lived.

What endures – though this, too, is perishable – is clout.

You earn clout but you can't really control it. If you get enough clout, the money and the publishing opportunities come to you. You start getting invited to contribute to an anthology or publishing house or speaker series. Clout enables you to write whatever you want, and it earns you higher advances. Clout is something publishers want, and something readers, too, want to have when they put your book on their shelves. Clout is related to fame: it works like word of mouth. Your "brand" – your byline – has credibility and people in the industry value your way with words.

Too many writers I know are eager to grab at clout by promoting themselves like crazy, often too soon in their careers. They shoot themselves in the foot by branding themselves when they haven't earned a reputation yet, or don't have more to offer than one item. They are impatiently seeking the aura of clout. It is true that some folks will buy books or review manuscripts if you grab their attention by wearing clown shoes. A sucker is born every minute. Clout can be attributed to an item, but as an author you need to earn clout toward your byline, and you get it for your ability to produce great ideas time after time again.

Clout circulates around those who are time-tested, proven, and focused on their craft more than their careers. Because readers don't buy careers. They buy books. If they buy more than one book by the same author, it's because the writer earned that sale by providing satisfaction that assured the reader they would get a repeat performance. This clout is earned more through what they actually did, than what they said they were going to do.

What is clout? It is not merely grabbing attention, or generating an audience. Clout is not about self-promotion or publicity or manufactured reputation. Clout is attributed to your reputation, and something that others (like your publishers) like to share in.

Clout is created by being good at what you do. Earning respect. Getting credentialed or attaining a degree. Gaining a reputation for making good on all that promotion and publicity you see other writers touting around. Clout is what readers attribute to you when they spread your name by word-of-mouth, and what publishers and other writers attribute to you when they add blurbs on your books, and what the genre attributes to you when you win awards and tributes. Your gold shines on them, so they drop your name because they feel it "rubs off" on them, giving them some gleaming kind of status by affiliation with your gold.

Did you catch my redundancy in the paragraph above? Clout is ATTRIBUTED to you. Given by others. You can only earn it by being good at what you do and that takes time. If you exceed people's expectations, though, you will get a buzz going. Writers often over-promise in their self-publicity, and shoot themselves in the foot that way.

Clout is actually a sort of performance, generating attention through not the reader or the writer but a third party, in concert with both. It works a little something like this: another person turns the spotlight on you, and the rest of the audience turns its head to follow the beam of light. Your job is to stand on stage and sing your heart out, over and over again. Keep them in the chairs. You probably shouldn't be singing songs that are all about yourself. You are the vessel through which the song is produced. If your product is appreciated and admired, the appreciation and admiration will be attributed to you: the generator of it.

How can you control the spotlight? How can you turn heads? Well, you can't really.

But a publisher is the one who points the spotlight on you. And you can use the audience as a sounding board to learn more about what you're doing that works.

If a singer on stage notices that people are cupping their hands around their ears, they turn up the volume. If the audience seems to be watching the singer's feet, the singer might dance even though he didn't plan to. By being attentive to the signals your readership is sending, you can get affirmation about what it is that "works" in what you're doing, and you can also discover traits in your writing that you hadn't considered before that you can draw focus and inspiration from.

Now, don't get me wrong. I'm NOT saying you shouldn't write for money or respect or to make your mother happy or whatever floats your boat. I'm not saying be a snob or just publish in literary markets or to only enter contests to win the accolades that come with awards. That's related to clout, but I'm talking about listening to what signals people are sending you to help recognize your innate writing talents so you can strategically develop them.

Cultivate an ear for reader response and look for ways to encourage readers to respond collectively to your work so you can grow.

For instance, I always thought of myself as just a writer of horror stories that weren't afraid of repulsing the reader. I enjoyed rubbing people's noses in things – and I still do. But it wasn't until I started getting reviewed that I realized I was often being more humorous in my genre stories than other writers were. Readers would send me notes, with jocular expressions like "You sick bastard! LOL!" It helped me to realize that my audience enjoyed the tongue-in-cheek things I was doing, so I began to try to grow that side of myself by studying comedy, looking into the market for humorous horror, and writing a gross-out comedy novella called Licker that didn't take itself serious at all. That book is now something of a cult hit and got some wonderful reviews. I now don't take myself so seriously, and I find that my readers actually prefer that (but I also don't JUST do comedy... and sometimes just to keep them guessing, I take contrarian turns on myself!).

It took me a decade to realize that I have as much clout to readers as an educator as I do as an author. Winning my first Bram Stoker Award gave me the clout I needed to get into graduate school, and I believe it also helped me land a tenure-track job at a university afterward. I was so happy having a job that allowed me to teach the genre I loved. But it wasn't until recently that I realized that as many people knew me for being a good writing professor as they do for being an insanely twisted horror author. So after thinking about this, I realized I could market my educational side just as consciously as I do my horror writer side.

By "market" I do not mean that I "cashed in" on my degree, but, rather, that I saw a way to cultivate my growth and explore new writing territory in a way that could reach an audience and meet their needs. This awareness of my own clout led me into publishing essays on the craft of writing in several reputable instructional guides, like the HWA's On Writing Horror or the popular book, Writer' Workshop of Horror – both of which every horror author ought to read. Later I even edited a popular how-to book on the subject of writing popular fiction, called Many Genres, One Craft: Lessons in Writing Popular Fiction. And this past year, I published Instigation: Creative Prompts on the Dark Side, drawing from some workshop activities I've actually proctored in the classroom, on top of a column of prompts I used to write for Hellnotes.

You probably have clout in things that have nothing to do with writing. Maybe you keep the best lawn on your block. Or are respected for volunteering to serve in the war. Or have the world's best pencil collection. You can write non-fiction books about these very things, or you could integrate your knowledge about these things into your stories. The old adage "write what you know" should come with a corollary: "write what you are known for." The reason you're known for it is that you are considered the authority on the subject. And the root of the word authority is...

AUTHOR.

The proof is in the pudding and I have learned over the years that I am sometimes the worst judge of my own strengths and weaknesses. I only know that readers and editors know better than I do about such things. I try to put their needs above my own and try to bend my own wishes toward what it is they are after when they pick up a title with my name on it. This is not about author branding or gaining attention or building a reputation, per se. Money, awards, hit counts, bestseller charts... these things are really just silly ways of keeping score. Quantitative evidence of repute, at best. But for me, writing is a quality issue. Quality stands the test of time. And reflecting (humbly) about my clout and trying to understand what it is that people like about me is really about enabling myself to continue to sing my lungs out on that stage known as the literary marketplace.

My parting advice to you: shout at the devil and spray the lung tissue proudly, persistently, and in a way that only you can do it.

Scott Nicholson is the international bestselling author of more than 30 books, including The Home, The Red Church, Liquid Fear, the After post-apocalyptic series, The Harvest, Speed Dating with the Dead, and many more. He's also written the children's books If I Were Your Monster, Too Many Witches, Ida Claire, and Duncan the Punkin, and created the graphic novels Dirt and Grave Conditions. You can find him at www.hauntedcomputer.com or sign up for his newsletter for new releases, free books, and giveaways: http://eepurl.com/tOE89

The Cheesy Trunk of Terror

Scott Nicholson

There was a wonderful downtown store called The Curiosity Shop that closed its doors this year. The Curiosity Shop sold gifts and collectibles, some new regional books, and assorted paper goods. At the back of the store, a set of creaky stairs led to a loft where used books, mostly paperbacks, were sold at half off cover price. In many cases, of course, the books weren't sold at all. Especially those in the horror section.

The owners said that nobody bought used horror paperbacks. The selection was pretty good, and by trading in some hardcovers I sampled the work of some writers who were new to me. Of course, most of the available titles were by V.C. Andrews, Anne Rice, and those fellows you may have heard of named King and Koontz. I also found the early work of people like

Douglas Clegg, Ramsey Campbell, and James Herbert. But there were some of the newer Leisure titles as well, already in the second-life stage despite being less than a year old. The section also contained a couple hundred of those forgettable, seemingly-interchangeable horror novels from the 1980s.

But that wasn't the best part. What really made prowling that dusty loft a joy was the "Cheesy Trunk of Terror." That's where the lousy paperbacks went to die. The trunk was one of those old reinforced cardboard things many of us trundled off to college, with the corners frayed and the fake brass worn. The store owners had so little respect for the books, they scrawled "25¢"on the cover in thick black magic marker. You could get an armful of them for the cost of a Big Mac.

The trunk always seemed to replenish itself, as if there were a secret compartment in the bottom and the books leaked through from some strange subterranean source. Most notable was that the trunk wasn't exclusively the domain of John Coyne, Ruby Jean Jensen, and Lisa W. Cantrell. If the store had more than three copies of any horror, mystery, or suspense book, the extras went into the mix as well. John D. MacDonald, Patricia Cornwell, and H.G. Wells appeared there. Even King and Koontz were no strangers to the trunk.

As a reader, the trunk was a treasure trove. As a writer, though, the trunk took on an entirely new meaning. The first time I stood over that trunk, I realized the implications of my own dedicated dream of having my words bound between covers. No matter how much I gave, no matter what amount of sacrifice, no matter my degree of success, my work was ultimately headed for the Cheesy Trunk of Terror.

The feeling was a bit humbling and discouraging. I even made a remark to the owner as I brought my selected pile to the checkout counter, something to the effect of, "Well, I wonder how long it will take for my first novel to wind up in there."

"When's it come out?" he asked.

"This summer."

"Then probably by fall," he said.

I gave the Cheesy Trunk of Terror a great deal of thought in the days that followed. Every writer believes that his or her work will resonate for centuries and will always appeal to audiences, no matter how far society may stray from the era of the book's copyright date. Every writer believes the work is worthy and special. We hope our books will continue to reach new readers, even in those resale circumstances where we receive no additional royalties. In short, we never want to be classified as "cheese."

After my discouragement faded, a different type of emotion dawned. The Cheesy Trunk is no more limiting for a book than a graveyard is for a human soul. It's not the product itself that matters, though most writers want to be paid for their work. Most important is the very act of dreaming, the pleasure of probing and tasting and sniffing this thing we all call existence. It's the job of milking a cow and making cheese if you're a writer, or consuming that cheese if you're a reader.

Sometimes we take everything too seriously, especially the "horror" label, which has been alternately maligned and defended in far more sentences than were ever penned toward the genre's greater glory. Some refuse to acknowledge a horror book that doesn't have "horror" brazenly printed on its spine, while others turn up noses at yet another reeking mound of innocent cheese. Some want dark fantasy and some want psychological suspense. Some want to abolish horror sections in bookstores. We're all different in our tastes and needs, yet we're all the same in our pursuit of emotional truth.

It doesn't matter if you're a writer selling a million copies or a reader who argues that horror requires supernatural elements. It doesn't matter if you're a critic who measures each new slot paperback against the literary classics or an internet gusher who proclaims every new writer the "future of horror." It doesn't matter if you have ten Stoker awards on the shelf or a library full of expensive limited editions. It doesn't matter if you mechanically crank out gore as if grinding sausage or if you hide your genre reading material behind academic hardcovers.

It's about doing the best you can with what talents you have, showing up day after day, reading what you want without justifying it to others. Give it whatever name you favor, call it dark fantasy, the H-word, terror, suspense. The labels may decay and the pages eventually crumble to dust, but that doesn't take away from the simple magic of a work's existence. It's about the words and it's about the feeling. It's about being there.

In the end, we're all in the cheesy trunk together. And the trunk is never empty.

Joe Mynhardt is a South African horror writer, publisher, editor and teacher with over fifty short story publications. He has appeared in dozens of publications and collections, among them For the Night is Dark, Dark Minds, Darker Minds *and* The Bestiarum Vocabulum.

Joe is also the owner and operator of Crystal Lake Publishing. He has published and edited Paul Kane's Sleeper(s); *Daniel I. Russell's* Tricks, Mischief and Mayhem; *Fear the Reaper; Kevin Lucia's* Things Slip Through; *Gary McMahon's* Where You Live; Horror 101; *Jasper Bark's* Stuck On You; *William Meikle's* Samurai and Other Stories; *and* Tales from The Lake Vol.1

Upcoming collections Joe has edited include Jasper Bark's Stuck On You and Other Prime Cuts, The Outsiders *(Simon Bestwick, Gary McMahon etc.),* Children of the Grave *(Joe McKinney, Armand Rosamilia etc.), and* Tales from The Lake Vol.2.

Crystal Lake Publishing also won the Publisher of the Year Award in the This Is Horror Awards 2013.

Joe's collection of short stories, Lost in the Dark, *is available through Amazon. He is currently working on* Lake of Fire, Painted Black, *and* For Those Below.

Read more about Joe and his creations at www.Joemynhardt.com and www.crystallakepub.com or find him on Facebook at "Joe Mynhardt's Short Stories."

Joe is an Associate member of the HWA, co-opted board member of his local writers association, and global moderator for MyWritersCircle.com.

How to Be Your Own Agent, Whether You Have One or Not

Joe Mynhardt

What I'm about to tell you is probably the best career advice I've ever come across. And just like me, you should really consider taking this serious, because whether you have one or a hundred stories published, you're stepping into the public eye now, and you need present yourself in a suitable light.

Basically, you need to be professional. Call yourself a writer or an artist, but the fact remains that in today's global village (you probably haven't heard that name in a while), you need to put your best foot forward at all times. You need to be your own agent. No one else has your concerns more to heart than yourself, so you need to market not only your stories, but yourself as well. People are watching you, and with social media today, people want to connect with authors, just like they enjoy connecting with your characters. You need to present them with something they can relate to (again, just like your characters).

Now, there are a lot of things to consider here, so I made up a list of 15 tips on being your own agent, in no particular order.

My Top 15 Tips on being your own agent, whether you have one or not:
1. How people see you online might not be the way you think they do. It's just like writing a book, you have to make sure the message or image you're trying to send

comes over properly. Do they see what you want them to see? If they do, you're on your way to building a strong image.

2.   Saving time is very important in this business. Do the best you can in what little time you've got. Make every second count. If you know what work needs to be done today, get to it. And find ways of making life easier for yourself. For example, I have FAQ sheet I can send interviewers (but I still give them the option of asking or adding their own questions); I have a long term and short term writing schedule (in order, telling me what needs to be done each day so I'm always ahead of schedule); I have a Word document with all links and promos for my books; I have a shortcut for every important folder on my computer (and know exactly where they all are); and I have a Book Launch folder for every book. All my data is being recorded, from dates to ISBN numbers and so on, because sooner or later you'll have to refer to them. These are just some of the things you can you. I'm sure you'll have some of your own, and would love to hear about them. Every second counts.

3.   Stay out of political or religious debates. Don't even be pulled into choosing sides. You should post personal stuff on FB or Twitter, since it is your page and people want to get to know you. Don't only post serious stuff. People love getting an inside look at an author's life. The key here is to always think what message you're really sending. What will be the long term effect it leaves on others? You won't find me talking about something I almost messed up, because it'll make me

look like an amateur having a go at a pro's job. I will however share some of my frustrations, just to remind them I'm not a machine, but a human who sometimes needs their support.

4.   When your agent, editor or publisher asks you to do something, tell them when you'll have it done and hand it in a day earlier. Editors like to make lists of people they can count on when time is short. If you're dependable, you'll always have projects coming your way.

5.   Make it as easy as possible for people to work with you. I worked with a great author a while back, but he was so difficult that I'll always think twice about contacting him in the future. Don't let one bad trait spoil what you have to offer. Also, don't ever think you know better than your editor or publisher. They won't always be right, but neither will you. It's like when people give you advice or point out mistakes in reviews. You should always be on the lookout for ways to improve or learn more from this business, and being open-minded is not only great for your imagination, but it's a great skill for any writer to have.

6.   Be active on social media sites, but always keep your eye on the clock. Wish people happy birthday and comment on their status. Draw them into a conversation, especially on your blog comments. Congratulate them on achievements. Make people notice you and remember you. I've actually met people while commenting on a mutual friend's status. You'll quickly realize if you and that person will get along.

7.   Which brings to a very important point. Don't be fake. If you don't really care about other authors, your readers or your publisher, you're in it for the wrong reasons. And it'll be a lot harder for you to make it in this industry, or to even find intrinsic value when you do find success. Build honest relationships that will be equally beneficial.

8.   Make the most of every situation. Whenever an opportunity to promote yourself or your book comes along, sit back for a second and think about what to do next. How many times have you kicked yourself in the past for not making the best of a situation or grabbing an opportunity? If a new review pops up, do you just link it once, or do you use it to revive your sales like it should be used? Once per social media platform should be enough (twice on Twitter), since you don't want to irritate your followers. If you do post a lot about your books, make sure you put some funny, inspirational and even personal stuff in-between. And just sharing the stuff others post doesn't really count.

9.   After almost 70 acceptance letters and a few hundred rejection letters, I know how it feels to be rejected by editors and publishers, and I'm sure you do, too. No one likes being brushed off, ignored or even disrespected. But it happens, and we should all get used to it. That does not, however, give you the right to do the same. Remember this before you reply to any comments or emails. Stay professional.

10. It doesn't matter how busy or swamped you are, don't act like you're the only one with a hectic schedule.

Welcome to the world of running a business. Yes, you're not just an artist or a writer. Learn to cope, but also learn when and how to say no.

11. Always have a story or two on hand, in case an opportunity comes knocking, even a couple of ideas you can pitch on a moment's notice. One of my biggest breaks came because I had two stories ready with only a few hours before the deadline. I made the pitch and the editor loved it. I jumped on that opportunity and rode its wave for the next year or so.

12. Back up your work. Please! Don't lose your stuff. Some people never recuperate after such a huge loss. I backup my work every Sunday, but during holidays, when I do a lot more work, I'll backup almost every day. I'll save my main writing folder on my flash drive and external hard drive. I heard of a guy who wrote his doctorate on his flash drive. He never backed it up or shared it with anyone. And we all know how long a flash drive can last. Sad but true. Always remember that when you send someone a story or sample chapter via email, that attachment will always be there. Emails are a great way of getting back old stories or chapters you might've lost.

13. Always try something out, whether it's a new method of approaching a story, a new writing schedule, point of view, themes that make you uncomfortable, screenwriting, comics, graphic novels or even a marketing strategy. Not every approach works for everyone, but you might just find something that works for you.

14. Don't be scared to ask questions... without being annoying, knowing when to back off, and staying professional. You'll always need help or advice, and there's always someone who can teach you something. Just make sure you help out wherever you can, as well. Asking questions is also a good way of showing people that you're serious about this business, as well what your interests are. Who knows what opportunities this can bring in the future? No one's asking you to travel to war-ravished countries or feed the orphans. Just show that you care. Get involved in whatever way you can.

15. Get over your self-doubt and increase your output. Writing slower does not mean writing better.

If all this seems too much for you, and you'd like to speak your mind whenever you want, perhaps writing under a different name would be best. There are a lot of successful authors out there who aren't recognized on social media or in public.

Also, none of this means anything if you don't write. Try to establish a routine where you get your writing done first. I like to finish all my offline work first, before going online, whether it's editing, writing a blog entry or working on a new story. It's not always possible, especially if opportunities come knocking or a book is being launched, but don't let these things grab your attention every day. Don't allow going online to turn into a bad habit that'll drain your imagination and time. You can't blame Facebook if you're career doesn't take off.

Lucy A. Snyder is the Bram Stoker Award-winning author of the novels Spellbent, Shotgun Sorceress, Switchblade Goddess, and the collections Orchid Carousals, Sparks and Shadows, Chimeric Machines, and Installing Linux on a Dead Badger. Her story collection Soft Apocalypses will be released by Raw Dog Screaming Press in July 2014. Her writing has been translated into French, Russian, and Japanese editions and has appeared in publications such as Chiral Mad 2, What Fates Impose, Once Upon A Curse, Strange Horizons, Weird Tales, Hellbound Hearts, Dark Faith, Chiaroscuro, GUD, and Best Horror of the Year, Vol. 5. You can learn more about her at www.lucysnyder.com.

Networking at Conventions

Lucy A. Snyder

The most important part of making a career as a fiction author should be obvious: you have to write well and tell an engaging story. But if you've been writing and submitting for a while, you've no doubt realized that simply being a good writer isn't all there is to it. Luck seems to play a distressingly large role in the publishing process. But the funny thing is that writers who actively seek out writing opportunities generally seem to be "luckier" than those who don't.

My first four book deals happened because I knew editors who were familiar with (and liked) my work. More to the point, I made my pitches to them when they had lulls in their schedules but hadn't gotten around to posting calls-for-manuscripts. HW Press has *never* been open to submissions, and CGP was closed to submissions when I made my deal for *Installing Linux on a Dead Badger*.

Plenty of other authors have taken advantage of insider information. Author Gary A. Braunbeck has done something that many claim can't be done: he's sold the majority of his books without an agent's help.

Before he was a novelist, Gary published a considerable amount of short fiction and wrote many stories for various Tekno Books anthologies. Tekno puts together anthologies for publishers like Ace; if you've read an anthology edited by Martin Greenberg or John Helfers, you've read a Tekno Books production regardless of the logo on the spine. These anthologies are invitation-only, and you will not be invited unless you're a pro writer known to the editors, or recommended to them by one of their existing writers.

Because of his work for them, the editors at Tekno knew Gary produced good fiction, met deadlines and was easy to work with. So, when Steve Perry told them he had started but couldn't finish *Time Was*, they asked Gary if he wanted to take over. And so Gary got his first published novel. Gary's other books have often come about because he knew editors and informally found out about their interests and gaps in their schedules etc.

Are you starting to get the idea that networking with other writers and editors is pretty important? Good. Because it's *hugely* important.

And a considerable amount of networking and publishing business gets done at conferences and conventions.

There are a plenty of conventions to choose from, and

the good news is that convention expenses are tax-deductible for working writers. But a tax deduction is no replacement for having money to live on; once you factor in memberships and hotel and travel costs, you can break your budget fairly quickly attending just a handful of conventions. Worse, if you're not choosy about which conventions you attend, you might have fun but come away without having done any significant business.

What Should You Look For In A Convention?

Essentially, you should attend conventions that have the highest number of people who write – and preferably *buy* – the kind of fiction you want to sell. Your goals past that will be a little different depending on the kind of fiction you write and where you are in your career.

If you're a beginning story writer with few or no publishing credits, your best bet is to focus on conventions that offer strong writing-related panels and workshops and steer clear of conventions that mainly focus on costuming or media. Look for conventions that offer publisher-sponsored parties, teas, and other events; they are prime opportunities to get to know people in the business.

Once you've got a few story sales to your credit and you've finished a novel manuscript, you'll be looking for slightly different offerings at a convention. Namely, you'll be focusing on conventions frequented by book editors and agents. And while you can make good contacts at regional conventions, be wary of the agents featured at smaller conferences. Some convention organizers don't do a good job of distinguishing between genuine professional agents and amateurs (or, worse, "agents" fronting for book doctor scams). In general, if an agent's office is in a small Midwestern town, he or she isn't going to do your career a lot of good. Larger conventions may offer pitch sessions with agents and publishers – these sessions can be a prime opportunity to make professional connections if not outright sales.

Once you're a working professional writer, you'll be going to conventions to meet with friends, your editors, and your agent. The convention's programming will probably be of limited interest to you – you've seen it all before – and it's entirely possible you won't enter a programming room unless you're a panelist. The rest of the time? You'll probably be in the bar with the other pros.

So, if you're a convention newbie and the people you hoped to meet are conspicuously absent? Head to the hotel bar, and keep your eyes and ears open. There's business afoot.

How To Network At A Convention

Obviously, you want to make a good impression, and appearances do matter (yes, even in science fiction). Focus on the fundamentals. Make sure you and your clothes are clean and in good condition (get some sleep!). Don't emit a strong odor, be it bad breath or expensive cologne. Wear the kind of clothes the other pros will be wearing; this will be business attire at most romance conventions, but it can be a casual shirt and jeans at an SF or horror convention. Be yourself and have fun, but don't show up for your pitch session wearing your entry for the costume contest (especially if you're going as Barney the Dinosaur).

Some authors can wear tee shirts emblazoned with the cover of their latest book without seeming obnoxious; not everyone who tries succeeds. A little self-promotion is healthy and expected, particularly if you're at an autograph table, but it's probably best to avoid turning yourself into a walking billboard.

If you've chosen writing as a profession or avocation, the chances are high that you're an introvert. Shy, even. Maybe the thought of going up to strangers fills you with anything from dread to panic.

Take a deep breath. Calm down. Networking isn't that bad, and like most other things, it's a learnable skill. All those editors and writers and agents you want to meet? Many of them are introverts, too. And while they're doing business, they're pretending to be extroverts, with varying degrees of success (so keep this in mind if people seem weird. They're probably just trying too hard).

Once you've pushed yourself past your comfort zone, your sense of social depth perception can suffer, and it's easy to inadvertently come on too strong and annoy the person you're talking to. Your risk increases a thousand percent if you're drunk, so when you're in the bar and you want to do business, it's best to stick to tea or soda. But by all means, if the editor's glass is dry and she's looking longingly at the martini menu, offer to buy her a drink.

Don't pitch at people unless you're in an actual pitch session. You're not looking to corner an editor, you're looking for a conversation; if you're doing all the talking, you're probably doing it wrong. The best way to be interesting is to be *interested*. Ask the editor about his or her ongoing projects (provided the editor didn't just discuss them in detail at the Q&A panel you skipped out on). But don't make them feel they're being grilled or being asked too-personal questions; the worst thing you can do is to come off as a potential stalker.

But if things go well, you can have talks that give you valuable information about who's looking to buy what (and who you perhaps shouldn't submit to). Furthermore, a good conversation with an editor or fellow author will make you feel energized and excited about your writing prospects. And the very best conversations may be the start of new lifelong friendships.

A Short List of Conventions

Hundreds of conventions happen every year throughout the U.S.; you can find local and regional conventions fairly quickly through the power of Google. Here's a short list of genre-oriented conventions that tend to attract a high percentage of professional writers, agents, and editors (although big conventions have more events, remember that when it comes to having a chance to sit down and talk with someone, smaller, more intimate conventions are often better):

Romantic Times Booklovers Convention – this weeklong convention is held in a different city each year and will be of most interest to working novelists who seek to connect with romance readers and to aspiring romance writers. Attendance often tops 1,000, and the convention offers a huge track of writing and publishing workshops, some of which deal with mystery, fantasy, and other genre topics. It's also comparatively expensive; registration alone can be more than $500.

RWA National Conference – this is the national conference of the Romance Writers of America, and it features workshops, pitch sessions, etc. It's a highly business-oriented convention and is hosted in a different U.S. city each year.

Worldcon (The World Science Fiction Convention) – Hosted by the World Science Fiction Society, this convention is in a different major city every year so that people around the world have the opportunity to attend. Attending members vote on the Hugo Awards. Recent Worldcons have had between 3,000 and 6,000 attendees; in short, it's a huge convention, and it covers the whole spectrum of SF.

World Fantasy Convention – like Worldcon, this is held in a different major city every year. Attendance is usually limited to about 1,000 people. It's almost exclusively a professional's convention, and usually has a strong secondary focus on horror as well as fantasy.

World Horror Convention – this usually alternates between cities in the West Coast and East Coast with occasional hosting in Canada and the UK. It's the professional gathering of the World Horror Society and frequently features pitch sessions. The Bram Stoker Awards are sometimes held at World Horror, but sometimes they have their own separate convention:

Bram Stoker Awards Weekend – when the Stokers ceremony is not held at World Horror, it becomes the centerpiece for a separate convention usually held in New York City or Los Angeles. Most of the attendees will be members of the Horror Writers Association, and there may be pitch sessions.

Necon – the Northeastern Writers Conference is best known as "Camp Necon". It's held in Bristol, Rhode Island every summer and it's a weekend dorm party for writers, artists and editors, most of whom work in the horror and dark fantasy genres. It's low-key and casual, and offers an unparalleled chance to spend quality time with top authors. Attendance is capped at 200, and memberships sell out quickly.

Readercon – this highly literary speculative fiction convention is held in the Boston area each summer. It attracts many professional SF, fantasy, and horror writers and editors, with an overall attendance of around 650.

WisCon – this Madison, Wisconsin convention focuses on feminist science fiction literature and hosts the Tiptree Awards. It strives to provide a welcoming atmosphere for minority and LGBT writers. Many pros attend this convention; attendance is capped at 1,000 and memberships often sell out in advance.

Context – held in Columbus, Ohio, this small, friendly convention focuses on speculative fiction literature. It attracts regional writers and publishers, and generally has an attendance of around 300.

Capclave – this Washington, DC convention focuses on

literary science fiction and fantasy and particularly emphasizes short stories. Attendance is usually between 300 and 400.

Norwescon – this Seattle-area convention has a mainly literary focus but also offers gaming, anime, etc. Recent attendance has often topped 3,000. The convention hosts the Philip K. Dick Awards.

Gen Con – this gargantuan Indianapolis gaming convention hosts a writing track that has had over 1,000 participants in recent years. It's an ideal place to network for opportunities in game writing and gaming novelizations, but plenty of magazine and anthology editors attend, too.

R.J. Cavender is an Associate Member of the Horror Writers Association of America and the thrice Bram Stoker Award® nominated editor of the +Horror Library+ anthology series and co-editor of Horror For Good: A Charitable Anthology, both from Cutting Block Press. He is the resident horror editor at The Editorial Department, managing editor of horror at Dark Regions Press, acquisitions editor at Blood Bound Books, and the pitch session coordinator for World Horror Convention. He is also the founder and host of The Stanley Hotel Writers Retreat.

Pitch to Impress: How to Stand Out from the Convention Crowd

R.J. Cavender

I've had some great experiences pitching and having projects pitched to me since first arriving on the convention scene in 2005. In the last few years alone I've taken pitches at The World Horror Convention in New Orleans, The Bram Stoker Awards in Long Island, and KillerCon in Las Vegas. Pitching a project is not the mysterious dark art most make it out to be, but it is your one chance to make a strong impression with an agent or publisher.

Here are a few cautionary Do's and Don'ts I've learned over the last few years, making it from one side of the pitch table to the other. Whether you've already booked your convention registration, or are just considering attending a writing conference, these tips will help you present the best possible pitch, and give your project a chance to stand out from the convention noise.

#1 – KNOW WHO YOU'RE PITCHING

Early on, I jumped into a few pitch sessions half-cocked, and really had no idea who I was talking to. I made a complete fool of myself. There's no greater waste of time for an author, agent, or editor than just barking up the wrong tree. So, it's important when planning a pitch session to KNOW WHO YOU ARE PITCHING. Do a little research and find out the sort of authors and projects they represent, and then consider if you have something that fits into that structure. Don't think for a moment that you can sway an editor or agent with your one-in-a-million idea if they don't represent that sort of work. If it's not what they do, it's simply not what they do.

#2 – BE DIRECT

Pitch your idea and be direct about your story concept and expectations. Have faith in your story and writing—sell the idea.

#3 – BE YOURSELF

Be yourself, but be the best yourself that you've got. Be well-groomed, be on time, and have a pen and notebook present. Be ready to go. Have a business card. Have a flash drive with your story. I sometimes ask for the first five pages of a story at a pitch session and have even asked an author or two to read their opening pages. Be ready for anything, or at least know where the nearest Kinko's or business center in the hotel is.

#4 – BE PREPARED

Spend some time with your pitch and be prepared enough to say and do everything that you'd like within the allotted time. Have a two-minute, five-minute, and ten-minute pitch in mind for the story. You should never theoretically run out of things to talk about concerning your project, so be able to condense it into a two-minute pitch or talk about it all night if need be. Be prepared to answer any and every question about your story and its characters. You never know what a long conversation about your story might lead to.

#5 – BE INVOLVED

Follow up if that's what is expected of you. Find out what will make it easiest on the agent/editor in that situation. If you're asked to send follow-up chapters of your work, do so as soon as you can. I've received follow-up emails from authors before I even make it home from a convention, and that's certainly a way to stay in an editor or agent's mind. Just refer back to #1 on this list and make sure that you're following up on a lead that's a substantial one.

In closing, I'd like to say that pitch sessions are bar-none one the best ways to get some face-time with people who can help your writing career. Have fun with the pitch session, but also treat it like you would a job interview. A face-to-face meeting beats out an impersonal query letter any day, so consider also how you'd feel working with the people you meet. I've started many longtime friendships and working situations with people I've met at conventions and in pitch sessions. It's a realistic next step that any author can take to further their career.

Writing might be a mostly solitary craft, but getting a book published takes networking and a team. So, it couldn't hurt to plan your next vacation to correspond with a writer's convention. A weekend of panels, readings, and conversations with like-minded people can do wonders to recharge the creative batteries. I always leave conventions with a stack of new business cards, an armload of books, and lots of new projects to follow up on. I bet you will too.

Shirley Jackson Award-nominated author Tim Waggoner has published over thirty novels and three short story collections of dark fiction. He teaches creative writing at Sinclair Community College and in Seton Hill University's Master of Fine Arts in Writing Popular Fiction program. Visit him on the web at www.timwaggoner.com.

You Better (Net)Work

Tim Waggoner

Large conferences like the World Horror Convention, the World Fantasy Convention, and Worldcon – as well as large regional conferences – can be great places for new and upcoming writers to learn from more established professionals, of course, and since fans also will be in attendance, these conferences are also marketing opportunities. But in my opinion, the most important professional reason to attend conferences like these is networking. You can do the other stuff – gaining knowledge, marketing and promotion – on your own, without the time and expense of going to a big conference. But while you could argue that a certain amount of networking can be done via social networking sites (they have the word *networking* in their name, after all), I'd argue that there's no substitute for meeting, talking, and getting to know – and be known by – people face to face.

I first started attending large writing conferences when I was in my late twenties/early thirties (I'm fifty now). I'd had a handful of short stories published by that point, and I'd come to the conclusion that I wasn't doing everything I could to advance my writing career. I'd arrived at this conclusion after reading a number of articles about – you guessed it – networking. One of the first conferences I attended for the specific purpose of networking was Marcon in Columbus, Ohio. I wrote to the organizers, introduced myself, listed my meager credits, and expressed my interest in serving as a panelist (even though I'd never been on a panel before). My reasoning was that if I was a panelist, the other writers on the panel would automatically see me as one of them (to a greater or lesser degree) and not a member of the audience. In other words, I wouldn't be just another fan. I figured that I'd get an opportunity to introduce myself before the panel began, which meant I could approach my fellow panelists any time after that without worrying that they'd see me as a stranger (or worse, a stalker!). Also, the panel content itself and the discussion that followed would give me something to talk about with the other panelists later, saving me from having to try to come up with conversation topics on my own. I also found out which authors were attending and, if I wasn't already familiar with their work, I made sure to read a sampling before the con.

I lived in Columbus at the time, and two of the authors in attendance also lived in the city: Dennis L. McKiernan and J. Calvin Pierce. I decided to do what I could to make their acquaintance. After all, if we lived in the same town, there was every chance I'd see them at other events in the city and maybe – if I was lucky – build some kind of relationship with them (a guy can dream, can't he?).

The conference organizers scheduled me for several panels (which to be honest, I didn't really expect) and while I wasn't scheduled to be on any panels with Dennis, I was scheduled to be on one with Jim (J. Calvin) Pierce. I don't remember what the panel was about or how it went, but afterward, I spoke with Jim, told him how much I enjoyed his book (which was true), and Jim – who happened to be heading off to meet Dennis for a drink, invited me to join them. I felt like I'd hit the networking jackpot!

A couple weeks later, Jim invited me over to his house to talk writing, and that evening he was heading off to his writers' group, which included not only Dennis, but Lois McMaster Bujold as well. He asked if I'd like to come along. As you might imagine, I said yes, please! I soon became an official member of that group, and I can't tell you all the ways it helped me grow personally as well as professionally. And all because I took the first step of trying to get on panels instead of just sitting in the audience (something that admittedly is a lot easier to do at smaller cons than the major ones).

One bit of advice the networking articles I read offered was that writers should strive to create their own "look," a certain appearance and style that sets them apart from the crowd, draws attention to them, and makes them memorable. A look can have other uses too. Maureen McHugh once told me a story about attending a Worldcon years ago at which Neil Gaiman was also in attendance. The two of them tried to leave the hotel to have lunch, but Neil – who was well on his way to superstar status even then – kept getting stopped in the lobby by fans who wanted to talk to him. He apologized to Maureen and asked her to wait a moment. He went to the men's room, removed his sunglasses and leather jacket (which was his look at the time), and returned. Neil and Maureen then exited the lobby without further interference.

"What did you do?" Maureen asked.

Neil smiled. "I became Clark Kent," he answered.

When I was trying to decide on my look, I considered a number of options. Finally I decided I would be the funny/weird tie guy. I bought ties that had pen designs on them (because I was a writer), and skull designs (because I write horror), etc. I wore them with button shirts, slacks, and black work shoes. It was a dismal flop. Writers, as a rule, are notoriously casual in their dress, and editors, agents, and publishers tend to dress more professionally. So since I wore ties, no one recognized me as a writer. Everyone thought I worked in publishing. The next time I went to a conference, I wore turtlenecks, jeans, and sneakers, and everyone knew that I was a writer on sight.

Should you have a "look"? I don't bother anymore. I just wear whatever I feel like, but I'm farther along in my career than a lot of writers. If you want to go for a look, I suggest doing what feels natural and right for you. Scott A. Johnson wears a kilt at cons. Alethea Kontis wear a princess tiara. I saw Teri Jacobs wearing a very cool Cthulhu necklace at a con once. Michael West has an extensive collection of black T-shirts with horror movie posters and characters on them. At the last Worldcon, John Edward Lawson wore an extremely cool 18th century style outfit, complete with chest ruffles (even cooler, it was the outfit he got married in!). Maurice Broaddus is a stylish dresser, and Jeremy Lassen is known for his awesome suits. I once saw

Maurice and Jeremy do a who's-better-dressed showdown in a hotel lobby at a con, and it was amazing!

One caveat I would offer is that at SF/F/H cons, some pros view dressing up too much as wearing hall costumes, which is something (in their view) that only fans do. So take that into consideration if you're going to go for a distinctive look.

One of the great advantages of going to a conference, especially a larger one, is that you might get a chance to pitch your novel to an agent or editor one on one. If you're lucky, there will be formal, scheduled pitch sessions you can sign up for. However, there will also be opportunities to informally pitch your project. You'll need to be assertive (but not overly aggressive) and talk to editors or agents after panels, at parties, in the bar or lobby. If you can find editors and agents, that is. They're so used to being stalked by hopeful writers that they're often careful not to remain in the open too long, lest they attract an endless crowd of project-pitchers. Here's where being a panelist can help you again. If you were on a panel with an agent or editor, that gives you a connection to them that you can later use as a conversation starter. I never start out pitching a project when talking to editors. I might ask how the conference is going for them, and I often ask questions about the current state of the publishing industry or what I, as a creative writing teacher, should be telling my students about publishing. These aren't mere conversational gambits. I'm genuinely interested in these topics, which I can have a real conversation about before any business talk begins. When an agent or editor is ready to entertain a pitch, they'll use this phrase: "So, what are you working on?" That's your cue to pitch away.

The worst informal pitch I've ever seen occurred a few years back at a party after an award ceremony at a conference, which was held at a bar a couple blocks from the hotel in NYC. I'd published a horror novel *Like Death* (recently republished by Apex Books in both print and e-book versions) with Leisure Books, and I sat down with my editor, Don D'Auria, to discuss, among other things, my follow-up (which would turn out to be *Pandora Drive*). We'd only been chatting for a short time before a young writer came over and asked if she could join us. I was acquainted with this writer, although not very well, but even so, horning in on what's clearly a private business discussion is considered extremely bad manners at a conference. Don and I were both a bit surprised at the writer's boldness, but we said sure, pull up a chair. We started talking about general topics, and the writer took every opportunity to interject the title of her unpublished novel into the conversation as awkwardly as possible, always using the same phrase. "Well, in my novel TITLE . . ." (I won't mention the title because I don't want to embarrass the writer publicly, but you can bet your ass I remember it. I heard it probably a few dozen times, and even if my brain one day succumbs to Alzheimer's, I suspect the very last memory to go will be the title of her novel).

She went on like this for a while, until finally Don excused himself and got up to go speak with someone else. The writer looked crestfallen, but she remained to chat with me a while longer. Eventually she left and Don returned to the table and sat back down.

"Sorry about that," he said. "I just couldn't take it anymore."

Needless to say, Don did not publish the writer's

novel, and as far as I know, it was never published. She was aggressive rather than assertive. And instead of having a genuine conversation, she employed a pat sales technique that she'd probably read about in some dumbass business marketing book. The result: she made herself look like an annoying wannabee in the eyes of one of the most important editors in the horror genre. Not the impression she wanted to make, I'll wager.

Enough with the anecdotes. Here are a few tips on networking at conferences.

Have a business card.

Even if you're just embarking on your writing career, you need to be able to give people your contact information. Don't put anything on the card you don't want to share with the world at large, such as your street address, home phone number, etc. If you have a website – and you should – make sure the URL is on your card.

Don't network drunk

It's easy to drink too much at a con, and writers aren't alone in this. I once had a drunk editor come up and start apologizing for taking so long to get back to me about a story she asked me to write for an anthology she was putting together. Problem was, she'd never contacted me about sending a story. I don't know for certain who she thought I was. My guess is she mistook me for British author Tim Lebbon, but you'd think that even drunk, the fact that I don't have an English accent would've tipped her off that she'd made a mistake. She definitely lost professionalism points in my eyes, and it didn't help that it was only mid-morning, either (in case you're wondering, she no longer works as an editor). A drink or two might help loosen you up and bolster your confidence – especially if like most writers you're an introvert. But don't overdo.

Don't be too stalky.
The con's program schedule can help you determine where and when that editor or agent you're dying to talk to will be, and if you're lucky, you may be able to chat with them after a panel or two. But beware becoming a stalker. If you start showing up everywhere your "target" is, you'll end up creeping them out, which might just get you a visit from hotel security.

Don't be (obnoxiously) pushy.
You want to be assertive enough that you can approach an editor or agent and start a conversation. You don't want to shove a 1000 page manuscript into their hands. And realize they're living people. Don't expect them to sit with you for six hours of in-depth conversation about your magnum opus. They need to eat. And pee. And sleep.

Don't stick with a clique.
If you have friends or acquaintances at a conference, it can be tempting to hang out with them all the time. Presumably you all like each other, so it's fun to hang out together, but it's also safe. You need to break out on your own now and again to make contacts, and who knows? Maybe even make a few new friends.

Network at different times and places.
Some people are morning people, some night people. Some hang out at the bar, some in the dealer's room.

Some go to parties, some avoid them like the Red Death. Whichever category you fall into, make sure you vary the times and places you'll be during the conference. It will maximize your networking opportunities.

Be yourself. Unless you're a jerk. In that case, try to be someone better.
The most important piece of advice I can give about networking is to try to relax and be yourself. The more genuine you are, the more editors and agents will be able to view you as a normal person instead of an overly desperate writer who's only interested in using them. They'll be able to relax around you and feel free to chat. Remember, agents and editors go to conferences, at least in part, to network too, so they expect writers to talk about their work. But no one likes a hard-sell approach.

Hopefully the tips I've passed along will serve you well the next time you attend a conference. And if despite my best efforts you end up making a fool of yourself, go ahead and blame it on me. After all, there's no such thing as bad publicity, right?

Theresa was born and bred in Birmingham and her career has been pretty varied; from Warehouse Packer, then bar work, to being a crap waitress then swiftly into retail, Admin, Professional Student and dosser until finally entering the Civil Service in 1999. She left the Service in 2012 to pursue a career as a writer.

Theresa writes humorous fiction including SF, Urban Fantasy & Horror. She has twelve anthology acceptances behind her. She also writes a number of book reviews and at her site www.terror-tree.co.uk Her collection of short stories, Monsters Anonymous, was released from Anarchy Books Sept 12. She is Publishing Director for Fringeworks Ltd.

She has loved horror, fantasy and SF all her life, thanks to her father who raised her on 50s Sci-Fi Universal Monsters, tango and popcorn. Her love of the bizarre, (including her dad) remains constant, to this day. She also owes a great debt to Rog Peyton from the BSFG who introduced her to alternative fiction at the tender the age of 14.

You can follow Theresa on Twitter @BarbarellaFem or find out more about her work at www.theresa-derwin.co.uk.

Class: Vaginas in Horror

Teacher: Theresa Derwin

Are you sitting comfortably? Pen and paper to hand? Right, so what are we learning today? This class will focus on -

Oi you at the back stop picking your nose!
And Gary? McMahon! Listen to me when I'm talking to you! What did I tell you about bringing your pet rat to school?
I don't care if it contains a thousand souls of murderers, don't bring him again.
Right, where was I? Vaginas in Horror -
Morris? Mark! Stop snickering at the back.
Are we ready class? Good, then I'll begin.

It all started with an assho- sorry class. I'll begin again. It all started February 14 with an online debate that got a little out of hand. But this debate was perhaps the culmination of growing tension within the genre throughout the years. February is historically 'Women in Horror' month and has been for some years; a month in which male and female horror writers across the spectrum celebrate the talent of women working in the horror industry, from actresses, to directors, to writers and beyond.

This year, the 'Women in Horror' website used an image as part of their advertising banner and website, this image being a pair of bright red lips with two little vampiric teeth peeking out, just visible. It was online this month of celebration that a voice of dissent accused the women in horror of using a vagina to promote their cause, thereby detracting from the issues. Furthermore, the individual rotated the lips and placed it next to a picture, close up, of a vagina next to it with arrows and designations pointing out the relevant parts of this anatomy. He, and it was a he I'm afraid, accused the 'Women in Horror' campaign of using sexuality as a means of making a point.

Twitter and Facebook exploded! Almost as much as it did a week or two later when the John Ross/Hugo awards debacle occurred. The individual was questioned quite rightly for his opinion and women across the web started using the image of lips in various guises as their Facebook and Twitter avatars and the world first saw the hashtag #vaginasinhorror. And I, my dears, groaned in dismay. Because, naively, I thought we'd moved on.

You see, who would be silly enough to ostracise fifty percent of their reading audience (assuming you accept that women also read horror) and approximately forty percent of the professional horror writing community? The clever horror author or horror fan nowadays would be smart enough to realise that networking is key to success in the industry, so why lose half of your readership/colleagues with stupidity?

There was a time, many years ago, when women were treated as an inferior species in the horror genre (bear with me), a victim, tart, Scream Queen, or eccentric who wrote the odd ghost story that wasn't really scary. Having recently watched the horror flick Trailer Park of Terror, it galls me that even now in 2014 there are horror films in which the female is objectified or her role is clichéd. In this particular film, the entire premise is that of the woman scorned, Norma (blonde hair, red dress) is seeking revenge on the male population through a deal with the devil. Yet despite her man-hating stance, it doesn't stop her seducing the unwitting arrivals at the trailer park following a crash. As for the other female roles in the film, they are merely ciphers, apart from Miss Number One Massage who for some reason is intent on ensuring her victim dies happy, if you know what I mean? The females in this film basically fall into two categories: victim or whore. And yes, I forgot the obligatory flesh eating monster.

So, have films progressed at all? Partly yes, particularly if we cite examples such as Ellen Ripley from the Alien franchise, Alice from the Resident Evil franchise and the stupendous French horror Martyrs. This has been a slow progression, but one evident since the 80s.

And there were of course strong women working in the horror industry at that time, but invariably were expected to present a certain persona in order to be accepted. Fans of the Hellraiser films will know the name Barbie Wilde, a woman in horror who has become famous through her portrayal of the female cenobite and later for her intense creativity and writing talent as evident from her stories (such as in Hellbound Heart) and her collection The Venus Complex.

Wilde's diversity though, is evidence of much more than her, ahem, diversity; it is necessity. It demonstrates that with the flux of the horror industry many artists and writers had to expand their repertoire working across creative boundaries in order to actually get work; particularly so it would seem, for female writers in the genre who have to become 'Jane' of all trades. The likes of Sarah Pinborough and Alison Littlewood have expanded their horror background to write dark fantasy and crime, whilst in the 1990s, prolific and well known horror/dark fantasy writer Laurell K Hamilton (of Anita Blake fame) started to 'sex up' her literature to appeal to the masses, the publishers and the fans. What started as a series with a strong, 'kick ass' female character soon became a series embroiled in its own mythology presenting an over sexed female lead dependent on a harem of men to secure her powers. Of course we then saw the emergence of the 'paranormal romance'. Female writers of urban fantasy, dark fantasy and horror were encouraged to add a dash of sex and spice to their supernatural stories in order to sell. And let's face it, what was the female horror writer to do in such a situation?

So you see the horror genre is littered as a whole with examples of women fighting for their right to be a 'woman in horror', and speaking from personal experience, it has not been an easy battle, though things have changed for the better. As an attendee of numerous conventions I have met some amazing fans, writers, actors, directors etc. of the genre and in the main, they're bloody nice people! Networking is an essential part of gaining work in the industry, however, it is more important when it comes to gaining insight and expertise. I remember asking a journalist, Lee, a well known fan at Alt-Fiction a few years back for a read through of a story I was about to submit to a publisher, my first story in around fifteen years as it happens. Lee kindly took the manuscript off me, and started to browse through. Then I saw his eyebrows raise in surprise. He couldn't hide his reaction. Something was wrong with the piece; I'd had a feeling I'd gone wrong along the way, but were it not for Lee's sound advice, honesty and own writing talent, I'd have never got that story published. The ultimate part of that experience was that I felt as though I belonged; I was respected, listened to and offered sound advice irrespective of gender. And that my friends, is why we have such a strong community. As a writer it is essential that we nurture these building blocks and secure the foundations layer upon layer until you have a solid relationship. Share stories, ideas, influences. When on Facebook, Twitter or at a convention it is just plain silly to ignore the potential of a relationship because of gender. It is even more inane, as I have unfortunately experienced and heard of from other female writers, to display inappropriate behaviour towards a female fan or professional in the industry. I have found many instances in which a female writer has been approached via Facebook messages and asked some unmentionable questions. This, dear class, is inappropriate behaviour.

Let's put it plainly; treat each gender with equity rather than equality and don't come on to a woman (or man, as it goes both ways) in such a situation because you think they're fit. If my experience of conventions are anything to go by, her or his mind is an attractive prospect too. And friendships are worth far more than a slap across the face. Just because someone likes to dress up, wear a corset or a little make-up, doesn't mean they're on the prowl. It means they're an individual with individual tastes in fashion, or perhaps it's their persona as a horror writer. Food for thought I hope. And next - I give a perfect example of what NOT to do in a convention circle.

Back in 2012 I attended a brand new horror convention, which I won't name. However those of you in attendance may remember that I was quite vocal at one point. It was at the end of a successful and enjoyable day that one of the organisers asked the guests to come up to the front for a photo. It was then that I literally 'saw' what was wrong with this picture. At the front of the convention room, stood a row of fifteen men including the moderators of panels, all very talented men in horror, including Joseph D'Lacey and David Moody. However, there was not one single woman included as a guest or moderator at the event. So raising my hand I piped up: "I'm not being funny or anything, but where are the women up there?" I was met with a few raised eyebrows and blank stares until I clarified: "This is a horror con and there isn't one female up there. How come?"

More blank stares and some embarrassed looks until finally one of the organisers, a woman in fact, replied, "I didn't invite any. They only write Mills and Boon sh**." Okay – I would have loved to have been a fly on the wall if that were said to Sam Stone.

Slowly, picture it now kids, I stood up, took a deep breath, and prepared to explode, until a hand held me back with a whispered "You've made your point", then a conversation started before I could get involved; looks of embarrassment exchanged across the all male guest entourage and mostly male audience. Then Michael Wilson of This is Horror rightly joined in the conversation and started to name the plethora of female names working in the horror industry, from Shirley Jackson onwards. But you can imagine my horror, particularly as a horror writer myself (and I can assure you there is no shortage of viscera in my work) at hearing a female horror fan speak those words. It is at that point dear reader, that I made it my mission to educate horror fans about the powerful and talented women working in the horror industry.

It is interesting that a number of the males in attendance, notably zombie author Sean Page, came across to me afterward and thanked me for speaking up. "I was thinking it too," a few said.

Following this incident I've been blogging incessantly about the issue of gender and genre fiction across the horror and SFF communities. Apart from respecting all within the community, it strikes me again that it isn't very clever to lose a substantial portion of your target audience and/or colleagues/friends.

It was at a later convention in 2013 that I was asked to be on a panel about horror, and I was excited about sharing panel space with David Moody and Simon Clark. However, the moderator came up to me and asked if I was the only woman on the panel. And furthermore, would I mind if he asked me the question on stage, which he did. It gave me great pleasure that fans and writers in the genre were beginning to notice inconsistency in representation at events.

So what gives? Why is it even an issue? After all, despite the things we are taught at school: boys and girls are different and boys can't learn girls subjects and vice versa, biology teaches us something else. In the Daily Mail of 5th Feb '13, writer Paul Harris reported on the gender issue in a piece entitled 'Men from Mars, Women from Venus? No, actually, we're all on the same planet'. 'Ever since the Dawn of creation,' he begins, 'it has been a comfortable assumption - men and women have completely different characters.'

He goes on to say that despite this assumption, we are, in fact, quite similar. And more! Biology can prove that there is no inherent difference between men and women. A study has found that 'we share a vast range of identical traits. Right down to weeping at slushy dramas (men) or being an aggressive executive who's good at maths (women).'

In the study in which more than 13,300 individuals

were questioned, on a range of 122 stereotyped/gender relative situations, there was 'little difference between the sexes.' It was furthermore proved that men and women in general valued the same attributes in future partners.

So, without getting too technical, it brings to mind theories such as the self-fulfilling prophecy and nurture verses nature. In short, are girls trained from an early age to like girly things? If this is the case, does this explain why the idea of a woman liking, nay, loving, something as dark and monstrous as horror is anathema to many?

An interesting question and I don't have the answers, however I would add, don't judge a book by its cover. Don't believe that a woman is inherently female in all ways and therefore can't scare you, because hell, have you ever read Shirley Jackson? In one of her most powerful novellas, 'We have Always Lived in the Castle', we come across one of the darkest female characters I have ever discovered in horror fiction. Strong, powerful, yet flawed and very scary, the female narrator of this piece will get under your skin.

So kids, what's the point of this lesson? Well, put simply, pick up a book by a female horror author and read it. I have a list of over fifty women in horror I regularly recommend to readers, and I'm just an email away. Google me; I'm not shy! Don't ignore that quiet person in the corner at a convention; it could be their first con and you may just hook up with the future Stephen King, Sarah Pinborough, Stephen Jones or Ellen Datlow of the industry. Take the proverbial saying to heart: don't judge a book by its cover.

Try a new author, don't assume it will be stunted or

flaccid horror if the author is female. Women can be scary too. Just take Ellen Ripley. Now there's a woman I'd like to meet.

Weston Ochse is the author of twenty books, most recently SEAL Team 666 and its sequel Age of Blood, which the New York Post called 'required reading' and USA Today placed on their 'New and Notable Lists.' His first novel, Scarecrow Gods, won the Bram Stoker Award for Superior Achievement in First Novel and his short fiction has been nominated for the Pushcart Prize. His work has appeared in comic books, and magazines such as Cemetery Dance and Soldier of Fortune. He lives in the Arizona desert within rock throwing distance of Mexico. He is a military veteran with 29 years of military service and currently returned from a deployment to Afghanistan.

Website: www.westonochse.com

Friendship, Writing, and the Internet

Weston Ochse

I was thinking the other day about my friends.

Not those people I went to high school with, or old army buddies, but the friends I've made in the writing profession. It's amazing really how close you can get to someone without spending any real time with them, and on some occasions, never having met them at all.

I started writing in the mid-90s. Very soon I fell into a group of troublemakers in the HorrorNet Chatroom (who have come to be known as the Cabal). Most of us (with the exception of Ray Garton, Tom Picirilli, Douglass Clegg and Paul Wilson who stopped in to harass us) were at the same place in our writing, struggling to find our voice and be heard over the great chorus of creativity. Honestly, every evening was like being a member of the Little Rascals. We were close friends, eager to speak with each other and able to tell secrets that we couldn't tell those closest to us.

Then I discovered List Serves and subscribed to a few. Darktales, MIT Writers and HorrorWriters were my favorites during those days. The lists weren't as interactive and lacked the immediacy of the HorrorNet Chat, but they served their purpose, allowing me to reach out to a growing fan base, discover new friends and enter into business enterprises. I became the editor of the online journal Bloody Muse because of this. I collaborated with this guy from Pennsylvania on what would become a Scary Redneck franchise. I met editors, I met fans, I met fellow writers and I met friends.

Know how you can tell which ones are friends? When you meet them in real life you're smiling like a giddy school girl and find that you have nothing to say because they already know all there is to know about you.

I remember the first time I met my Cabal Mates. I was sitting in the bar of the Drake Hotel in Denver drinking a Fat Tire wondering what the hell I'd gotten myself into (my first Convention). Suddenly a bunch of inebriated ne're-do-wells stumbled into the bar. After awhile, one came over to my table and asked if I was Weston. Five seconds later I was being introduced to the members of the Cabal and it was like we were old friends. The feelings of acceptance and friendship I experienced were those you usually felt only after years of terrestrial friendships; or after a traumatic or life-changing event.

Why was I so happy to see these folks?

I'm not the *end all be all* of knowledge, nor am I some great Buddha coming down from a Tibetan mountaintop to dispense wisdom, nor am I a Jungian psychologist who can tell you what dreams are made of, but I think I have this one figured out. I think it comes down to this. What we do in the backyard and in the grocery store and in our living rooms rests firmly in the realm of the normal and is a part of the lives of our friends, neighbors and family. But the out-pouring of our souls, the writing if you will, that we do in front of our computers is as personal an activity as there is. We interrogate our imagination with words and plots. We delve into the hoary depths of our fears and report what we've seen. Sometimes we are embarrassed with how our minds work. We don't understand why we write what we do and we can't stop.

Our family loves us. We have friends from high school and college and our jobs. We have our favorite checkout line at the grocery store. We know people in our towns and they know us. But for all the love and all the friendship and all the *kum-ba-ya how ya doin's* that we exchange with our barber and the cute girl in aisle three, they cannot understand where the viciousness, the horror, the weirdness, the many-tentacled beasts, the vile murder, the unrelenting mayhem, the putrid grotesqueries, the rapes, the disembowelments and the just plain evilness comes from.

We're afraid that they'll associate what we write with who we are; and sometimes they do.

Leave behind whatever psychosis makes us do what we do. That's for another article down the road. The fact is that we write this vile stuff and we love it. These friends I spoke of earlier, those who I never met, but felt close to – they all had one thing in common. They accepted me for what I wrote, gave me encouragement to keep doing it, and understood the catharsis inherent in the writing of it. I was able to get closer to these strangers about something very personal and dear to me than I was to my family or friends.

This isn't an indictment on my family and friends. They're normal people and should live normal lives, thinking normal things, doing normal tasks.

Who are we to try and make them understand what they can't understand?

And guess what? We don't have to.

Because of the magnificence of modern technology, we're able to reach out and touch people of our ilk at any hour of the day or night, on message boards, chats, lists, MySpace accounts, Live Journals, Facebook, Twitter, blogs and instant messages. No longer are we alone in what we do. There are entire communities out there who accept and encourage us.

I wonder how writers communicated before the internet. My wife tells me of this thing called a letter. Days, sometimes weeks, would pass before a single thought could be conveyed. What a lonely existence it must have been. So let me take a moment and thank all of my writing friends. Thank you for being there, for accepting me and encouraging me. There are those of you who I feel closer to than some members of my own family. And one day perhaps we'll even meet.

What about you? Do you share your soul? Do you reach out to like-minded people? Or do you keep your muse locked in a musty closet, chasing spiders to eat, and herding dust bunnies as playmates?

JOHN PALISANO is a two-time Bram Stoker nominated author. His short fiction has appeared in venues such as the Lovecraft eZine, Horror Library, Terror Tales, and many more. His novel Nerves was released by Bad Moon Books. He is also a contributor to FANGORIA magazine. Check him out at:
www.johnpalisano.wordpress.com

How to Fail as An Artist in Ten Easy Steps: a rough list, off the top of my head, by confirmed repeat failure...

John Palisano

DISCLAIMER: Any list is just a list, and not a guide. No one's advice is a be-all, end-all. No one's path is yours. Find your own way. While you're on your journey, have a little fun. Just like this list. Don't take things too seriously all the time – only when you have to.

1. Don't be any good.
We all want to get out there. We're human. We seek validation. Friendships. Lovers. Acclaim. Glory. But hold your horses, skipper. Make sure your stuff is as good as can be before you share it. That can be a tough moment to figure out, but you'll probably be close. It's a fine line between believing in yourself and not. Just make sure your stuff's up to snuff. If you put it out prematurely, you may damage your reputation. Never a bad idea to grab a few confidants and get another

opinion (see 4 and 5.) It's okay to fail in the beginning several times before something clicks. Really.

2.   Don't promote yourself.

In college, there were some absolutely astounding filmmakers and writers I knew. Some of them had a weird outlook. They never wanted to send out there stuff, or submit it. Sharing it was like pulling teeth for them. They had zero faith in themselves, despite many of our constant praise. They wanted to keep their art pure and not become salesmen. While that's perfectly understandable – most artists are not natural salespeople, especially of their own works – but waiting for someone to discover you is a sure road into obscurity. If you have ambitions, you'll have to find a way to get your work out there without becoming obnoxious. Not easy, but necessary.

3.   Promote yourself!

Okay! So not promoting yourself isn't a problem. You've got it covered. Your elevator pitch rolls off your tongue like butter. Every social media site swarms with your latest releases. Not only have you flown your freak flag high, you bought a second, made posters, bought internet ads, magazine ads, reviews, and you're just totally consumed to the point where everything you say and do has to do with your super-duper passion. But you know what? A lot of people will tune you out. You have become the living embodiment of spam. We all know of lots of celebrities and products we hear of all the time. And hate. Barraging people with your stuff probably isn't going to make people more or less inclined to hand over their money for it. Either they will, or they won't.

Don't beat people up over and over again.

4.   Listen to everybody.

You've got your stuff ready. You've been over it a hundred times. You love it! Your Mom loves it! Your spouse or lover thinks it's brilliant. So does everyone on MyTwitFace! You've done it. You're ready. Climb to the highest digital roofs and scream out loud, "Look, everybody!" Screeeeecch! Make sure you get some unbiased opinions on your stuff. Listen carefully. If more than one person finds something amiss, it's worth considering. If different people dislike different aspects, well, get some more opinions. It may just be a matter of taste. Another big thing: if you can get someone successful to check out your stuff and give you an honest opinion, you're ahead of the game. Just remember: successful people aren't always great teachers, or great judges of other people's works. Sometimes, though, they really have their finger on the pulse and can be invaluable for up and comers.

5.   Don't listen to anybody!

What the heck! I just told you to listen to everyone. As I mentioned before, this can sometimes be great, but it can also be destructive, given certain situations. I can't tell you how many times I've been told to give up, get a real job, told my art was a 'hobby' (as if!), along with a ton more borderline abusive things. In one critique group, one guy was so mean I folded for almost two weeks at one point. It took all I had to get back up on the horse. In the end, use your judgment. Is the person coming from a sincere and knowledgeable place? Or are they just a bitter, cynical jerk? Do they really have the tools and experience to offer you a valid opinion? Or is it just that: an opinion? Sometimes it's the latter.

6. Follow the rules.

"If you're on time, your late." That was a mantra I heard again and again in the film industry. They'd give you a call time, but expected you there earlier. There were a lot of dos and don'ts told to me by others. Lots of fear mongering. Sometimes, though, it was sneaking around the rules that got me ahead in ways just playing by the rules would not have accomplished. Sometimes this has gotten me in trouble, though. Before that, though: you need to apply this to your creations. Is your work too safe? Too similar? Does it not really stand out? Is it not special enough to warrant attention? Maybe going out on a limb will make all the difference, breaking down doors, and helping you stand out in a sea of others.

7. Don't Follow the rules!

So you didn't follow the rules, like old John said. You submitted your story in medieval fonts. With artwork. You sent your album of ambient noise guitar to a network show. You sent along that one-long tracking shot feature-film about 90 minutes in the life of a tree to the Short Film Festival. And they rejected you. Well, it's always good to follow submission guidelines. They're there for a reason. If you're making a programmer or an editor's life hell, you're likely not going to be asked to the party. Sure: rules are bent here in extreme situations, but it better be extraordinary. Otherwise, paint within the lines. Maybe think of it as 'focus' rather than 'limits' if you need to.

8. Be impatient.

"Did you read the book I sent you this morning?" "Have you watched my film?" "What'd you think of my double LP with 24 EDM reinterpretations of 'Chopsticks'?" "When's my review coming out?" These may be valid questions, and they may mean the world to you, but pushing people who may help you can close the door faster than you'd think. Most people get into the arts and love feedback. Some arts, like writing, can take ages to get responses and feedback. Know that going in. Take up another hobby. Or better yet? Keep working on your art and making new stuff while the other stuff makes its way out there. For me? I balance writing with music. Fiction is glacial. Rock n' roll is instant. Somehow, they meet in the middle and keep me from going completely to 'unhinged' on the dial.

9. Be a sore loser.

"And the winner is?" says the presenter. "Not you!"

So what do you do? Tear up the program in dramatic fashion, like one fellow I saw. Or applaud and clap and move on. Don't go on the web and start slagging the winner. Keep it classy. Awards are great and fun, but aren't the only gauge of how successful your work is. There are many other venues for that. Your readers, listeners, viewers. Worry about them first. If you're connecting with an audience, no matter how small, focus on that, and not on a little plastic coffee cup with your name on it and 'Best Joe Of The Month' – there's always next month, and the one after that.

10. Be a winner.

Okay, so what the heck is this one? "Be a winner"? I thought this was on how to fail. Let me explain. There are a lot of people out there who are afraid of success. It's a very real fear. I've seen it happen more times than I care to report. "Fear of success" happens a lot. Folks sabotage themselves. Screw things up on purpose. It's understandable, though, isn't it? Success is scary. If you get a hit, then what? How will you cope? Maybe you feel you're really a fraud and don't have more than one thing in you. Maybe you don't want to be disappointed. It's a weird, weird phenomenon. And real, believe it or not. If you think this is you? Work it out now before you hit it big, okay? The rocket ship of your success isn't going to wait – it'll be gone into the stratosphere without you.

So there's my silly, light-hearted little list. I hope you read it with the spirit in which it was intended. There are some serious bits in there, though, so I hope it's slightly useful, too. And here's a little extra. Let's go to eleven, shall we?

11. Be yourself.

You often hear about artists finding their voices, but it's so true. When Bruce Springsteen was heralded as the new Bob Dylan, he vowed, "I don't want to be the next anybody." Neither do you. Only you can make the stuff you want to make. Only you sound like you, play like you, sing like you, write like you, paint like you, see like you. Your biggest competitor is yourself because you need to find and present the best you have to offer.

No go to it, and have a hell of a time on the way.

Mark West's short fiction first began appearing in the small press in 1999 and was collected in Strange Tales from Rainfall Books. Following publication of his novel In The Rain With The Dead he fell into a writer's block that lasted until Gary McMahon demanded a novelette from him – that was The Mill and kick-started his writing. He's published over seventy short stories, two novels, a novelette and his Spectral Press chapbook sold out four months prior to publication.

Mark lives in Rothwell, Northants (which serves as the basis for his fictional town of Gaffney) with his wife Alison and their young son Matthew.
Website – www.markwest.org.uk
Twitter - @MarkEWest

Writer's Block

Mark West

I started writing fiction when I was eight, attempting to expand the Star Wars universe and put me and my friends alongside Han, Luke and Chewie. I wrote through my teens and twenties – shorts and novels – and was finally published in the small press in 1999. Once that initial acceptance came, it seemed to open a floodgate and I wrote a lot of stories. I submitted most of them too and was very lucky that the bulk went on to appear in small press zines.

I continued to write shorts, I wrote a novel or two and then, in 2005, my son was born. I still don't know if it was that earth-shattering event (I was very glad to see him, don't get me wrong), or the one a couple of years earlier that would go on to inspire "The Mill", but my writing engine seemed to have sprung a leak.

I'd made my final revisions to my novels "In The Rain With The Dead" and "Conjure" before he was born, and had it in my head that I would take a few weeks off, but soon those weeks turned into months. Six months, in fact, went by and I hadn't written anything except for a few pages of notes. I began to panic and – trust me when I tell you this – panic is the absolute last thing you should do.

You see, a writer needs to write. He or she might do something else (I work as a finance manager, for example), he or she might have other hobbies, but at some point, the creative process is going to start feeling short-changed. Stories are running in your head, you keep seeing things in the world around you – "ooh, that'd be good for a character trait" or "wow, I could use that alley as a great location" – and yet they're not going anywhere.

Now there can be a whole host of reasons for writer's block – you've written yourself into a corner, you don't know where to go next, you've run out of ideas, your ideas are terrible – but since this is my article and I know my story best, I'll tell you about it. But I think the lessons learned can be extrapolated into your own issue.

My output up to 2003 was cheerfully gruesome – I was a teenager in the 80s and embraced Clive Barker and the splatterpunk movement wholeheartedly and that flowed through into my writing. Of course, some of my stories were quieter, I used ghostly elements from time to time, but I enjoyed gore. In 2003 (after I'd written "In

The Rain With The Dead"), we lost my sister and her passing was a real blow. It also affected my writing, in that I edged towards the supernatural with "Conjure" and the thought of writing blood and gore after that didn't really feel right to me.

After my son was born, I started making notes for a project that involved snuff films. It didn't work and I didn't make the connection, so I started something else, an apocalyptic novella. I wrote lots of notes for it, thousands upon thousands of words, but I couldn't get it to work, I couldn't get it to sing. And the more it lay there, quiet and immobile, the more I whittled that the story writing thing I'd enjoyed for so many years had broken. It upset me, it depressed me and the more I worried, the worse it got.

With hindsight, I can see what the problem was. There was something on my mind – the death of my sister – and I needed to explore that, to make sense of where I was and where I needed to be. I had to figure out what I wanted to do and say (I know, this sounds pretentious but bear with me) and that, on the whole, was about the human condition and not about people getting their arms or legs chopped off. I was experiencing grief, I was experiencing the overwhelming human tornado of fatherhood, that was what I needed to talk about.

That all came later, when I wrote the piece of work that broke me out of my block. At the time, I only knew Gary McMahon online and we were talking one day and I mentioned my block. He'd suffered one too and he asked me to write a story for an anthology he was putting together. It was all lies, of course (he told me much later), but he asked and I was compelled to deliver and I sat down and I thought about what I wanted to do. He told me, the only guideline that I got, to scare him, to write something that moved him and frightened him. So I worked through my usual process, what scared me, what moved me, what frightened me? And there it was – I was frightened of losing someone, I was moved by grief and that was what I needed to write about.

"The Mill" came out of that process and set the template for everything that has come after – there can be as many pyrotechnics as the story needs, but it has to be rooted in reality, it has to have an element that scares or frightens me and that, at the end of the day, makes it more human. It also helped that somebody was waiting for it and I really didn't want to let them down.

So my block was combated by Gary McMahon, lovely man that he is, asking me for a story. Not everyone is going to have that option, obviously, but there are lessons I learned.

A block can be caused for as many a number of reasons as you can think of. But if you bear the following in mind, hopefully you can work your way out of it.

You've written yourself into a corner? Start again, it's as simple as that. Go back and re-work the character and his activities, or jump forward and work on a new bit, or try and decide if this is what you want to do. Sometimes, you know, it isn't.

Is this what I want to write? Only you can tell that but if you've always written one way – lashings of gore, yay! – but now you're turned off by the whole idea of it, try something new. Challenge yourself.

My writing stinks. Sadly, nobody will be able to convince you otherwise, but a good test is to write something and put it away, leave it time to breathe and settle. Go back to it a fortnight or a month later, read it with fresh eyes and if it still stinks, try it again. If, as I believe it will, it doesn't, use that discovery and start working again.

But, you cry, I haven't got any ideas.

Well try this. Pick a subject, any subject. Take something you fear, put that into the mix. Take something that scares you, put that into the mix.

For example, you see an anthology call that's looking for terrifying stories set in the outdoors. "Oh no," you think, "I can't do that."

Break it down.

What experience do you have in the outdoors? Have you ever gone camping with friends, or on a bonding course with work colleagues? You have? Well, there's your setting.

What do you fear? Being alone, being put with people you don't know or like, being outside, being trapped in a tent/cave? Let's say it's being alone, for sake of argument.

What scares you? Being incapacitated, being pursued, death? So let's take being pursued.

You now have three key items for your idea – it's set in the great outdoors and your hero is there because he's on a bonding course with work. He wakes up one morning and everyone is dead, or gone, with no clues either way. Then he sees someone approaching the campsite, a normally dressed man who starts to run towards him. Our hero takes flight.

Of course all of this seems very easy now and you can write yourself into a corner, you can run out of ideas, you can be stricken with terrible self-doubt (you wouldn't be a writer if you weren't). But keep your head, take some deep breaths, have a think and then try the exercise. What comes out of it might be rubbish but, if you've written one tale, you can write another…

"If you've got a writer's block, you can cure it this evening by stopping whatever you're writing and doing something else. You picked the wrong subject."
– Ray Bradbury at The Sixth Annual Writer's Symposium by the Sea, 2001

Adam Nevill was born in Birmingham, England, in 1969 and grew up in England and New Zealand. He is the author of the supernatural horror novels Banquet for the Damned, Apartment 16, The Ritual, Last Days, *and* House of Small Shadows. *In 2012* The Ritual *was the winner of The August Derleth Award for Best Horror Novel, and in 2013* Last Days *won the same award. Adam lives in Birmingham, England, and can be contacted through www.adamlgnevill.com.*

Going Underground

Adam Nevill

NOBODY SAID IT WAS EASY:

Easy never came into getting published as a horror writer. I completed my first novel, *Banquet for the Damned*, in late 2000. I began writing the novel in 1997. But by the summer of 2002, every agent who accepted fiction in the *Writers and Artists Yearbook* had turned down my letter of introduction. It took two years for all of the rejection letters to come back. "No horror" being the usual refrain, or "too many authors already". And as no publisher took unsolicited manuscripts, that was that. Game over. By that time, I'd forsaken a career in television a second time. I was living on a shoe-string (again), enduring an existence above an old pub in East London, working nights as a security guard, and going mad with sleep deprivation and despair. As a lesson in futility, this is not unique. This all happened before the current digital age, when anyone can publish their novel straight to eBook, but however your book gets to market these days, I think the core lessons I learned below are as relevant as ever if you want to stand out and resonate.

GO UNDERGROUND:

I went underground. A master in my chosen field of horror, Ramsey Campbell, recommended I send my novel to one of his UK publishers, a small press. The year was now 2003. The small press, PS Publishing, accepted *Banquet for the Damned* within a week and produced a beautiful limited edition hardback that garnered critical acclaim and gave me a small profile. Without the advice on the appropriate place to send my novel – to someone not just receptive to the genre, but enthusiastic about it, who would actually read my horror novel – *Banquet for the Damned* would have remained an uneaten meal, moldering on the pantry shelves of my hard drive. Had it been the eighties when horror was box office, the story may have been different with the bigger publishers, but I'd written a huge supernatural horror novel in a publishing climate that had no interest in horror. Why did I write it? Because that was the novel I was *driven* to write at that time.

But my rightful place was the underground, of which I knew nothing, and I needed help from those who understood the great opportunities that exist in the underground. Don't fear the underground. The underground is your friend, and increasingly in the rapidly changing world of books, the underground can be your savior. For quality and innovation, and for precursors to future trends, even for first class book design and packaging, what emerges from the genre underground often puts what is published above ground to shame. The underground won't support a career, but it can start one if you have the patience to serve an apprenticeship down there.

Even if your chosen field is out of vogue in mainstream publishing, there will be a world of small presses in which to cut your teeth. Small presses actively look for new voices. Dedicated well-read fans of the genres actually own the small presses (and that's not something you can take for granted with the majors). I'm not talking about eBook platforms that publish every single thing sent to them in the hope that one title will go stratospheric. This isn't about volume, I'm referring to dedicated small publishers who are curators of the genres they love. Start below, down there, *La Bas*; it's very satisfying to emerge from the underground with a profile and to then attain more mainstream success.

CALL THEM LEGION FOR THEY ARE MANY:

As well as researching the small press scene, get involved in the actual genre community. Go to open nights and signings and groups and conventions. Opportunities to contribute to small press anthologies will arise and you will meet established authors, the reviewing community, and guest editors. You are no longer just an attachment on an email coming out of the void; you become more than another outline with three sample chapters. One circuit of a dealer's room and you'll see a miniature book fair of small dedicated publishers, cover artists, websites, and calls for subs. If you have ability, people in that world will soon notice. If you have the requisite passion, but need tuition and advice, there are panels and workshops at cons in which accomplished writers give their time. Support the scene and it'll support you.

THE FAUSTIAN PACT:

The other part you really have to get right you will do all on your own. Forget about deals, careers, professional writing for a moment, or even for a few years. The writing is what counts. And I have a very old school approach to writing because it's the only one I know: read the canon of the field you want to contribute to, acquire the craft of good writing through practice and tuition, develop a voice. If it takes ten years or longer, so be it. *Apartment 16* took four years to write and *The Ritual* another two after that. There was no deadline, deal or publisher waiting for either book, or even any readers beside my Dad. And during most of that time, little had changed in publishing: no one was publishing horror in the mainstream beyond some series fiction in the US and the big names from the seventies. So why did I write them: because I was *driven* to. After the two novels were complete and delivered to my agent early in 2009 (my agent took me on because he'd read my first small press novel), publishing in the UK had just begun to return its capricious eyes back towards supernatural horror in fiction after the success of *Let the Right One In*, and *The Birthing House*. I had waited it out. There was even an auction for *Apartment 16* and *The Ritual*. How times had changed over a decade.

But I believe the commercial success of these two novels, the critical reception, the foreign rights deals and film options, that have exceeded all of my expectations as a former small press writer, have only happened because I spent so long gestating, evolving, developing, and rewriting those first three novels over a decade,

423

while also contributing short stories to small presses to build profile. I did it the old fashioned way. In total, it took fifteen years to *make it*; fifteen years with writing, and reading better writers, as the main purpose of my life.

So I also highly recommend completing a book, and rewriting it until you don't feel you can rewrite it anymore, before approaching a publisher. Don't be afraid of drafts that go into double figures. Take four to six weeks off, or even longer, between drafts. Meantime, write short stories between the drafts. Good writing that endures always comes from rewriting, but learn *how to* rewrite from professional writers on good courses. Rewriting is not just about tinkering with grammar, extending or deleting material, it's about saying what you need to say in the way you want to say it. It's going through every single line over and over again, and then studying the paragraph, and then going back in... But you have to be able to identify what is wrong with a sentence in the first place before you can change it. My early work was incoherent; two poets showed me how to rewrite, and how to think about language differently.

Why be another literate adult who gets lucky with some craft in a fad that is *hot right now*? Or one that loses patience and just self publishes first drafts straight to eBook? Be as much of the *real deal* as you can be. Writing should be a purpose for life. Writing well comes from the repetition of hard work and application. Eventually it will deliver dividends at some level. There is no shortcut to being good at something. But when you become good at something, the satisfaction and joy is considerable.

The strange and special ingredient in fiction that

transports the reader is innate. But once your incrementally hard-won craft and your innate imaginative quality have combined, your work will resonate. You may never be able to properly articulate that special innate quality, that is unique to you, until you have read widely in your chosen field – the canon – and acquired the craft. At whatever level you are published at, your work will then get word-of-mouth and you'll find ideal readers and achieve peer recognition, or even a bigger audience. But also learn to manage your expectations without becoming demoralized. Success isn't necessarily only measured in commercial terms.

Always try and write what you feel *compelled* to write. And if what you are writing makes you feel uncomfortable or even ashamed, then stick with it all costs... it's where the most affecting writing often comes from, particularly in horror. If I don't feel I'm close to damaging myself by the time I finish one of my novels, I know the writing may run the risk of being flat and unaffecting for the reader. But when you hit that zone that is all your own, well... there's nothing quite like it. Euphoria awaits.

For those about to go underground, I salute you!

Steven Savile has written for Doctor Who, Torchwood, Primeval, Stargate, Warhammer, Slaine, Fireborn, Pathfinder, Arkham Horror, Risen, and other popular game and comic worlds.

His novels have been published in eight languages to date, including the Italian bestseller L'eridita.

He won the International Media Association of Tie-In Writers award for his Primeval novel, SHADOW OF THE JAGUAR, published by Titan, in 2010, and The inaugural Lifeboat to the Stars award for TAU CETI (co-authored with Kevin J. Anderson).

SILVER, his debut thriller reached #2 in the Amazon UK e-charts in the summer of 2011. It was among the UK's top 30 bestselling novels of 2011 according to The Bookseller. The series continues in Solomon's Seal, WarGod, and Lucifer's Machine, and is available in a variety of languages.

His latest books include HNIC (along with the legendary Hip Hop artist Prodigy, of Mobb Deep) which was Library Journal's Pick of the Month, the Lovecraftian horror, The Sign of Glaaki, co-written with Steve Lockley, and has recently started writing the popular Rogue Angel novels as Alex Archer. The first of which, Grendel's Curse, is out in May.

He has lived in Sweden for the last 17 years.

Website http://www.stevensavile.com

Be the Writer You Want to Be

Steven Savile

I've had a lot of good advice over the years, that's what happens if you hang around a bunch of talented folk long enough, some of it has to rub off eventually. Basically if they cast enough pearls this swine's going to pick a few up. I mean it'd be rude not to, wouldn't it?

Your humble introducer for this book, Mort Castle, said something that stuck with me for a very long time. I was young, impetuous and wanted to be someone. Mort very sagely said, "You want to be in this for the long haul, kid. That means it's not a sprint. It's like a long lonely walk in the desert." And he was right. Sure, there's a burning desire to see your words in print, to hold a book in your hands and go, "Look at this, I did this, this is me." You want people to see your genius, to understand, because, I mean, it's you and they need to know just how brilliant you are. But if you do the mathematics, if you take your time, write 3 brilliant short stories in a year and keep that going for what would be a fairly decent working life, let's say you start getting it right around the age of 30, and write until you're a cheerfully retired 65, that's 35 years producing 3 brilliant stories a year. That's 105 brilliant short stories over the duration of your career. Not good ones, not so-so ones, but brilliant ones. That's a body of work to be proud of. Say you manage one brilliant novel every three years in the same time, suddenly your body of work is 12 brilliant novels and 105 brilliant short stories. I mean holy crap that's some doing. That's the work of a genius

427

that, when you put it all together and look at it. That's grandmaster stuff. And it's achieved at what feels like a crawl taking the time to do it right, to say exactly what you want to say, to be exactly the writer you want to be.

The second piece of advice that lodged in my brain was from Tim Powers, who quite honestly I think is one of most singularly talented writers in the field today, and Tim says to me, quite earnestly, "Steve, when you die and go to heaven St Peter's not going to look at you and say, 'Why couldn't you be more like Stephen King?', because we've got a world of people trying to be the next Stephen King. He's going to look at you and say 'Steve, why couldn't you be more like Steve Savile because we've only got one of him.'" Yes, of course, we fumble our way through this writing game often blagging it, wearing our influences in our words, but there comes a time when our voice needs to shine out, and that's a vital part of being the writer you want to be, and a big part of having the career you want to have.

I was pretty driven as a young writer back in my early 20s. I was goal motivated. I set out targets I wanted to hit. For instance I'd read that pretty much every author I admired had their first book out when they were 27, so I wanted my first book on the shelf age 27. I made it, but not with anything I'd have expected if you'd asked the 19 year old me who set the goal. It was a kid's adaptation of Return of the Jedi complete with puzzles. Sometimes we take strange paths to get to where we want to be.

The third piece of advice I've treasured came from Kevin J Anderson, and this one is wonderfully simple. "If an editor approaches you for an anthology and its theme is fluffy pink unicorns, and you say you'll do a story, then write the best damn fluffy pink unicorn story you can, or don't agree to do it." We were talking about writing for hire at the time. I was mulling over the Warhammer trilogy, which, despite being fantasy novels are some of the most overt horror I've written in years, being very much a homage to the old Hammer House of Horror vampire movies. It was such a wonderfully straightforward point, but so true. The thing is you never know who is going to find your fluffy pink unicorn story and it be the first time they encounter you. If you blow their socks off with the most amazing fluffy pink unicorn story they are going to perk up the next time they see your name, but if you phone it in and write a pretty tepid fluffy pink unicorn story you've lost them probably for life.

If you know anything about me, you'll probably assume this is a case of do as I say, not do as I do, because, quite honestly the last 9 years of my life since I walked out of the classroom for the last time and took the leap to full time writer, it's fair to say my output has been staggering, especially when you consider I would write maybe 2 or 3 short stories a year before that, and would labour over a novel for a couple of years with very little expectancy of it ever seeing the light of day. Something happened the day I signed the deal for Warhammer and suddenly had to deliver 3 novels in 270 days. That worked out as over 300,000 words, and they wanted a couple of 10k stories in the mix to introduce me to the fans. It meant writing 1,000 words a day ever day, without fail, for the best part of a year. No days off. No getting out of the chair until the 1,000 words were done. It demanded a discipline I'd never had before, and was driven very much by fear. After all there's a penalty clause on these contracts where basically you can hit a point where you're so late it's not worth finishing the book, because you'll be paying them to take it off you.

From that point my career has been slightly insane. The first novel, Inheritance, debuted in 2006. As of writing this I've published in the region of 3,000,000 words since that day... in 9 years. That means somehow I've maintained a published output of 1,000 words a day, every day, for those 9 years, and it's been across the most bizarre spectrum of things, from doing Top Trumps books for kids about predators and creatures of the deep, to novels about the Elder God Glaaki, an Arthurian Knight on a quest for the Devil's Cup. I've written for a hip hop legend, I've ghosted under a house name and I've been fairly lucky with my own thriller series. I joke that I'm the bestselling novelist you've never heard of, in part because of things like writing the story for Battlefield 3, which sold about 20,000,000 units last count, but you get the idea.

There was a reason my output changed so drastically: fear and hunger. But I'll come back to that.

I used to be the kind of writer who thought every idea I wanted to turn into a story needed to be unique, important, and special. To be worthy of saying. I'd forgotten (or never understood) that a major part of a writer's job is to entertain. What that meant in reality was I'd discarded hundreds of very workable ideas in search of the one. It's like looking for your soul mate, only because you know they're not out there you're making them up yourself. But I won't try and pull a fast one, I'm still a bit like that, or at least part of me is. You see, no matter what work I have on the docket, I always make sure I'm doing something purely for my own soul, something that's not a commissioned piece, something just for me. And it's always got to be a piece that feeds the writer I want to be.

Okay, I said I'd come back to it. Fear and hunger. I'll be honest, they are great motivators. So if you're reading this, obviously the final piece of advice I've got for you is don't go and get a well-paying job, don't get comfortable, comfort is the enemy. If you've got one, give it up, because if you're not starving you're not doing it right (okay I'm lying, don't give up the day job. Don't starve. I really don't advise it. We live in such a precarious environment, especially if we're looking at it long term in relation to healthcare, to pensions and growing old comfortably. Writing is a mug's game unless you're one of the lucky few. For the rest of us, if we run the numbers of hours spent working on a book vs. income from a book most of us are probably scraping minimum wage, but it's hardcoded into our DNA, we want to put ourselves through this. We need to). In the 9 years I've been a professional writer the world has changed so much, and so quickly, but other writers in this book will be giving you advice on how to cope with changing markets, becoming a hybrid author, marketing yourself on the internet and building your platform, keeping deadlines, being professional, having a shower before convention appearances, all the fun stuff. Me, I'm going to offer the one piece of advice I cling to: be the writer you want to be. Because this is your life, you're one shot at it, and long after the stories are forgotten by others they're on your bookshelf to remind you why oh why didn't I write the best fluffy pink unicorn story that I could?

AFTERWORD

Joe Mynhardt

So we come to the end of this journey, but, like any good series, we'll start hoping for another season, and then demand one.

I hope you found some useful information in this book, even if we just reminded you how much you love the genre – get the wheels spinning again. One of the best On Writing tips I've ever received mentions taking a few minutes every day to just sit and think about where you are in your career, and what opportunities are staring you in the face. I'm sure you'll be able to find a lot of ways to make extra money, if that's what you're after. We didn't even cover all aspects in this book, so think even wider than the reach of this book. Perhaps you know someone in the horror gaming industry (hook me up, okay). Following this advice has led to a lot of great ideas (including this book). It's also great for relieving stress and avoiding that feeling of being overwhelmed. I get that sometimes, but staying organized helps a lot.

I'll leave you with a couple of thoughts, just a few things I've picked up over the years:

- Take care of yourself, your body and your mind. Being a writer is a life-long commitment. I'd rather write a little every day and live a long life, than push myself and live in pain, and eventually die from stress. You'll have days where you'll have to just grit your teeth and work through personal problems or fatigue (much like the day I'm having right now), but some days you'll have to listen to your body. You're human after all. Just like our characters, we also have our flaws.

- Hang out with fellow authors.
- Be a sponge.
- Find your goal. Find out what you want out of this writing business and go for it. Full speed. All or nothing.
- Never give up. Just keep moving forward. Little by little every day.
- Set yourself short, medium and long-term goals. Make sure every day is spent working towards them. Every day! Even just a little bit.
- Say 'Yes' as much as you can, but know when and how to say 'No'.
- Stay in practice. Write every day, read every day. It'll do wonders for your imagination.
- Support your fellow authors and small press publishers. You can't expect the entire world to read just your books, right? And in the end, what it's all about, is telling stories. Not just yours.
- Like with every job, make sure you have more good days than bad. It's not always easy, that's for sure. Tapping into your emotions and fears, finding out and being so damn honest about who you are really takes it out of you, but you have to make sure you enjoy it.
- Find a routine that works for you. Try everything. I change my routine every few weeks, sometimes with each new project. This is probably what has kept me at a safe distance from writer's block.

- Don't do it alone. It's lonely enough being a writer.
- One of the major differences between a successful writer and a perceived failure, is determination. Don't give up. Pay your dues. Learn from every failure, every missed opportunity, every single rejection. No matter how many they may be. Just imagine that great success story you'll be able to tell your fans one day.

A special thanks to everyone involved in this book, the authors who donated their articles, Ben Baldwin for the cover, and R.J. Cavender (you know why). A special thanks to Emma Audsley for joining the team throughout this project. It was a monster, to say the least.

We've done our part, now it's up to you, dear friend. I hope to see you on the road to success. Who knows, if I spot your name enough and enjoy your contribution to the horror genre, I might just be contacting you.

All the best,
Joe Mynhardt

"First, find out what your hero wants, then just follow him!"

– Ray Bradbury

"Reality is merely an illusion, albeit a very persistent one."

– Albert Einstein

"Don't forget - no one else sees the world the way you do, so no one else can tell the stories that you have to tell."

– Charles de Lint

"It is more than probable that I am not understood; but I fear, indeed, that it is in no manner possible to convey to the mind of the merely general reader, an adequate idea of that nervous intensity of interest with which, in my case, the powers of meditation (not to speak technically) busied and buried themselves, in the contemplation of even the most ordinary objects of the universe."

– Edgar Allen Poe

"We think too small, like the frog at the bottom of the well. He thinks the sky is only as big as the top of the well. If he surfaced, he would have an entirely different view."

– Mao Zedong

"Rejection slips, or form letters, however tactfully phrased, are lacerations of the soul, if not quite inventions of the devil—but there is no way around them."

– Isaac Asimov

"Description begins in the writer's imagination, but should finish in the reader's."
– Stephen King

"Some people never go crazy. What truly horrible lives they must live."
– Charles Bukowski

"Whether you're writing about vampires, zombies, werewolves, demons, witches, ghosts or serial killers, the tone, the mood, the settings, the characters, and the plot should be so uniquely personal that only you could have possibly written it. That is the only reason anyone should ever write any story, ever, because you are the only person who could have written it."
– Wrath James White

"It's poor judgment', said Grandpa 'to call anything by a name. We don't know what a hobgoblin or a vampire or a troll is. Could be lots of things. You can't heave them into categories with labels and say they'll act one way or another. That'd be silly. They're people. People who do things. Yes, that's the way to put it. People who *do* things."
– Ray Bradbury, The October Country

"I try to create sympathy for my characters, then turn the monsters loose."
– Stephen King

"Trust dreams. Trust your heart, and trust your story."
– Neil Gaiman

"A serious adult story must be true to something in life. Since marvel tales cannot be true to the events of life, they must shift their emphasis towards something to which they can be true; namely, certain wistful or restless moods of the human spirit, wherein it seeks to weave gossamer ladders of escape from the galling tyranny of time, space, and natural law."
– H.P. Lovecraft

"Give them pleasure - the same pleasure they have when they wake up from a nightmare."
– Alfred Hitchcock

"Don't tell me the moon is shining; show me the glint of light on broken glass."
– Anton Chekhov

That is part of the beauty of all literature. You discover that your longings are universal longings, that you're not lonely and isolated from anyone. You belong."
– F. Scott Fitzgerald

"I have seen the dark universe yawning Where the black planets roll without aim, Where they roll in their horror unheeded, Without knowledge, or lustre, or name."
– H.P. Lovecraft, Nemesis

"The boundaries which divide Life from Death are at best shadowy and vague. Who shall say where the one ends, and where the other begins?"
– Edgar Allan Poe

"The sinister, the terrible never deceive: the state in which they leave us is always one of enlightenment. And only this condition of vicious insight allows us a full grasp of the world, all things considered, just as a frigid melancholy grants us full possession of ourselves. We may hide from horror only in the heart of horror. ("The Medusa")"

– Thomas Ligotti

"All our fears add up to one great fear, of the body under the sheet. It's our body."

– Stephen King

"Experience: that most brutal of teachers. But you learn, my God do you learn."

– C. S. Lewis

"Alone. Yes, that's the key word, the most awful word in the English tongue. Murder doesn't hold a candle to it and hell is only a poor synonym."

– Stephen King

"The death of a beautiful woman, is unquestionably the most poetical topic in the world."

– Edgar Allan Poe

"[Horror fiction] shows us that the control we believe we have is purely illusory, and that every moment we teeter on chaos and oblivion."

– Clive Barker

"If you don't know it's impossible, it's easier to do."

– Neil Gaiman

"The brick walls are there for a reason. The brick walls are not there to keep us out. The brick walls are there to give us a chance to show how badly we want something. Because the brick walls are there to stop the people who don't want it badly enough."
– Randy Pausch in his 'Last Lecture'

"A wise man will make more opportunities than he finds."
– Sir Francis Bacon

"I have the heart of a child. I keep it in a jar on my shelf."
– Robert Bloch

"Either write something worth reading or do something worth writing."
– Benjamin Franklin

"Life is a journey, not a destination."
– Ralph Waldo Emerson

"It is so shocking to find out how many people do not believe that they can learn, and how many more believe learning to be difficult."
– Frank Herbert

"I read to see myself in other people's lives."
– Stephen Sondheim, PASSION

"A mind that is stretched by a new experience can never go back to its old dimensions"
– Oliver Wendell Holmes

439

"I'm going to marry my novels and have little short stories for children."

– Jack Kerouac

"Any man who keeps working is not a failure. He may not be a great writer, but if he applies the old-fashioned virtues of hard, constant labor, he'll eventually make some kind of career for himself as writer."

– Ray Bradbury

"Logic will get you from A to B, imagination will take you everywhere..."

– Albert Einstein

Connect with Crystal Lake Publishing
Website (be sure to sign up for our newsletter):
www.crystallakepub.com

Facebook:
www.facebook.com/Crystallakepublishing

Twitter:
https://twitter.com/crystallakepub

We hope you enjoyed this title. If so, we would be grateful if you could leave a review on your blog or one of the many websites open to book reviews. Reviews are essential for a successful book. And remember to keep an eye out for more of our books.

THANK YOU FOR PURCHASING THIS BOOK,
AND KEEP WRITING/READING

Other Books by Crystal Lake Publishing

Fear the Reaper

WARNING:
THIS IS NOT JUST A BOOK

This is a journey into the life of Death; a journey through this world and the next on the words of twenty one of the best horror writers around.

Will you follow them to stare into the eyes of the Grim Reaper? Can you handle the true story of the birth of Death, or the minute details behind catching or escaping Death, becoming Death? Dying? These are not just stories but horrific experiences of pain and death: the deaths of lonely people, famous people, entire worlds, and the death of innocence and the pain of those left behind as they wait their turn, wondering what it will be like – no one is safe from the Reaper!

FEAR THE REAPER includes stories by: Taylor Grant, Joe McKinney, Rick Hautala, Gary Fry, Ross Warren, Marty Young, Stephen Bacon, Dean M Drinkel, Richard Thomas, Sam Stone, Eric S Brown, Mark Sheldon, Steve Lockley, Robert S. Wilson, Jeremy C Shipp, Jeff Strand, Lawrence Santoro, E.C. McMullen Jr., Rena Mason, John Kenny and Gary A. Braunbeck. Includes a poem by Adam Lowe.

Introduction by Gary McMahon.
Artwork by Ben Baldwin and Will Jacques.

Edited by Joe Mynhardt.

Available from Amazon, Smashwords, Barnes & Noble, Createspace and the Crystal Lake Publishing website in paperback and various eBook formats.

For the Night is Dark

The Dark is coming! Call your friends over. You don't want to go through this alone.

You will be taken back into the past, down to the depths of the ocean and across the borderline between our world and the next. You will see snapshots from the lives of small children, old-time cockney gangsters and aimless stoners. You will journey into the darkest house on the darkest street, wander hospital basements and take a flight in the comfort of first class. You will meet Mr Stix.

This tome includes stories by some of the best horror writers around: G. N. Braun, Carole Johnstone, Armand Rosamilia, Daniel I. Russell, Scott Nicholson, Gary McMahon, Joe Mynhardt, Kevin Lucia, Tracie McBride, Stephen Bacon, Benedict J. Jones, Blaze McRob, John Claude Smith, Tonia Brown, Mark West, Robert W. Walker, Jeremy C. Shipp, Jasper Bark, William Meikle and Ray Cluley.

Edited by Ross Warren
Artwork by Ben Baldwin

Are you scared of the dark? You will be.
Available from Amazon, Smashwords, Barnes & Noble, Createspace and the Crystal Lake Publishing website in paperback and various eBook formats.

Jasper Bark's Stuck On You

Warning! Do not buy this book, gentle reader.

No really, we mean it. Move along, click away from this page and go look at some Dino porn instead. We're not kidding. The only reason we published it is because award winning author Jasper Bark has got some serious dirt on us. Honestly, there's no other reason to put out something this depraved.

This is the sickest, filthiest and most horny novella you're likely to read this year. It will turn you on even as it turns your stomach. Think you've seen everything there is to see in horror and erotica? Think again! Just when you think this story can't get any lower it finds new depths to plumb.

Why are you still reading this?! Oh God you're going to buy it aren't you? You can't help yourself. You're going to click on that purchase button and download this little bad boy.

Well don't say we didn't warn you...

Available from Amazon in eBook format (paperback short story collection coming July 2014).

Kevin Lucia's Things Slip Through

Welcome to Clifton Heights, New York. Just another average Adirondack town, and nice enough in its own right. Except after dark, or under the pale light of the moon. Or in a very private doctor's office at Clifton Heights General Hospital, where no one can hear you scream. Or on a road out of town that never ends, or in an old house sitting on the edge of town with a mind - and will - of its own. Maybe you shouldn't have left the interstate, my friend. Maybe you should've driven on to the next town. But you didn't. You saw our sign, turned down our road, figuring on just a short stay. And maybe it will be. Or maybe you'll never leave. Anyway, pay a visit to The Skylark Diner. I'll be there. Pull up a chair and let me tell you about our town. It's nice enough, it really is. Except after dark. Or on cold winter days when no one is around, and you're all alone...

"An impressive debut collection from one of the horror genre's best new authors. Lucia is a true craftsman of the horror story, with a fine sense of the genre's best traditions." – Norman Prentiss, Bram Stoker Award-winning author of *Invisible Fences* and *The Fleshless Man*

"Lucia's *Things Slip Through* serves itself up as both a short story collection and a complete, cohesive novel all at once – a chimeric concoction of honest, heartfelt, and truly frightening prose that should not be missed. Highly recommended." – Ronald Malfi, author of *Floating Staircase*

Available from Amazon, Smashwords, Barnes & Noble, Createspace and the Crystal Lake Publishing website in paperback and various eBook formats.

Gary McMahon's Where You Live

Horror is everywhere...

It's waiting behind a closed door, sitting in an ordinary chair, or following you on a country walk. Perhaps it's washed up on a tranquil beach, hanging at a local skate park, recorded on an MP3 player hard drive, or even embedded somewhere deep within the design of something as simple and innocuous as a supermarket barcode.

Horror is everywhere, in the shadows and in the light.

It takes on every shape, comes in every conceivable size.

But most of all it's right where you live.

"Gary McMahon is a spellbinding storyteller." – Graham Joyce

"Gary McMahon's horror is heartfelt, his characters flawed and desperate..." – Tim Lebbon

"Gary McMahon is one of the finest of a new breed of horror writers." – Steve Rasnic Tem

Available from Amazon, Smashwords, Barnes & Noble,

Createspace and the Crystal Lake Publishing website in paperback and various eBook formats.

William Meikle's Samurai and Other Stories

In Samurai and Other Stories you'll find numerous ghosts, many Scotsmen, a big blob, some holy relics, some unholy relics, a Mothman, a barbarian, some swordplay, a shoggoth and people that nobody expects.

This collection by William Meikle brings together stories from the past decade in an exploration of the perils of exploring dark places, both external and internal.

Includes: Samurai, Rickman's Plasma, Home is the Sailor, Turn Again, Inquisitor, The Scotsman's Fiddle, The Toughest Mile, The Havehome, The Yule Log, Living the Dream, The Shoogling Jenny, The Haunting of Esther Cox, Dancers, The Brotherhood of the Thorns, The Young Lochinvar, and A Slim Chance.

Available from Amazon, Smashwords, Barnes & Noble, Createspace and the Crystal Lake Publishing website in paperback and various eBook formats.

Paul Kane's Sleeper(s)

The sleepy English locality of Middletown is about to get even sleepier, as a strange malady starts to affect the population. It spreads quickly, causing the authorities to quarantine this small city, and seek out the only person who might be able to help: Doctor Andrew Strauss. However, Strauss has a secret, one that has linked him to this place all his life, one that has linked him to a particular person there, though he doesn't yet know who. But he's not the only one hiding things – and as he ventures into Middletown to collect samples with an army escort, a mixture of UK and US troops, cracks soon begin to appear in the operation. Especially when his team come up against the most terrifying threat humankind has ever known... From the imagination of the award-winning and bestselling author of *Who's Been...?* and *RED* (optioned for film and turned into an award-winning feature script), this chilling reworking of another well-loved fairy tale reads like a heady mix of *The Andromeda Strain*, *Inception*, *Outbreak* and *Quatermass*, and is a tale that's bound to delight genre fans the world over.

Available from Amazon, Smashwords, Barnes & Noble, Createspace and the Crystal Lake Publishing website in paperback and various eBook formats.

Daniel I. Russell's Tricks, Mischief and Mayhem

A little girl brings home more than she bargained for after winning a stuffed bear at a carnival side show. After saving her family from one kind of predator, a protective mother releases an Australian legend hungry for blood and flesh. In his diary, a killer of historical notoriety tells the story of what really happened that night...in the dark...Tricks, Mischief and Mayhem is the debut collection of short stories from Australian Shadows Award finalist Daniel I. Russell. Spanning nearly ten years, this macabre showcase contains the best of Russell's published short fiction and five brand new tales.

Includes: Living Haunts, The Blood Pit, By the Banks of the Nabarra, A Picture Tells, The Lady of Potter's Field, Roots, The Bell Jar Heart, Prosthetics, The Vending Machine, Disproportional, Creeper, It Comes But Once A Year, The Love Revolution, Fluffs, Following Orders, Linger, Devolution, Broken Bough, Nobody Messes With Venus, Tricks, Mischief and Mayhem, Seeing the Light, and God May Pity All Weak Hearts.

Available from Amazon, Smashwords, Barnes & Noble, Createspace and the Crystal Lake Publishing website in paperback and various eBook format.

AUTOGRAPHS

Printed in Great Britain
by Amazon.co.uk, Ltd.,
Marston Gate.